Richard K. Geyer
1988

FROM MOUNT KENYA
TO THE CAPE

Ten Years of African Hunting

FROM MT. KENYA TO THE CAPE

Ten Years of African Hunting

Craig Boddington

1987

SAFARI PRESS
P.O. Box 3095, Long Beach, CA 90803, USA

This one for Brittany.

Second Edition

ISBN 0-940143-07-0

TO THE READER

Safari Press, America's premier big-game publisher, brings out new books on a regular basis. If you would like to be advised of our new publications, please send us a card giving your name and address.

SAFARI PRESS
P.O. Box 3095
Long Beach, CA 90803
USA

TABLE OF CONTENTS

FOREWORD

Africa has long been the big-game hunter's Mecca. But what is it like today? Craig Boddington will tell you in this very readable new book. Unfortunately, there have been major changes since the better known works on African hunting were written.

The East African hunting of the storied past has indeed ceased to exist over the last ten years. Radical political change and civil war have eliminated many of the traditional hunting grounds of East Africa. Only in Tanzania is big-game hunting still available. Meanwhile, such other traditional favorites as the Chad, the Central African Republic, Angola, and Mozambique have been closed to hunting. Today's hunter is quite limited in choice. The traditional peripatetic safari has given way to hunting from fixed camps or from ranch homes. Today's hunting grounds are found in Zimbabwe, Zambia, Botswana, South-West Africa, and South Africa. Ethiopia and the Sudan are possible but at times questionable.

The Big Five can no longer be taken since black rhino are strictly protected, at least against the rifle of the legitimate sportsman. Elephant hunting is still available but in a rather limited way and at substantial cost. It is true that buffalo, lion, and leopard can still be shot, but to get more than two of these species on a single safari is almost impossible. The plains game, yes; there is still good hunting to be had, but one's bag is more restricted than it was in the days of the roving safari, and the total number of species that can be had on one hunt is more limited.

Why, then, does Africa continue to attract hunters in substantial numbers? As Craig Boddington points out, there are very few one-safari-only African hunters because "the sights, the sounds, the smells, the very feel of the hunter's Africa will forever call, and once the hunter has been there, his soul will never be content until under the Southern Cross once again."

Loss of the opportunity for more than a fleeting taste of the old East African safari has not dimmed Boddington's enjoyment of what does remain; not only the sights, sounds, and smells, but also the experience of contacts with native tribes and with the matchless variety of African game species. Add to those the everchanging panorama of African scenery: vast mountain ranges, immense forests, arid deserts, lush riverine deltas, and thousands of miles of rolling plains and bush.

The lure of the campfire is still there with its comradeship and evening recall of the day's events. The professionalism of the P.W.H. and of his African trackers still remains to be marveled at and admired. The thrill of the stalk has in no way been lost, while the need to plan and to concentrate on the nature and the content of the hunting bag does contribute to the selectiveness of the safari. The taking of superior trophies is achieved more through concentrated effort than by chance encounter. In this respect African hunting has perhaps become more like what we are used to in North America, where one may expect on a given hunt to encounter relatively few species.

One's goals have to be set in advance. One's plans and preparations have to be aimed at a few top trophies. The opportunity for chance encounters with other species may be less but not necessarily lost.

In this atmosphere Craig has maintained a suspenseful story throughout. Page by page, the reader looks forward with increasing expectancy to the uncertain outcome of a stalk. When it has succeeded, the reader joins Craig in his satisfaction. If the stalk should fail on the last day, one shares his disappointment, while realizing that the game was well played and worth the time and effort.

The book is, of course, a writing achievement of the first order, as might be expected from a man like Boddington who has hunted so widely since boyhood and has developed in such a significant manner the talents of the professional outdoor writer. While not intended to be a "how-to" book, this volume nevertheless is as good a guide as may be found today to what one can expect from an African safari in 1987. Though the author believes that hairbreadth adventures are largely the result of poor planning and execution, they can and do happen at times, and the reader will enjoy those incidents.

Finally, Boddington's advice on how to select the hunting area today, the best and most reliable manner of booking, and the proper weapons and equipment to take are as authentic and reliable as one could have from any source.

I very much doubt if any American hunter who has not yet been to Africa can read this book from cover to cover without reaching the decision that he had better book a hunt right now, while sport of the quality that Boddington describes is still available.

John H. Batten
November 1986

xi

INTRODUCTION

Just 10 years have passed since I planned my first African hunt. It seems a lot longer since that Bicentennial year, for indeed the last decade has brought many changes, not only to me personally, but also to the world of the hunter and to the world as a whole—and many of those changes have occurred across the face of Africa. In the summer of 1976, as I planned my first safari, I was a Marine lieutenant out to fulfill a boyhood dream. Like so many hunters, I wanted to see Africa once, and I knew that, having seen her, I would get her out of my system and be done with this fantasy that had plagued me for so long.

Of course I was wrong. Only those who have never experienced Africa believe that she ever relinquishes her spell. Fifty years ago, when Ernest Hemingway returned from his celebrated safari with Philip Percival, he was asked what his next plans were. The answer was simple: "Make enough money to go back to Africa." No one ever said it better. The sights, sounds, smells, the very *feel* of the hunter's Africa will forever call, and once the hunter has been there, his soul will never be content until under the Southern Cross once again.

Financially, I would surely be better off if I'd never heard of Africa; the "high cost of lions" that Ruark wrote of 30 years ago has grown ever higher. Professionally, as an outdoor writer, I would surely be in no worse position had I stayed in the whitetail woods and quail hedgerows, for indeed there is little market today for serious accounts of African hunting—the days of The *Green Hills of Africa* and *Horn of the Hunter* are long gone. Unquestionably my life would have been simpler had I never undertaken that first trip 10 years ago, for I've spent a great deal of my time simply figuring how I could afford to return—and return to Africa I have, again and again, and no doubt will continue to do so. For whatever the cost—in any coin—the experience has been worth it all and more. This book tells of that experience, 10 years and more than a dozen safaris. It isn't a "how to" book, although perhaps there will be some useful information herein. It isn't a book of derring-do and close brushes with fanged death, for in truth Africa is generally dangerous only when you make a serious mistake, and therefore it is inestimably safer than an L.A. freeway, where your life depends upon so many steady hands all at once. It is an accurate, and I hope interesting account of one man's experience in several parts of the hunter's greatest paradise.

In 1976, the hunter's map of Africa was a bit different from what it is today. The desert hunting in Chad was a recent memory. Recent, too, was the memory of hunting in Angola and Mozambique. Tanzania had been closed to hunting longer than any of those three, and Ethiopia was at best uncertain. Zambia was just coming on as a safari destination, the opportunities to hunt South Africa were but a shadow of what they are today, and in its eleventh year of terrorist warfare, Rhodesia could open just a fraction of its fine game country to hunting safaris.

The Central African Republic—it was an Empire then—and Sudan were much as they are—specialized safari destinations and a bit uncertain. South West, too, has changed but little—a fine, scenic area for a plains game safari. In 1976, for the hunter in search of a one-shot safari that would allow him to experience as much of Africa as possible, there were really but two choices—Kenya and Botswana. After agonizing deliberation on my part, Kenya won out, no doubt simply because of the tradition of a Kenya safari. In truth, Kenya's game in its closing days wasn't what it had been in Ruark's or Hemingway's day; had I chosen Botswana or Zambia—largely an unknown entity then—there is a chance I'd have taken every major species on my list, and even a slight chance I wouldn't have returned to Africa so quickly or so often.

But Kenya it was, and perhaps it was the luckiest decision I made, for within weeks of my hunt, Kenya safari was no more, and if I didn't have all the trophies I might have desired, I did have the experience of a traditional East African safari that may never be again. This book, then, will start under Mount Kenya and will travel from there to the hot coastal plains of Tsavo, where Colonel Patterson once dispatched the maneaters. It will travel south to Rhodesia's dense thorn, farther south yet to the Namib Desert, then east to Zululand's lush hillsides; back north into the Kalahari, west again to the Orongo Mountains, northeast to the Luangwa Valley, west to the Kafue Plateau and then south to the cool green hills of Matetsi; north to the Bangweulu Swamp, then back west to the emerald-green Okavango Delta, and south again to the windswept Cape Mountains. Finally, it will travel north to the watershed of the mighty Limpopo, the great hunting grounds of a century ago and more. It's a long ways from the Limpopo to Mount Kenya, but in many ways it was a trip back to the beginning of my African experience, for it was shared with the professional hunter who began my African obsession.

The book will end there, on the Limpopo, and that seems a fitting place to rest, for in the days spent there I felt transported back to the beginning. But that hunt on the Limpopo is only a stopping place. Lord willing, the ending remains far in the future, and there is still so much of Africa left to see. To the north, the high blue hills of Ethiopia beckon, and off to the west, the great forests, only the edges of which I have seen. Elsewhere across that vast continent are so many little corners that I'd like to see—and so many that I'd like to see again.

It's often said that African hunting isn't what it used to be, but then, few things in this world are what they used to be. Africa can't be as it was in Selous' day any more than the American West can be as it was in Jim Bridger's. Fortunately or unfortunately, I never saw Africa in Selous' day, or Hemingway's, or Ruark's. I've seen it only in my own time, and I have nothing to compare. What I've seen of it I've seen in the last 10 years—and it's magnificent. There is a burgeoning human population, it's true, and there is rampant poaching which must be controlled. There is also political unrest with no conclusion in sight. But there are also vast regions of virgin bush, forest, savanna, and desert—places where, each night, lions still roar and hyenas laugh and you move closer to the fire—and not just for warmth. Places where impala leap in the sunlight, kudu slip through the dappled shade, and vast herds of buffalo come to water. Africa is there, and it remains our globe's most captivating continent. Those who will can pine for the good old days, but I'll enjoy all I can of what there is now.

Los Angeles
January 1987

CHAPTER I

THE SLOPES OF MOUNT KENYA

The Land Cruiser wound its way north out of Nairobi, through the rich farming country that might have been called the White Highlands just a few years before. I dozed as we hummed down the well-maintained highway; the previous two nights had been virtually sleepless both from anticipation and in the aftermath of transoceanic flight. Now that the Great Adventure had finally begun, the jet lag released its hold—and I remember very little of my first few hours on safari!

I awoke with a start when we pulled into the little hamlet of Nanyuki, far up into the foothills of Mount Kenya. During the long year of anticipation that had followed booking the safari, I had carefully reread all of Ruark and had read every other book on East Africa I could find. *Nanyuki*—the very name lifted the hair on the back of my neck, and I'm sure I expected to see Peter McKenzie, or at least Karen Blixen, strolling along the sidewalk.

Of course, towns are much the same wherever you find them. Nairobi had been a big town—city, if you will—and it had been crowded and hurried, not unlike the cities my wife, Sharon, and I had left behind. The bazaar and curio shops had held our attention—for a time—but there were literally dozens of small shops, and they were all identical. The Norfolk and New Stanley hotels had provided a thrill just from their historical names, but they, too, had been disappointments; they were, after all, just hotels. So it was with Nanyuki: The thrill was provided by the name alone; the town was what it had always been—a small community supported by the local farming industry.

Ah, but the mountain! Mount Kenya was very real, and no matter how many daydreams had aggrandized it, that pinnacle of stone and ice was up to the challenge. Much of south-central Kenya is high country;

1

Nairobi itself sits more than a mile above sea level. On to the south are the Masai Steppes, and across the border into Tanzania rises Mount Kilimanjaro. Off to the west is the high Mau Forest, and to the north-west the rugged Aberdares. But in all of Africa there is no mountain like Mount Kenya. In the Kikuyu language it's *Kerinyagga*, literally the "home of God." And if God chose to live on a mountain, I suspect he'd pick a mountain such as this.

Whereas Kilimanjaro presents a gentle, rounded silhouette that has formed the backdrop for countless paintings and photographs, Mount Kenya knows no subtle curves. It rises starkly and abruptly out of the dark forest and emerald bamboo that ring it—a craggy pinnacle of black rock and eternal snow. Mount Kenya is located virtually on the Equator, so it's climate allows the dense hardwood forest to grow to nearly the 12,000-foot level, and the bamboo grows several thousand feet above that. From Nanyuki we turned east, climbing into the forest belt and heading towards our first camp.

The Mountain is home to relatively few species of game, but those that are found there can grow to magnificent size in the impenetrable

Mount Kenya rises out of the highlands near Nanyuki, a pinnacle of rock and ice surrounded by a belt of impenetrable bamboo and, lower down, dense hardwood forest—home to superb buffalo and bushbuck, a few eastern bongo, giant forest hog, and long-horned forest rhino.

forests. Some of Africa's finest buffalo come from the slopes of Mount Kenya, and the forest rhino—the few that remain—are famed for their long horns and short tempers. I had no rhino license but had come to the Mountain to look for buffalo and the superb Masai bushbuck found there. The forests and the bamboo are also home to a few eland, zebra, and waterbuck, plus the odd duiker and oribi. The great prize, Kenya bongo, shares the forest with the buffalo, but is no quarry for the beginner. And beginner I was as the Toyota left the traveled roads and bounced up a steep track ever higher into the forest. In the years since I have enjoyed the exhilaration of pent-up anticipation as every safari begins—but there can never be another first safari, nor can the excitement that accompanies each new sight and sound on that first one ever be equaled.

Dark caught us on the narrow track, and with it the evening chill. Camp would be at 7,000 feet, advised Willem van Dyk, our professional hunter, host, and mentor for the next 21 days, and he advised my wife and me to pile plenty of blankets on the beds. Craggy of face and stocky of build, Willem wasn't a picture-book professional hunter. But nearly a year before, over the telephone, he had given me straight talk about his operation and my chances for the game I wanted to hunt. Somehow, and I'm still not sure how, he had won out over countless pretty brochures, and the all-important, never-to-be-equaled first safari had been placed in his hands.

During the passing months he had been good about correspondence. Not great, but good—and, I would learn as the years passed, better than most! With a 21-day safari planned and lion and buffalo chosen as the primary species, Willem had booked us first into Block 74 well up on Mount Kenya, then into Block 26 hard on the Tanzania border east of Tsavo National Park. The two areas were to be vastly different safaris in terms of country, game, and outcome. I have always suspected that Willem chose the Mountain primarily because that style of hunting suited him, not simply because it was the best place he knew. In truth, it suited me as well—cool and pleasant, yet both physically and mentally challenging to hunt. It was the kind of place that required not only hard work but also a bit of luck to hunt. As we rolled up the Mountain towards camp, our hunting luck had yet to be tested.

Untested, too, was the full measure of our faith in Willem. Though quiet by nature, he had patiently answered all our endless questions, and he and his pretty wife, Rosemary, had patiently squired us through Nairobi's endless shops. We had had a bad moment initially when the

Olympic Air jet deposited us into Nairobi in the early dawn; there can be no panic like that of the first-time African hunter who arrives to find no professional hunter awaiting him at customs—unless it be that of his spouse, a bit uncertain about the whole proceedings in the first place. Ten minutes of terror, and then Rosemary was there to smooth things over while Willem finished with his previous client. Some hours later, over lunch, more panic as Rosemary found a discreet way to tell us that the remainder of our deposit, payable in advance—and paid to our agent *well* in advance—had not arrived. But all that was behind us now, and we felt in good hands.

We felt better yet when we rounded a final bend in the track and the headlights bounced off green tent canvas and a seeming sea of smiling black faces. Nowhere have I been more welcomed in a hunting camp—that was a part of the Kenya tradition that has been largely lost. We shook hands all around, trying to remember names but knowing we would not, at least not at first, and haltingly repeating our first words in Swahili—*"Jambo, jambo."*

The night was cold as we sat close to the fire, sipping a local beer and watching the African sky—magnificent everywhere, but spectacular from the altitude of Mount Kenya. After a short wait, just long enough, the headman, Mbogo, rang a silver bell to announce our first meal on safari—medallions of bushbuck, as I recall—served on china in the dining tent. James, the first cook, and Miichai, his assistant, bore witness to all the legends of Kenya camp cookery. Advice to trim down *before* the hunt had been well-meant, and should have been well-taken!

Willem's advice to pile on the blankets was well-taken, for it was cold on the mountain. Not freezing cold, but cold enough for sound sleeping under several layers of wool, and cold enough that hot tea in the predawn chill never tasted so good. Buffalo was the order of the day that first morning, and for the rest of our stay on the mountain. To hunt them we would arise in the dark, eat a light breakfast, then bounce the Land Cruiser on up the Mountain well ahead of dawn. The buffalo on Mount Kenya have been harried for a dozen of their generations, and their survival on those well-traveled slopes is a credit to the wariness of their breed.

Like so much of Africa, Mount Kenya is changing quickly. The cultivation moves farther up the mountain yearly, and it is preceded by woodcutters, removing both timber and fuel wood from the very heart of God's home. The buffalo have retreated ever higher, spending most of their days now in the impenetrable bamboo and coming down into

A hunting camp on Mount Kenya had to be one of the most pleasant experiences in the hunting world. The mornings were cold, warming to "just right" at midday and cooling off to a nice, crisp evening. At midday it was perfect to lounge in the shade; in the evening a warm fire was required.

the forest only at night to feed. In the morning we would hope to get above them and catch them as they fed uphill. In the evenings we would hunt bushbuck and waterbuck and hope for the slim chance of catching buffalo on an early feed. It was steep country with thin air, and the hunting was all on foot—more similar to mountain hunting in the American West than I had imagined, and much more challenging than I had expected.

That first morning we left the Toyota and hiked up a narrow game trail through stands of ancient hardwoods. The underbrush was strikingly green, and there was just a slight thinning of the forest before the bamboo took over completely. It was there, along the indistinct edge between forest and bamboo, that I saw my first Cape buffalo—indeed, my first African animal.

There was fresh spoor along the narrow track, and the oddly familiar cattle smell was fresh in the air. We were just minutes behind these buffalo, but the bamboo was so close that it seemed certain we were already too late. We were, for those buffalo; we followed the spoor to a damp,

5

grassy hollow, a rare opening beyond which the bamboo closed like a solid wall. There we rested for a moment, blowing from the 10,000 feet of elevation. And there, in a small depression, like a whitetail buck who had lain still during the drive but could wait no longer once the movement stopped, was a fine buffalo bull. Black and dirt-scabbed, he rose from the sparse cover like a flushing grouse, but it was no grouse that turned to face us at 20 yards' distance.

Eventually I would learn that he wasn't a great bull, at best an average bull—perhaps particularly average, since he has never grown in my mind's eye. His boss was mature but not impressive, and his horns spread just beyond his outstretched ears with little downward hook. The .375 swung on him, but it was the first day and on Willem's whispered "Not big enough!" there was little regret in lowering the rifle. The bull, seemingly embarrassed by being caught out, trotted away for a few steps, then turned and peered at us again. Finally, with mud shaking from his flanks, he turned and vanished into the bamboo. A great bull he may not have been, but he's a well-remembered bull. I have often

The forest belt is an extremely dense hardwood forest, huntable only on foot. Movement is fairly quiet, but visibility extremely limited. Above the forest the bamboo takes over, an impenetrable wall of vegetation that's nearly impossible to hunt in.

Buffalo hunting in dense cover such as is typical on Mount Kenya is extremely exciting and extremely difficult. An unobstructed view of a whole animal is rare, and judging trophy quality, then getting a shot requires a bit of luck as well as skill.

wondered, hindsight being as it is, if I would have lowered the rifle so readily had I known the miles I would tramp in search of his equal—let alone his better. I'd like to think I would still have let him trot so casually into the trackless bamboo, but then we'd all like to be a bit better than we really are. The truth is I'm not so sure . . . .

It was never to be so easy again. In fact, to this day it has never been so easy with buffalo. From that point we tracked, only to lose them in the hopeless bamboo or jump them at close range in stuff too thick for a shot. It never occurred to me that it was dangerous work, nor have I ever found unwounded buffalo to be anything more than simply wary—but it was damned difficult work, with shifting mountain breezes, few openings, and buffalo that knew exactly how the game was played. I was hunting in Russell Birdshooters those first few days. My journal entry from the third day reads:

"Buffalo again. Lots of fresh tracks but none sighted. Found good area, so maybe tomorrow. Boots making much noise in forest. Hunting in tennis shoes from now on. Van Dyk says that would be a great relief to him . . . ."

The mornings were always buffalo, but we varied the evening's hunt. Mount Kenya produces some of Africa's finest bushbuck of the large Masai race, and we didn't want to leave the area without one. The waterbuck came as a gift, actually, a chance sighting while we were hunting bushbuck, and he had the distinction of being my first African trophy.

We had seen a couple of good bushbuck in a second-growth clearing well down the slopes, in sight of William Holden's Mount Kenya Safari Club, though many miles distant. Together with our Wakamba trackers Muindi and Musili, Willem and I took a short hike along a grassy watercourse. It was ideal bushbuck country; we had just spotted a nice buck feeding along the opposite slope when Muindi raised a hand and pointed. Far down the valley four female waterbuck fed in the lush grass. We moved a bit closer, and there to the left was the bull, a defassa waterbuck with no white rump-ring and with fine horns for Kenya. Musili carried a makeshift bamboo tripod; the range was long, but with that for a rest not uncomfortably so. The .30-06 seemed horribly loud in the still meadow. The bullet hit with a slap, but the bull was off instantly. I shot behind him as he ran, then placed the third shot correctly when he paused at forest's edge. I had read that waterbuck smell terrible, and indeed they have their own smell—but this one smelled like the finest perfume to me, and looked even better than a fashion model who might wear that perfume.

There was just a bit more luck due us that evening. On the way back to camp just ahead of dark the blurred form of a duiker crossed the road in front of us. Knowing it was hopeless, we stopped the truck and peered into the shadowy trees just in case. For some reason he stopped just inside the first cover, and I had just enough light to get the crosshairs on him. He was one of the best East African duikers ever taken, but I didn't know that then. I did know he was big for his kind, and I thought, now that the ice was broken in spades, we'd have things all our way.

Not even close. We'd had our good luck, and now we'd have to have the bad—very bad—before more good would come our way. The next day was the day of the wounded buffalo.

We found him well after sunrise, grazing contentedly in a brushy *donga* just below the bamboo. We had tracked him to there, stalked him from above, and had him cold turkey. The brush was too noisy for a close approach, but we got within 60 yards and knelt down behind a great log. My .375 was an old friend, a rifle I'd had since I was 16 in preparation for just this occasion. The scope sight had never varied, and it had been rechecked on the first day. There was plenty of time: time to evaluate the horns, time to get a good rest, time to align the sights perfectly—and time to flub the shot.

Second-guessing is easy; the most likely thing is that I didn't pay attention to the sharp downhill angle and never got the bullet inside the ribcage. Once it's over, kicking yourself is easy, too. But I can still see those crosshairs plain as day, and the easiest thing of all would have been to make the shot properly in the first place. But I didn't.

At the shot the buffalo swapped ends, giving a good crossing shot. I fired again, hit again, but God knows where, and then the rifle that had never failed before jammed tight as a tick. Vaguely I was aware of Willem rising beside me and I saw his over/under .458 come up while I frantically tried to work my bolt. There was a great sound, like the ringing of a giant bell, and I turned to one of the most astounding sights one could ever witness. The Kreighoff double, having discharged both its barrels simultaneously, was turning a slow circle about 10 feet overhead. Willem, with a live weight approaching 200 pounds, seemed to be completing a somersault about 10 feet farther back from where he had started. And the buffalo, unfortunately for everyone, had just been swallowed by the bamboo.

We waited for a time, both to allow the bull to stiffen and to give Willem a chance to get his vision back. He appeared to have broken nothing, but bad headaches and double vision would plague him for several days. I was always glad he never had to shoot again on that safari—but in any case he never again loaded more than one barrel on his double.

A half hour or so passed, a long time when you're waiting to finish something that you know you started poorly. Finally, though, Willem reckoned his head was as good as it would get, and we started up into the bamboo. Until now we had avoided going into the bamboo after the buffalo, allowing them to win the game if they made it that far. I'd kept quiet, but I hadn't been sure if I understood the rules. Ten feet into the bamboo I understood them completely. The pale green closed around us, and only the ground beneath and the maze of bamboo stalks remained. It was mostly hands and knees, but the trail of the bull's passage was clear at first. The blood was sparse, but in the soft ground there was no problem following. The bamboo shut out most of the daylight and all the visibility, but ahead ran a narrow tunnel created by our buffalo and others. To the sides visibility was no more than a few feet. We moved carefully, Musili ahead on the track, Willem just behind, and I behind him. Well to the rear Muindi followed with Sharon—far enough back, we hoped, that the legendary buffalo trick of lying in wait would be played against me instead of her. I asked Willem how we could find him in that stuff, and he grinned—a little lopsidedly. "Actually, the idea is for him to find us."

We followed for two hours and seemed to gain little. The blood remained constant, a drop here and a drop there, but finally our bull's tracks mixed with those of another, later herd, possibly spooked by our approach. The bamboo had opened a bit, but the track was becoming vague and uncertain. We found just the occasional drop of blood now, then cast about aimlessly amid many tracks to find the next drop.

After the palm-sweating, back-breaking agony of the bamboo, the best thing would be to say that we took the bull in full charge as he lay in wait. The next best thing would be to have taken him—or found him dead—in any configuration whatsoever. The truth is that we lost him, and the further truth is that, from the blood we could find, it's unlikely my two .375 solids had done him any serious harm. Willem's shots missed, typical performance when a twin-barreled gun doubles, since the vibrations make both bullets go haywire.

I took it hard, and took it harder yet when I missed a fine bushbuck that same evening. It would have been an easy shot—had I seen the animal. But he was black animal in black shadow, and despite Musili's directions, I never saw him until he ran.

I have a feeling I was less than perfect company that evening. Sharon set me straight. Over the years we would have many differences and eventually would part, but she was dead right that night. She told me I was trying too hard, and I was.

There were many dreams at stake on that trip, and a lot of scrimping and saving and extra work had gone into it. Unless you have the advantage of independent wealth, that's the case with every major hunting trip, and quite naturally every part of you wants it to be a success. You want it so badly that you simply can't allow yourself the natural mistakes—the bad shots, the blown stalks and the screwups. But they're part of hunting, too, whether it's in the grouse cover on your back 40 or on the trip of a lifetime. If you take the bad along with the good, then the good is all the more enjoyable. But if you can't accept the bad, chances are that you'll have more than your share of it. I was trying too hard, working overtime to convince myself that everything was wonderful and that I was having the time of my life—and to convince Willem that I was not only a good hunter, but also a great guy. In short, I was well on my way to becoming a problem client. I gave it some hard thought and realized I had to loosen up. It didn't happen overnight, but within a few days I really was having the time of my life—without hav-

10

ing to work at it! Perhaps I would have settled down on my own in a few days. Most hunters do, and most professional hunters are used to the start-of-safari antics. Or perhaps I had badly needed Sharon's blunt advice. Certainly I've never forgotten it.

The next morning we tried for buffalo again early, then moved very slowly through some open forest looking for bushbuck, alternately sitting and then moving a few hundred yards. The forest was truly magnificent—huge trees that blotted out all but a few shafts of golden sunlight, and overhead unfamiliar birds and the beautiful black-and-white colobus monkeys. Seeing bushbuck wasn't a problem; even seeing record class bucks was an everyday occurrence. But Willem wanted only the best the area could offer, whether it be the most common or the most rare of animals.

I think it was that morning that we stalked up on the giant forest hogs—two very large boars rooting in some dense forest. I hadn't purchased a license for one, and indeed had no desire to shoot such a singularly ugly beast—but seeing them was worth the morning.

That evening we hunted bushbuck in the same fashion, moving slowly and stopping often. That was the night of the rhino, the "whoof" and the parting brush coming too close and too fast as we crept along minding our own business. There had been a time in Kenya when we could have stood and shot it out without incurring the wrath of the game department, but no longer. We ran, very quickly and with no words exchanged, and we put the largest tree we could find between us and the equally startled rhino. He was a fine bull, one of so few left on the Mountain, and he turned off into the forest without giving us more than a glance. We breathed hard for a time, then continued.

In the morning we trailed yet another herd of buffalo to the edge of the bamboo, lost them as usual, and circled back to the truck for coffee and biscuits from Willem's chop-box. Njomo, our driver, was glad to see us. He'd been penned in the cab of the truck since daylight by a big herd of buffalo that insisted on grazing in circles where he was parked. Of course, some of the tracks were the platterlike spoor of outsize bulls.

Our luck on the Mountain never really changed, but we finally wore it down a bit. On our next to the last evening we drove back to the spot where I'd shot the waterbuck. It was a more open area that offered better visibility, and we'd seen more bushbuck there than anywhere. Just where we planned to go, another Land Cruiser was parked sideways in our path—even in Africa, it seems, hunting pressure is inescapable. Kenya law allowed two resident hunters to share a given hunting block

Boddington's Masai bushbuck was taken high up on Mount Kenya. With 17-inch horns, he still ranks as one of his best—and most prized—African trophies.

with a professional hunter and his clients. Ninety-nine times out of a hundred there is no possible conflict in such large tracts of land, but this was the hundredth. We had little choice but to try a totally new area.

The forest was open here, and the open forest allowed heavy underbrush. Bushbuck tracks were thick, but as we still-hunted slowly I couldn't understand how a shot would be possible. It almost wasn't. We heard a bushbuck bark, then crashing ahead of us suddenly stilled. Slowly we pushed forward around an island of impassable nettles. The brush opened, then a tangle of vines blocked all view.

Muindi pointed ahead, but I couldn't see. Willem pointed, then directed me. I still couldn't see. In fact, there was nothing to see—just a faint shadow of brown against the brown-green of the vines. But finally the outline of a head took form, and I followed it down the neck and fired where the shoulder had to be.

12

Whatever it was bolted at the shot, and I began to kick myself yet again. But Musili quickly found blood, and a few steps farther on lay a magnificent 17-inch bushbuck nailed through the shoulders.

Like most first-time African hunters, I didn't know what I really wanted to hunt then. In fact, I wanted to hunt everything, and to some extent (shameful but true), I would judge the success of the safari by the size and variety of the bag. Later I would learn that those meant little; under some circumstances a man might cull common game such as impala and warthog by the dozen, but other species would always be earned. Few of the antelope tribe are earned in the same coin as the spiral horns, and the lowly bushbuck—most widespread and most common of this elite group—started my education properly. There are some animals that one will always hunt. Buffalo fall into that category—common enough that there is no guilt in the taking of yet another, but as exciting as any animal that walks. For me bushbuck are another—not as exciting as buffalo, but challenging in the way a whitetail is challenging. Common, abundant, but wary and cover-loving—a trophy worthy of more attention than it has ever received.

The next morning Willem sent the big Bedford truck and most of the staff on their way to Voi to set up camp, keeping just Muindi, Musili, and Njomo in our "fly camp." North American outfitters couldn't stay in business if the bulk of their clientele learned what "fly camp" meant in Kenya. Perhaps it's just as well all that is past now—it seemed almost a sin to hunt in such comfort!

That morning the buffalo won the game once more, beating us to the bamboo by minutes. But that night we got the drop on them, fair and square. We caught a small herd just coming out of the bamboo a few minutes ahead of dark. They were about 25 yards away through scattered trees, and we watched them until full dark—but there were no good bulls.

That was the end of our time on the Mountain. Oh, we would try again in the morning, but by now we knew luck was against us. We had been fortunate in our few successes, but buffalo wasn't in the cards. It was time to breathe our last of Mount Kenya's clean, cool air and hope that a change of scenery would bring a change of luck as well.

13

CHAPTER II
THE TSAVO PLAIN

The Masai was dry that year, too dry for March. Thunderheads to the south held promise, but the short rains of January and February had missed this area. We had driven southeast from Nairobi, dropping quickly in elevation and soon passing from cultivated land into the red dust of the Masai Plain. There were a few Masai along the road, distinctive in red cloaks, ocher-smeared pigtails, and the long-bladed spear that was an item of apparel as much as a weapon. Even as the last quarter of the Twentieth Century progressed, little change had come to the Masai.

Willem stopped briefly by the Wakamba Reserve, a roadside village of tumbledown shacks, so that Muindi and Musili could give some money to their wives. That was wives—in the plural—for each man: Muindi had three and Musili just two. They were good men, both of them, and they'd been hunting with Willem for many years.

Raised on a farm in the Kenya highlands, Willem had begun hunting professionally in the early Sixties, shortly after independence and the nationalization of his family's farm. He started hunting in Tanzania, and in the beginning he traveled to the Wakamba, Kenya's hunting tribe, to seek a few good men to hunt with him. When Tanzania closed hunting in the early Seventies, Willem moved the operation back to Kenya. Eventually that would end, too. Today van Dyk is in South Africa, a land his grandfather left at the turn of the century. He's still hunting, following his trade, but his back is to the sea now; there's no place left to go. At least he could continue hunting. I've always wondered what has happened to the great black hunters and trackers now that politics has decreed no need for their craft.

Taught by their fathers and grandfathers the tracking wizardry that a white man cannot even understand, let alone emulate, Muindi and Musili had perhaps been accomplished poachers in their youth. Today

15

they were chief trackers and gunbearers, an honored profession at which they were highly skilled and for which they were, by Kenya standards, extremely well-paid. They laughed much, and Willem joked with them in the 'Kamba tongue. There was no question, from the gunbearer elite down to Mwangia, the porter, as to who was in charge of the camp and the safari. Van Dyk was the boss, and a firm boss. But there was much mutual respect in his camp, a genuine affinity all around, with much trust flowing up and down the chain of command. We sat quietly in the Toyota, sipping a Coke from the cool-box, and when the appointed time approached, the men reappeared, waving good- bye as we rolled on southeast towards Voi.

The highway from Nairobi to Mombasa on the coast passes along the northern edge of Masailand, with the rise of the Masai Steppes visible on the skyline. It passes north of Amboseli Game Reserve, then bisects the great Tsavo National Park. At the right time of year there can be much game viewed from the highway, but not that year; the concentrations were well to the south, under those storm clouds and wherever else rain had already fallen. We stopped briefly at Mtito Andei, a whistle-stop within the park, and bought some postcards and such. Sharon found a superb carving of a bearded Kikuyu elder, a bust about 10 inches tall. She was a great haggler, and the Africans enjoy serious haggling—I suspect they are sadly disappointed by tourists who pay the asking price. Eventually the price became right, a few Kenya shillings for a truly fine piece, and we went on.

At Voi we checked in with the District Commissioner, Willem carefully signing into the massive logbook. That was the end of the hard-surface road; ahead lay two hours of dirt track more or less due south. The Bedford truck had preceded us by a day and a half, and headman Mbogo was charged with having the camp ready for our arrival. It was hot and dry in Voi, but the storm clouds to the south were getting closer.

The red dust plumed up behind the Toyota. Willem drove fast but with a firm, steady hand, and Block 26 approached rapidly. We passed a few villages, well-kept mud-and-wattle huts with carefully swept yards and loose chickens and goats, and a steady trickle of pedestrian traffic between settled areas. There was one school along the road, a new structure of brick—red brick from the red Kenya soil—and dozens of children in the schoolyard. Between the villages was nothing but thornbush, yet we saw no game. I didn't understand that; I had expected that African plains game would be like Wyoming's pronghorns—literally

16

The eland is a huge antelope, about the same size as a moose but amazingly agile and particularly wary. The East African or Paterson's eland is the smallest of the eland group. Like oryx, both males and females grow horns—but the great mass of this old boy quickly identifies him as a superb bull.

everywhere. It would take years before I understood that African man and African game don't coexist like Americans and whitetail deer, that game would be present only in specific areas set aside for game or where the economics favored the development of game. Right then I knew that the weather was hot and humid, the thornbush stark yet beautiful in its own way, and I hoped there was some game where we were going.

We collided with the storm clouds about a half hour from camp. Huge raindrops pelted the windows and raised little puffs of red dust as they impacted on the roadside, then spatterings of mud as the dust turned to goo. It didn't rain long, but Willem viewed it as a good sign. The area was too dry, and rains now would improve our prospects within a few days.

Block 26—we were in the northern fringe of it now. About 800 square miles of thornbush bordered by Tsavo National Park on the west and Tanzania on the south, it was fine elephant country, and in the days

17

when elephant hunting was open it produced large numbers of big tuskers. It was fine lion country, too, and home to a tremendous variety of plains game—impala, Grant's gazelle, gerenuk, warthog, fringe-eared oryx, zebra, hartebeeste, lesser kudu, giraffe, buffalo. Some animals would be resident year-round, but the herd animals—the great cats' main prey—would follow the new green as the rains progressed. Willem had a way of being painfully honest without totally dashing his client's hopes. Right now, he told me, the concentrations of game—zebra, buffalo, wildebeeste, and the lions that would follow them—were off to the west deep inside the park. These rains were a good sign, since they would bring new green and the great herds would eventually come. We had two weeks, so the unspoken question was, "Would any of this happen in time to do us any good?" Unspoken, because I wasn't sure I wanted to hear the answer.

The country here was largely dead flat. Ahead lay a few rocky hills, the *kopjes* so familiar in much of Africa. Willem pointed to the largest one. "That's Mount Kasigall. It isn't really a mountain, more like a big rockpile. But it is the commanding terrain feature in this area, plus it's about the only year-round water source locally. We'll find our new home at its base."

And so it was. The old Bedford had made it, and the camp was all set to move into. Centered around a huge baobab tree with Mount Kasigall looming overhead, it wasn't as pretty as Mount Kenya had been, but it was a fine place to camp. James, the first cook, had just baked some fresh bread as we arrived, and it was still piping hot when he brought us a loaf and a tin of butter along with tea. To a member of the Wonder Bread generation, fresh-baked bread is always a treat—but no one, my grandmother included, could top the bread James baked in his tin oven on a good bed of coals.

We had arrived a bit late for serious hunting, but the camp needed meat and I was chomping at the bit to get out and see some country. Philosophically, Willem was probably more serious about trophy selection than I was, and I was fortunate to have chosen him. I didn't know the difference between good trophies and just average trophies, and many times I would have settled for less than the quality that Willem insisted on. After a decade, many of those Kenya trophies are still on the wall and still rank high in the books, and I'm much more proud of them than I would be of lesser animals. But there was a much more practical reason why Willem insisted on only the best. Just a year before, at admittedly low prices, I could have purchased licenses for several impala,

18

warthog, gazelle, hartebeeste, zebra, and such. Only on the hard-to-come-by species would I have been limited to one permit, so shooting for the pot and for lion baits with little regard for trophy quality would have been possible and economical. A few months before, during what would be Kenya's last year of hunting, the rules had changed dramatically. License fees and subsequent trophy fees were increased tremendously, and with very few exceptions only one animal of a species could be taken. It required a change in tactics, for there could be just one impala taken, just one gazelle, just one zebra. Willem understood this better than I did, and he had laid his plans accordingly.

Grant's gazelle, for example, were very poor in that area. Actually, they weren't Grant's gazelle at all, but were the much shorter-horned Peter's gazelle, virtually indistiguishable from the typical Grant's race except a bit more pale and much less impressive in the horn. Willem had determined that a really good trophy wasn't possible, so we would quickly look for something representative and use my one gazelle for camp meat.

Over the next two weeks we would see few gazelle in the area, so the one we found was surprisingly accommodating and actually quite good. He was in a small herd with several females and a couple of smaller males, all feeding along slowly in their alert, nervous fashion. We made a short stalk, and he fell to a single shot from the Ruger .30-06. There was nothing truly remarkable about any of it, except that it was the first animal in a new area, it was the exact animal we had gone out to find, and he had gone down cleanly. The rifle had felt good, and the shot had gone where I had called it. Just maybe, it seemed, we had turned a new leaf. The gazelle's liver that night, beautifully grilled by James, seemed to cap a day that had brought nothing but good fortune and good omens.

The next day was spent largely on an exploratory trip to see the country, check the water situation, see what animals were most abundant, and of course and always, look for lion tracks. On our way into camp the previous day we had passed through a light shower, but as we got deeper into the hunting block well south of camp it was obvious that the area had received heavy rains.

It was obvious, too, that my misgivings of the previous day were uncalled for. Rain or no rain, the area was full of game; the deeper we got into the area, the more animals we saw. Off across a pan, skittish oryx with their rapier horns; zebra fading into the thornbush; giraffes picking leaves from the tallest acacia; impala and hartebeeste in plenty—this was very much the Africa I had imagined and had come to see. The track followed the contour of a low range of hills, and we stopped on a little knoll to glass. To our right, the ground fell away to thornbush-studded plain, with the Tsavo Park boundary somewhere out there in the shimmering mirage. To the left, more broken ground, the kind of country where we would look for lesser kudu in the days to come. To the south, open plain and thornbush as far as the eye could see; Tanzania was somewhere out there. From our vantage point we could view oryx, giraffe, zebra, impala, gazelle, and hartebeeste all in one vista. But we weren't really hunting that day; we were answering questions, so we moved on.

Close by the park boundary—a wide, well-kept dirt road—were many elephant, small family groups and large herds. We took time to take a few pictures but disturbed them as little as possible. One herd had a great bull, perhaps 80 pounds of ivory per side, long and beautifully curved in the fashion of East African tusks. A cow made a mock

The fringe-eared oryx is the smallest of the oryx tribe. This bull with 31-inch horns is a fine specimen, the best seen of many. Boddington used his Ruger .30-06 to reach out for this bull. Oryx are extremely tough, and are one African species that can be very hard to put down.

Elephant on the open plains is a rare sight in today's Africa, and good ivory in such a herd rarer still. Legal elephant hunting had been closed for several seasons when Boddington hunted Kenya, and although herds like this were a common sight, evidence of heavy poaching was just as common.

charge, causing Willem to jam the Toyota into reverse, so we kept on going and left them in peace.

There was new green close by the park, drawing out the elephant and the other plains game, but the waterholes we checked were still bone dry. As the day progressed, we crisscrossed the area, checking for sign and stopping to glass occasionally. There was good news and bad news; virtually all of the antelope species were present in the area, including eland, and more would be coming in daily. There were lion tracks, but those we saw were very old, baked into the ground during the last rain—maybe two to three weeks before from the look of the grass. There were no buffalo whatsoever, and nothing to do but wait and hope some moved in.

Since it had been a dry year in this part of Kenya, van Dyk reckoned a good warthog would be hard to find. Warthogs must have daily water, and their numbers drop quickly in a drought. Although we had seen a few other pigs, Willem didn't hesitate when he saw the glint of ivory through the brush. The boar was running, antenna-tail held high, and I couldn't hit him. I missed, missed again, and kept on missing—much to the delight of van Dyk and his crew. Finally I connected, rolling the pig in a great cloud of dust and drawing resounding applause from my audience. "You know," van Dyk commented, "you Americans tend to be very good shots at long range, but not too good on running game. Now the Germans, they love to shoot the running pigs." He performed a caricature of man standing exaggeratedly upright, head back, stiffly swinging a rifle on a moving target. "Just like in the Black Forest." He grinned slyly. "This is one animal that we can take another of. We'll try to get you some more target practice if we see another good one."

This was a very nice warthog with nicely matched teeth, and my horrible shooting—somehow carefully arranged by van Dyk—didn't matter as much as it had on the Mountain. Oh, I'd done some creative swearing while I shot at the warthog; a few choice phrases might have really impressed my troops back home. But I wasn't mad now, or particularly embarrassed. I was worried, though. "Much more target practice like that and I'll run out of ammo before this thing is over with." Van Dyk laughed, and then I attempted my first joke in Swahili. Holding up a .30-06 cartridge for Njomo, Muindi, and Musili to see, I told them all was well, that I had *mingi sana risase*—very many bullets—and we all laughed, and it was all right.

We had overnighted in Nairobi on our way down from Mount Kenya, and the next morning Sharon had come down with a nagging stomach ailment that would plague her, in varying degrees of intensity, for the rest of the trip. Over the years I've learned that camp fare is far safer than anything you can eat in town, but at the time we figured just the opposite and she was paying the price. I stayed well throughout, but from that point Sharon spent a good deal of the time in camp reading, resting, and trying one patent medicine after another. Turnabout is fair play, though. After leaving Kenya we went on to Egypt to see the pyramids and the Karnak temples. Sharon was feeling pretty good by then, but I made the horrible mistake of having fish in a Cairo restaurant, and it was my turn—I was certain I was going to die, and was actively looking forward to the end.

Our game plan for the rest of the hunt was simple. There were several species of antelope that we wanted, and some, such as a big impala or eland, might be found literally anywhere in the block. Those animals would be stalked if and when we saw a good one, but they wouldn't be specifically hunted. Others, like the lesser kudu or oryx, would most likely be found in a particular area. We'd plan more specific hunts for them. And of course, wherever we went, we would be looking for lion tracks and planning where to hang a bait.

On later hunts, I would hunt with professionals who literally saturated an area with cat baits, and I would hunt with others who were more sparing. Our block was a huge area, and widely dispersed baits do cause a logistical problem—if you can't check 'em, there's no point in hanging 'em! Still, I think we might have done better with a few more baits than we ended up with. Willem agreed, but with the licensing situation, there was nothing to be done. I had but one zebra, regardless of whether I was willing to pay for more or not, and I had two Coke's hartebeeste on license. These were literally the only lion baits available, so they would have to be allocated with utmost care. If things happened to fall into place, part of an oryx or eland could serve for bait, but the really desirable trophies would have to be taken as the opportunities arose, not when we happened to need a piece of cat food. Aside from being a sound game plan, it was literally the only one available.

That day we were presented a magnificent stroke of luck in the form of a fine eland, largest of the antelope tribe but surprisingly wary and skittish. This one was a real gift, a record book bull taken from a big herd that chanced to cross our trail close by the park boundary. His horns were long and massive and had a gnarled ridge that followed the spiral, truly a fine trophy. That evening we would find that there's more to an eland than his horns! This huge beast simply must be Africa's finest-eating game, to my taste even better than the delicate gazelles. We

The impala is one of the most common animals in many parts of Africa—but finding a trophy ram is often difficult. On the Tsavo plain it took a lot of looking to find an East African impala of this quality. Trackers Musili, left, and Muindi, both of the Wakamba tribe, are pleased this animal is finally in the bag.

butchered him on the the spot, and every scrap was hauled back to camp to be eaten fresh or dried as *biltong*, the air-dried jerky that is used in place of money over so much of Africa. Even the tripes were saved—or eaten raw on the spot by Willem and his enthusiastic crew. Sorry, but I had to draw the line on that one. It was late in the morning by the time the eland was skinned, butchered, and loaded, so we drove back to camp with our prize—and made many points with the crew.

During the next few days we hunted hard for just about everything. We looked over literally hundreds of impala and many score of oryx, but saw none that pleased van Dyk. In truth, we saw plenty that would have pleased me, at least at the moment, but they weren't good enough for van Dyk. We looked through some good lesser kudu country, but so far had seen nothing, not even a female. Gerenuk, too, seemed scarce in the area. These lovely giraffe-necked antelope, often called Waller's gazelle, are so typical of East Africa that I wanted one desperately. But I think we saw only one small male and a couple of females in the first week in the area. Both the gerenuk and the lesser kudu had me worried.

Of course, the lion situation was a constant concern. After a day or two Willem decided we should get a bait up, whether we had tracks or not. Rather than at the park boundary, where we were checking for tracks regularly, he wanted to bait in the hills off to the west, a long shot but an area where he had pulled in some fine lions in years gone by. It was also an area where we would be hunting lesser kudu, so checking a bait there wouldn't alter our hunting plans. This first bait would be the zebra, the only zebra we could shoot, and I wanted it to be a big stallion.

Everybody, hunter and nonhunter alike, appreciates the beauty of a zebra rug, but few understand how anyone could shoot an animal so similar to the horse. That is, at least, those who have never tried. Zebra are wary and they're spooky, and in the brush the level of camouflage afforded by those seemingly-bright stripes is astounding. Taking just any zebra isn't a particularly tough trick, 'tis true. But if you care about markings—and you should, considering the license fees for zebra—and if you care about sex, as many do, Africa's striped horse can offer an interesting little hunt.

We made several abortive stalks before we got into position on our chosen herd, and we spent several long minutes making sure which was the stallion as the animals stood in belly-deep yellow grass. Finally Willem gave the go-ahead, based simply on the attitude of this animal that we had singled out. He was quartered to us—and indeed he was a "he"—at about 200 yards, and the 180-grain Nosler from my Ruger

The steinbok is common in plains regions literally from one end of Africa to another. They're a beautiful little buck, and are usually taken at long range.

took him down cleanly. We skinned him quickly. In theory, lions don't care whether their meat is still wrapped or not—and of course I wanted to save the skin, an absolutely perfect black-and-white skin with no trace of shadow striping.

In those closing days of Kenya's hunting it cost me about $250 in licenses and trophy fees to shoot that zebra. The license, probably a quarter of that figure, had been purchased in Nairobi prior to the start of the safari. The balance would be paid after the hunt was over, and that second portion, perhaps as much as $200, would go to the tribal council representing the people of Block 26. I wouldn't be surprised if there was some corruption involved, but in theory it was one of the best game management systems I've seen in Africa; it made it worth the locals' time to make sure there was game there for the safari business.

My zebra would ultimately cost me $250, plus God knows how much in shipping, tanning, and such. His demise might actually have helped his herd. The sad part was that, at any of several dozen shops in Nairobi, I could have had my pick of zebra hides, already tanned and ready to hang, for as little as $70. And it's a sure thing that no game department, tribal council, or anyone else save the poacher, his protector in the government, and the shop owner (with the last two generally being the same person) would see any of the money. Kenya had Africa's most developed safari industry, and in its day Africa's most enlightened and most sophisticated game management. But it also had Africa's most organized poaching, and that ultimately proved too powerful. Poaching and legitimate hunting can never coexist, and in Kenya the poaching won out.

The twelfth of March was a red-letter day. I had seen many fine oryx by then, or at least many that looked just fine. There are four African oryx and one more in the deserts of Arabia. With all subspecies both males and females have horns, with the length often going to the females but horn girth always to the males. All oryx are the very devil to judge. This particular breed was the fringe-eared oryx, so-called because of prominent black tufts on the eartips. Light brown to dove-gray in color with attractive black-and-white facial markings, the oryx is a beautiful animal. Stout of build, much like a donkey, it's one of Africa's few fierce antelope. Strong of heart, it's hard to put down with even a well-placed bullet, and it knows how to use its long, straight horns, as so many lions have learned the hard way. These, the fringe-eared oryx, have the shortest horns. At one time a head in the mid-30s might have been possible, but today anything approaching 30 inches is very, very good. Of course, I couldn't have called an oryx within six inches, and I really didn't know what van Dyk was looking for—I only knew that we'd seen a great many oryx and I couldn't tell one from another!

And then, far off across a pan, there were four bachelor bulls. And any of them were better than anything we'd seen. Even I could tell that after some careful study, but Willem knew it in a glance. Even at 800 yards they were nervous. We cut the motor and waited, and eventually they settled down and grazed in and out of the thorn, only partially visible in the increasing midday heat waves. Cover was sparse, so van Dyk told me not to hold out much hope. I didn't have much—we'd made several stalks on oryx over the previous few days, and had never been close to taking a shot. But we hadn't been totally serious, had been only shopping with no intent to buy. This time, if we could get close enough, we would finish the oryx business.

I crawled out on my side, the side away from the distant oryx, and van Dyk followed. With the truck left in plain sight, we circled away using the sparse cover as well as we could. It was a hot morning, and the sun was well overhead by now. I remember sweating heavily, and I remember gasping for air several times on that long crawl. Once, at 400 yards, we almost committed. But just as I slipped the safety the herd moved a little, and there was now some thornbush we could use to get closer.

At 250 yards we reached the end of the line. We were crouched behind a tiny thorn tree, but only a few blades of grass separated us from the four bulls. We had been watching a fine bull on the left with an unusually wide spread. I took a rest across a spindly branch, ignoring the thorns digging into my arm, and set the crosshairs on his shoulder. Willem gripped my arm and whispered, "Do you want length or spread?"

"Length," I replied, and I still feel that way—I prefer oryx with long, nearly parallel horns, while others like horns that diverge with a wide tip-to-tip. Nobody's wrong, of course, but this was a time where a choice could be made.

"Then take the second from right. He isn't wide at all, but he might be a bit longer."

I shifted the crosshairs quickly, and at the shot the oryx scattered like quail. I couldn't tell which was which, let alone get off another shot. Njomo brought the truck up, and with a sinking feeling in my stomach I joined the search for blood. Musili found it quickly, good bright blood, and a few yards farther we could see it had pumped from both sides, an exit wound as well as an entrance. The shot had gone as called, through the lungs but a just a shade high, and the oryx was down 200 yards farther on. He was a beauty, the best we'd seen, with lovely parallel 30-plus horns.

We rolled into camp that noon with the horn honking and enjoyed a lovely lunch of cold rolled breast of eland—perhaps the finest cut of meat I've eaten before or since— then took a nap to let the edge go off this particularly hot day.

By midafternoon we were in a cool glade of hardwoods, trying to sort out a large herd of impala. We'd gotten just a glimpse of the herd ram, then he'd taken his ladies and gone into the thick stuff. These were East African impala, potentially much larger in the horn than the southern variety, and van Dyk was determined to get one typical of this large race. In previous years I could have—and probably would have—taken several of these pretty reddish antelope, using them for baits and for camp meat, and saving the best for a trophy. Now I could take just one, and though there were plenty in the area, rams that would satisfy my mentor were scarce.

At a quick glance, this one had looked good. Through the trees we had seen him several more times, and each time he had looked better. He must have had 30 females with him—a greedy fellow—and the brush was impossibly thick where he had taken them. We had followed as well as we could, but now were at a stalemate. A hundred yards to our front was a long brushline. Just beyond it was a cliff of crumbling moss-covered rock, sloping up quickly to a low hill mass. Somewhere between the brushline and the cliff, now unseen, were our ram and his harem. There were baboons in there as well, and they knew we were here. From the racket they were making, everything else in the woods knew as well.

If the impala went out to the left we'd never see them, but if they came out to the right—and it seemed most likely they would—then there was one narrow opening in that brushline where a guy just might have a quick shot. If they ran, no chance at all, but if they filed past, and if somebody could tell the shooter when the ram was coming through, there would be a chance.

So we waited endlessly. I had my rifle rested over the fallen log and the crosshairs trained only on that narrow opening; van Dyk, to my left, had his Zeiss 8x30s trained into the brush, hoping to pick up horns in enough time to warn me.

It took a long time, but it worked like clockwork. Eventually the ewes started through the gap, one at a time, and Willem was able to tick them by. As they went I practiced on each—pick it up at the edge of the gap, find the shoulder, very short swing, then squeeze. The space was about a full body length, perhaps four feet, and there would be much less than a second to make the shot.

I lost count of the females, but finally Willem could make out horns two or three back in the bunch. I got ready, slipping the safety and hoping I, too, could see horns and be certain. I could. I picked them up before the target was clear, and had the crosshairs on his shoulder before he cleared the brush. He came quickly, more quickly than the does, but I was swinging well with the front of his shoulder and the crosshairs were steady when the rifle crashed. The ram fell right there in the opening, without a twitch, and Willem, who never swore, said,

"F---, man, how did you make that shot?" I didn't know, but I felt I'd finally hit my stride. Indeed, I was not to miss a shot, or need a finishing shot, again in that trip—but how I wished I could have had another chance at that buffalo at this stage in the safari!

The days passed all too quickly, and we could watch the new green spring up. Daily, too, we could see that more game was coming into the area. There was a small lion in our block now, probably a very young male. He was traveling alone, and he was a busy young fellow. We cut his tracks by the zebra bait, just passing by with no meat taken, and we found a young oryx that he'd killed. That was the same day that we saw

When the author took this lovely lesser kudu, Kenya was the only place the animal could be hunted. Today Kenya is gone, but the animal may be hunted in both northern Tanzania and southeastern Ethiopia. Professional hunter Willem van Dyk worked hard to show Boddington this bull—and he was worth the effort.

Hanging a bait is typical practice for most safaris that inlude cat hunting. A zebra—one of the staples in a lion's diet—is one of the preferred lion baits. A small male eventually fed here, but the big lions never came.

a beautiful cheetah hunting along the edge of a meadow, and it was also the same day that we surprised a big pack of African hunting dogs, perhaps the most fearsome predators on the continent. We picked up a fine steinbok at noon, a lovely terrier-size antelope. Creatures of the sun, steinbok can be found in the openings, leaping and jumping in the midday sun when other game has sought the deepest shade.

We had seen just one lesser kudu, a female, and now our hunting was becoming ever more specialized—lion and lesser kudu, and little else. We had hung a hartebeeste about a mile from the park boundary, where the breeze would blow its scent deep into Tsavo. Typically we would head into the hills early, take a quick look at our first bait, now gone off badly, then hunt carefully for lesser kudu. When the heat was up and the animals had gone to shade we would head towards the park boundary, checking that bait and checking along the boundary road for lion tracks.

We had checked the zebra bait fairly early, then headed towards some brush-covered hills that in years past had held good numbers of lesser kudu. A lone hartebeeste stood at the end of a long meadow, and in the slanting morning sun it looked like there was something terribly wrong with him—mange perhaps. He ducked into the brush at our approach, so we followed quickly, planning to dispatch him if he was indeed as sick as he looked.

We plunged through the brushline and Willem pulled up short. Just 75 yards away, picking her way carefully through some tangled vine, was a lesser kudu female. We waited and looked, and behind her, just hints of shape in the brush, were two more. Then they moved a bit, and sunlight glinted off the horn of a fourth animal. We waited them out; their path would bring them past an opening, and all three females had stepped daintily through it. The male held up, just a hint of shape behind tangled brush. Finally he stepped clear, and the vertical crosshair found the first white stripe on his shoulder.

He made three jumps after the shot, then piled up. Though we had been hunting them hard, I had never before gotten a good look at a lesser kudu. They're a marvelous animal, perhaps the most beautiful of all the spiral horns. Not imposing like a greater kudu, but with the same pleasing combination of gray and white, yet with a daintiness lost in his larger cousin. This was a mature bull with the double twist, though not a great bull. Still, we never saw another male, and to this day I'm quite happy to have this one on my wall . . . .

We were getting short on time now, but the lions were coming. There were fresh tracks on the boundary road that morning—going back out of our block—but the bait was unmolested. Now we had to put all our cards on the table, so we set out at midday to get another hartebeeste and hang our last bait. The wind had come up, and it was overcast and cool. Nothing was moving, and for once we simply couldn't find even a hartebeeste.

Finally a lone bull stood facing us, staring out of some brush across an open pan at some incredible distance. I was getting a bit cocky now; it seemed I couldn't miss with the .30-06, and I saw no reason not to take the shot, it being the only opportunity we'd had. It seems I truly was on a roll, for I distinctly remember holding a full hartebeeste high and two body widths into the crosswind. Willem knew it was luck when the bullet caught him squarely on the brisket as he faced us. I knew it, too, but I wouldn't admit it. Muindi, Musili, and Njomo were much impressed—it was witchcraft to them.

We hung the bait as close to the park boundary as the law would allow, spacing it out from our other hartebeeste by a mile or so. Now all the baits were out and, except for a gerenuk and perhaps a dik dik, all the licenses were filled. The cards really were on the table, and we had four days left to hunt. There was nothing we could do but wait and hope. Well, perhaps there was *one* more thing.

With van Dyk's blessing, that night I went to the campfire of Muindi, Musili, and old Ngili, the skinner. I entreated them to speak to their ancestors and see if they might assist us in this matter of the lion. We sat around their small fire, squatting on bleached zebra skulls picked up for the purpose. Beer was drunk and snuff passed, with some of each carefully spilled on the ground so the ancestors could have their share. Much solemn conversation flowed in the Wakamba tongue, and eventually Ngili concluded that the old ones had been made aware of our plight, but only time would tell whether they could help or not.

The next morning there were fresh tracks by the second bait, but still no meat taken. It was a small lion, but miles from our bait in the hills so it seemed unlikely it was the same animal. That evening, finally, we saw a fine gerenuk, and I took him with a fairly long shot. He was in a brushy area that we had glassed for gerenuk three or four times already, but somehow van Dyk knew this was where we would find one if we kept looking.

In the gray dawn of the following morning we drove the boundary road. There, just a pale shadow in the red of the road, was the beast we had been looking for. Lion! Or lioness, I should say, returning to the Park after a night's hunt. There were eight in this pride, all females. We watched them cross in front of and behind the truck, and sped away when one big lioness made a mock charge. The gender was wrong, but the lions were moving in, and quickly.

We drove on down the boundary, looking for tracks, then stopped for a moment to glass a long stretch of roadway ahead. Like distant thunder, a lion roared off in the Park, and was answered by yet another. *Ngruma*, the Swahili word for "roar," is one of few words that does the sound justice. It was the only roaring we heard that trip, and it would be years before I would hear it again—but it's a sound that stays with you always, and is one of the many things that calls you back to Africa time and again, just for the off chance of hearing it once more.

One lion was off on the plain, the other was answering from a low range of hills just to the west—the wrong side—of the boundary. We were within a mile of both cats, but could do nothing. They were adjacent to our baits, and the wind was right, so the game was far from over.

That evening we covered some ground, just looking at game and making a count of both species and animals. It wasn't a particularly good evening in terms of game movement; I think our count came to just over 400. But there were 12 species that evening, a great variety for anywhere in Africa: hartebeeste, zebra, giraffe, gazelle, impala, gerenuk, oryx, warthog, steinbok, dik dik, elephant, and even a hyena slipping off into the brush.

The next day we made one last trip into the hills. Our zebra bait had never been taken, and the law required that it be cut down before we left the area. We saw our cheetah again, plus a very large herd of oryx. We were up on a hill, a fine vantage point, and the oryx were down below. Two youngish bulls had squared off and were doing the best job they could trying to kill each other with those sharp, deadly spears. They would rush together, not unlike wild sheep, locking horns with a tremendous crash, but staying together and using powerful neck and shoulder muscles to push each other, neither able to quite gain an advantage. Red dust flew and finally the fight moved into the brush where we could no longer see, so we retired and left them to settle their squabble one way or the other.

The signs of poaching weren't severe in this area. There were a few elephant skulls scattered about, but this had been one of Kenya's best blocks for good ivory until the closure of elephant hunting, so the skulls could have been from legally-taken elephant. That morning we did find a fresh hartebeeste carcass, dead within the hour. It was still warm, and there seemed not a mark on it. Then I saw a small hole, not quite right for a bullet, on the animal's neck. We cut inside carefully, and there was the iron head of an arrow and several inches of broken-off shaft. The black smear of fresh poison still dripped from just behind the arrowhead. I wish now that I'd kept it as a souvenir, but instead we turned it in to the game warden when we passed back through Voi. That afternoon, our next-to-last, we sat out a severe thunderstorm in camp, watching the lightning and listening to the rain pummel the canvas. We were finished, really; we had had our safari, and I was resigned to the fact that I couldn't have a lion. I was getting used to the idea, and I was happy with all the other fine trophies.

My journal entry for the following day, our last day, is short and to the point. "3/20—Tracked seven lions from 10:00 to noon. Caught up with them short of Park boundary—two young males. Decided not to shoot."

That's too simply put, but at the time I was too overcome with conflicting emotions to put it any differently. We had decided this last day

Often called the "giraffe antelope," the gerenuk or Waller's gazelle is a species unique to East Africa. This one is a southern gerenuk, now huntable only in Tanzania. The very similar northern gerenuk is now hunted only in Ethiopia.

would be an easy day—cut down the baits, look at a few more animals, and pack up for tomorrow's long drive back to Nairobi. That was the plan until 10:00 a.m., when we hit fresh lion tracks headed, for the first time, into our area instead of back towards the Park. We tracked on foot, plunging ahead quickly into the midday heat. There were five lionesses and, from the tracks, two good-size males. Our hopes, rising all morning, were dashed for the first time about an hour onto the track. They made a great swinging circle, ultimately making a beeline straight for the Park. We followed a bit farther to be certain, and when we were sure Willem suggested we cut across, pick up the truck, and follow them the rest of the way out just in case.

The funny thing was, with the Park less than a thousand yards ahead, they hadn't crossed. We blundered into the first lioness resting in the

Willem van Dyk, skinner N'Gili, and the author with the results of a two-week hunt on the Tsavo plain. Lion, the primary quarry, wasn't in the cards—but with African hunting, it's good to have something to come back for!

shade by a little waterhole, partially filled from the previous day's rain. Then we got more careful and began ticking them off, looking for the two males. The first male was young with no mane at all; to my eyes he was indistinguishable from the lionesses.

The big male was the farthest into the brush, and we saw him last. He was mature, and he was big in the body. But like his little brother, he was virtually bald. We had all the time in the world to make up our minds. It was high noon now, the heat of the day. The lions weren't really happy with our presence, but they were sleepy and comfortable and had no pressing plans. "There's your lion," said Willem van Dyk, wanting it to grow a mane as badly as I did. "I can't tell you what to do. Many clients these days settle for maneless lions, and some even like them. The decision must be up to you alone."

The crosshairs settled on him several times, but he wasn't the lion I had come for, nor the lion I wanted for my den and my memories. I couldn't squeeze the trigger, and eventually he tired of the game and faded off into the brush with his pride, at long last heading towards the safety of the Park.

It was a quiet trip back to camp that afternoon, and a solemn crowd of black faces as Musili recounted, in their language, what had transpired. Later, in Los Angeles, Willem would confide that he was

35

glad I hadn't shot. At the time, he left me alone with my thoughts, and my thoughts were unclear. I didn't know whether I had done the right thing, and it was several years and several safaris later before I became certain that it had indeed been the right thing. Muindi, Musili, and Ngili were even more confused. To them, a lion was a lion, and their ancestors had lived up to their part of the bargain.

I studied my Swahili dictionary for a few moments, then found the words to tell them that, indeed, their grandfathers had been most generous in giving me a chance at this lion. But I wanted a *"doumi m'kubwa,"* a big male, and I showed them with gestures the kind of mane I sought, and I told them I didn't mind not shooting this lion, for now I could return so we could hunt together for this lion's grandfather. With that, they brightened up considerably, and once more it was the happy camp that it had been for so many fine days.

That night Sharon and I were summoned to the campfire of Musili, Muindi, and Ngili, the aristocracy of the camp staff. There we found the entire staff gathered and three zebra-skull stools set aside as seats of honor for van Dyk, Sharon and me. Formally we thanked the ancestors for our last-minute chance at the lion, and we acknowledged that they alone had been responsible. More beer and snuff were passed, with appropriate portions spilled on the ground.

Ngili, as the eldest and having the special status of skinner, acted as spokesman as they got down to the business of the evening. We had been good clients, we were told; we had shot well, and I had helped load the animals and fix flat tires. We were each handed carefully-crafted fly whisks with ironwood handles, the whisks made of oryx and eland tail. Mine had small circles of elephant bone inset into the handle, and dangling from the polished wood was what appeared to be the dewclaw of a lion. Willem showed it to me, explaining that it had been carved from the dewclaw of my eland and was to remind me that I had earned my lion even though I had not shot him.

It was a fine farewell speech, and the presents were lovely. We were deeply touched, and we promised we would return to hunt the lion with them again. I intended to, but unknown to all of us hunting in Kenya had just a matter of days left to run. Now, a decade later, the rumors persist that Kenya will reopen. I no longer believe them, but if it ever happens that's still a promise I'd like to fulfill.

CHAPTER III
ON THE SABI RIVER

The late 1970s were quite possibly the lowest ebb of African hunting, at least in recent times. All of East Africa was gone—Kenya, Tanzania, Uganda, and Mozambique. Ethiopia was not open, Angola was finished, C.A.R. was on-again, off-again at best, and Zaire was, as it has remained, more a rumor than a fact. There were a few bright spots, however. Hunting in Sudan was in its heyday, and business was rolling along in Zambia and Botswana. South West Africa and South Africa were becoming ever more popular, and the safari industry and game ranching industries in the latter were growing by leaps and bounds.

Rhodesia was known to offer some fine trophies, but the hunting there was under a cloud of uncertainty. Ian Smith's government was winning the long terrorist war, at least on the battlefield, but the politics were getting ever more complicated, and the survival of Rhodesia into the 1980's seemed unlikely. To some extent, it was the very uncertainty that made Rhodesia attractive—especially if one's budget was limited! Some of the best areas, including the vast Zambezi Valley, could not be hunted. In fact, during the war years Rhodesia—now Zimbabwe—was largely a destination for plains game safaris. As always, it was fine leopard country, but the best lion, buffalo, and elephant areas were far too unsafe for safaris.

Since it was mostly a plains game hunt, and since the clients would have the inconveniences of traveling in mine-proofed vehicles and lodging in fortified positions, hunting in Rhodesia was truly a bargain in the late seventies. Cut off from foreign exchange for more than a decade and with the end of the war finally in sight—regardless of who won—more and more large landowners were looking at the safari business as a means of survival in the increasingly uncertain future. That was where Roger Whittal found himself as the decade drew to a close.

As the owner of 100,000-acre Humani Ranch, fine bushveld country on the Sabi River in southeastern Rhodesia, he'd managed to hold things together through a decade and a half of terrorist warfare, and he'd managed to keep himself and his family alive. Like so many land-owners, he needed the hard cash that hunting could bring.

Teaming up with him was Barrie Duckworth, formerly of the Rhodesian Game Department. Young, tall, and handsome, Duckworth fit the Hollywood image of the professional hunter to a T. Working elephant control in the parks, he had shot his thousand elephant long before he was 30, yet he had a boyish shyness that made him tremendously likable.

Some friends in Los Angeles had recently hunted with these folks and had come back raving about them and about the fine hunting that Humani Ranch offered. In the months since the Kenya safari I had done an overseas tour in Okinawa, leaving the active Marine Corps at its conclusion. I was in Los Angeles, writing free-lance and working with a booking agency arranging hunting trips. The price and the opportunities in Rhodesia were too good to pass up—and I was more than ready to see more of Africa.

The terrorist war had become particularly ugly in the last year or so. The end was in sight, and each side was jockeying for last-minute positioning. The planes had been shot down over Kariba and the survivors butchered, and I'd be lying if I said that wasn't on my mind when Sharon and I climbed into the Air Rhodesia Viscount for the short flight from Johannesburg to Bulawayo. The plane was painted flat, nonreflective gray, and our pretty seatmate was kind enough to point out that the paint helped confuse heat-seeking S.A.M. missiles, a most comforting thought. She also prepared us for the very fast descent without lights, but she was good enough to offer us a ride into Bulawayo—which was gratefully accepted!

Her name was Midge Joubert, and she had been shopping in Jo'burg. She and her husband of just a few months, burly Dave Joubert, had a farm outside of Bulawayo, and he also was embarking on a side business of professional hunting. Over the years we've stayed in touch, and while I've never hunted with Dave, a number of friends have. As a hunter I hear he's good, but I'll remember him always for his kindness in seeing us to our hotel that night. In truth, we were safer in Bulawayo than we would be at JFK—but it didn't feel that way at the time!

The next morning we made the appointed phone calls and learned that Duckworth himself would meet us in Bulawayo and fly to Chiredzi with us. We had expected him to meet us at the Buffalo Range airport at Chiredzi, so we were actually getting better organized than we had expected to be! Barrie came by at midmorning, quickly took charge, and we were off to southeast Zimbabwe, the lowveld country. The only problem was Air Rhodesia's refusal to check Barrie's fragmentation grenades. His 7.62mm F.N. and loaded magazines were no problem, but they drew the line at the grenades, much to Duckworth's dismay.

At Bulawayo we transferred to a Cessna for the quick trip up to Humani Ranch. We flew low over the trees, and I was struck by how different this country was from Kenya. Characterized by mopane woodlands, most of the Rhodesias—Southern Rhodesia (now Zimbabwe) and Northern Rhodesia (now Zambia)—are vast regions of thornbush, with few natural openings. The savannas of East Africa simply don't exist, and the country is much more similar to the oak forests of Appalachia. For a man who loves to glass, I expected it would be tough hunting, and in that I wasn't disappointed!

Sturdy Roger Whittal was there to meet us at the dirt strip on Humani, and in a matter of minutes we were moved into the sprawling old farmhouse and Anne Whittal was making us feel at home. A dentist friend of mine from Los Angeles, Ron Norman, had arrived a few days earlier and would be on the ranch through most of our hunt. One of the hands, Hilton Nichols, had taken Ron to another property to look for a blue wildebeeste, so we wouldn't see him until late. But we would see some of his handiwork. The big news on Humani was Ron's huge leopard, taken just the evening before. I saw the skin and the skinned carcass, and I couldn't believe my eyes—this cat was bigger than any mountain lion had a right to be. On Roger's cattle scale, whole, it had weighed 226 pounds! That thornbush is prime leopard country, and many good ones have come off Humani over the years. However, that's also cattle country, and the cats are hunted hard. If they live, they get smart and secretive. It's a fine place to get a big leopard to this day, but getting one is time-consuming and requires intensive effort. Leopard were still on the endangered list then, and it was uncertain whether Americans would ever again be able to import the hides. For that reason leopard wasn't very high on my list, nor was anything else in particular. There was some chance for buffalo, but the herds had been nearly wiped out because of hoof-and-mouth disease—not because the buffalo had hoof-and-mouth, but because it was thought that they might, and throughout the lowveld most of them had been eradicated by the government. Humani had a very few survivors, and they were starting a slow comeback. The area did have excellent kudu, some sable, tons of impala and zebra, klipspringer, duiker, some eland, and, along the river, fine Limpopo bushbuck. I still wanted a buffalo, and we would try to get one. But this time I hadn't established a lot of priorities, and instead intended to take things as they came and enjoy the country. As it happened, fate would do a fine job of establishing the priorities for us.

Ron Norman came in late and, of course, was congratulated on his leopard. In fact, the congratulating lasted a good deal longer than it should, and the alarm went off much too early. Today would be a day for looking around, checking for buffalo tracks, and perhaps putting out a bait or two for leopard.

We found buffalo tracks quite readily, a small herd crossing into some particularly dense woods. We tracked them for a couple of hours, but the wind was wrong and the animals extremely spooky. At one point we could see hooves milling among the trees, and several times the dust as they ran, but there was really no chance on this herd. Like most first days, though, it gave Barrie and me a chance to size each other up. I don't know what he thought of me, of course, but I liked him—he was a good hunter, a good host, and good companion, and I have never revised that first-day opinion.

Late in the day we did knock over a couple of impala for leopard baits. Impala were amazingly abundant in that area; in some stretches of bush we were literally never out of sight of at least one herd. Oddly, though, among all those impala the trophy quality was consistently average. Southern impala, unlike East African, are for some reason one of the easiest of all African species to put "in the book"—but not in southeastern Zimbabwe. There you'll look long and hard for a really good one. In this area, taking an impala was hardly a trick, but Barrie's method of baiting fascinated me. We staked the impala out on the ground, whereas everything I knew or thought I knew said to put the bait in a tree. In that region there are no hyenas, and lions are quickly hunted down as cattle killers. It seems there is no reason not to put a bait on the ground! I wish I could say the system works, but we were never to get a nibble on any of our strategically placed baits. That doesn't necessarily mean they wouldn't have worked. It might simply mean that a hungry cat didn't happen to find our baits!

Next to impala, greater kudu were perhaps the most common game on the ranch. It was expected that sooner or later a big kudu would fall into place, so we didn't hunt for them specifically. Indeed, we saw kudu every day—but we didn't see big bulls every day. The sable, on the other hand, was a potential problem. The bush was thick and there were miles of it, and the total sable population on the ranch probably didn't exceed 100. In retrospect, it's amazing that we saw as many sable as we ultimately did.

The first one was spotted on the first day, a lone bull, coal-black and fully mature, but his head was in yellowed leaves and he left before we had a decent look at him. This was early June, the beginning of winter in southern Africa. The country was much like the eastern United States in the early fall, with the leaves dead but most not yet dropped—actually the worst combination of circumstances, both noisy underfoot and still too thick for good visibility. In the next few days I would see a lot of animals with their heads hidden by leaves—and most of them seemed to be sable antelope.

It seemed that there was one very large herd of sable on the ranch, just a couple of smaller herds, and a scattering of lone bulls. It was early in the hunt that we found the big herd for the first time. We were driving along, not looking for sable, and they were feeding in the trees across a rare clearing. Barrie and I bailed out and worked our way through the grass, looking for a good bull. He was there, not a great bull but more than passable, and I will never forget him.

He stood facing me, coal-black with deeply ridged scimitar horns that seemed to sweep back forever. The distance was close, 100 yards, and the crosshairs seemed oh, so steady at the base of his throat. The .375 roared and he ran to the left, vanishing into the trees. With a tremendous clatter the whole herd—mostly unseen 'til now—was off. I wasn't concerned; it was just a matter of stepping into the brush and finding my bull dead. Except that he wasn't there, nor had the big Hornady softpoint left a drop of blood. In fact, I'd missed him clean, as far as we could tell—no blood, no sound of impact, no visible sign of a hit. We looked, and I'm willing to accept that I missed him. But to this day I'll always see the crosshairs steady as a rock on that bull's chest . . . .

We spent an hour looking for sign, then followed after the herd. There must have been 50 sable running together, and after my shot there were too many pairs of eyes to get close that day. We called it off, but now we knew where the big herd was living, and we could try them again another day.

Before we did, though, we had another go at a lone bull. This one was a twin to the one I'd shot at—heavy-horned, very black, with length about 38 inches, typical for the southeastern lowveld. Barrie knew I was gun-shy now, and he wanted me to get in close. We had spotted the bull moving in and out of some thick trees, and in order to get a shot at all, we had to get in very close. Lord, did we get close! He was a black patch in deepest black shadow, and at one point I could almost have touched him with my gun barrel—but for the life of me I couldn't tell how he was standing. Finally, at about 15 yards, he bolted like a whitetail jumping from his bed. My one shot hit a tree, and that was the end of that sable . . .

We trudged back to the truck, approaching from a different direction. In the bush it was easy to forget there was a war on, but the Rhodesians—black and white—couldn't forget it. Barrie's two trackers and our army-assigned bodyguard had stayed by the Land Rover with Sharon while we made our slow stalk in the heat of the day. They had seen people coming from an unexpected direction—us—and had laid down a quick perimeter, motioning Sharon to lie down. We strolled into the clearing with two old Enfields and a German G-3 trained on us . . . .

Later that afternoon we got onto the big herd again. They were feeding slowly through some mixed cover of dense mopanes cut with grassy meadows, and their tracks had crossed the road less than an hour ahead of us. We took the spoor and gained quickly, but the fickle wind gave us away. The herd jumped in thick cover, and all I could see was dust and a forest of scimitar horns.

We followed, drifting off parallel to the tracks to get the wind right, but these sable were well-spooked now and they knew we were after them. Just once the herd held on a small knoll, but there was no way to pick out a bull as they milled just before stampeding again. With the shadows starting to lengthen, Barrie suggested that we give them just one more try, then break off and head for the ranch.

This time they had gone some distance. We were just to the point of giving up when we came to the head of a long, narrow open valley. Barrie scanned ahead quickly, smiled, and turned to me. "I don't know what to say about these sable, but do you want a lovely kudu bull?"

There, at the far end of the valley, was a truly magnificent kudu with four cows. It was the height of the kudu rut, and his neck was swollen and his horns were thrown back. The slanting sunlight played on his vertical stripes and glinted off his horns, and he was clearly the best we had seen.

I found a small tree to rest against, gripping it in my supporting hand and laying the fore-end of the old .375 across my outstretched fingers. For a few seconds the crosshairs wobbled from one end of the bull to the other, but then I got my breathing under control and placed the

The dense riverine bush along the Sabi River was ideal bushbuck habitat, and in the troubled Seventies also provided a haven for terrorists crossing in from nearby Mozambique.

horizontal wire well up on his shoulder for the distance.

The solid "tunk" of the bullet hitting flesh came back to us as the bull faltered, then regained his footing and dashed into the cover with his cows. We ran after him—it was too close to dark to wait. He hadn't gone far, but he wasn't down yet. The .375 crashed again, and we walked up to admire one of Africa's most beautiful antelope.

This one was particularly fine, not because of his horn length, which was actually quite good, but because his horns were massive throughout and beautifully shaped, with tight spirals that formed a lovely V. He was a prime rutting bull, too, with full winter coat and long neck mane of silver and black. I've seen a number of bigger kudu since, and have taken several others—but it's that Rhodesian bull that is hanging on my wall.

By the time we had taken pictures and Barrie had hiked back to get the Land Rover it was nearly dark, and our troops were clearly getting nervous. We stayed with the kudu and were much relieved when we heard Barrie's motor whining as he churned through the brush. We loaded the kudu whole—no simple task, for it was a big-bodied bull. Then, as we drove out of the meadow in the last ebb of twilight, Barrie pointed out a wide game trail that wound down out of the hills and across the opening. Even in the dim light I could see that it was trampled flat by the passage of many large animals, and it struck me that it must be a cattle path.

"Terrorist highway," Barrie explained. "This is one of the routes they use when they come in from Mozambique. They usually don't do much mischief in these parts; they're really just passing through on their way to the TTL—Tribal Trust Lands. But this is no place to be this time of night. You'll want to hang on; I may drive a bit fast."

He picked his way carefully to the road, and then he did indeed drive a bit fast, overdriving his headlights and moving into the curves by feel as much as by sight. On lonely roads the Rhodesians always drove fast, theorizing that forward momentum just might carry them beyond an ambush. We never had a chance to test the theory—and that was just as well—but it was clear that it didn't always work. All the vehicles had heavy plating welded underneath to shield the passengers from mines, but the plating assumed the blast would occur under one of the wheels.

A matter of weeks previously, and not too far away, this very Land Rover had rolled into an ambush triggered by a command-detonated mine—a mine set off by a terrorist who had touched two electrical wires together at just the right instant, sending an electrical impulse to the hidden charge. The blast occurred directly underneath where I was sitting, and enough slipped between the plating to blow off the legs of the passenger. He was a young American, not a hunter but a recent high-school graduate who had come to Rhodesia to work on the ranch and see a bit of Africa. I suspect he was a courageous young fellow who might have done great things had he lived. Terribly mangled, he had gotten off two well-aimed magazines from his F.N.; his fire and the driver's had broke the ambush and forced the Terrs to "take the gap"—break off and run into the bush. But help had been too slow in coming. He died from shock and blood loss before arriving at the hospital.

The Land Rover had been repaired, and now I was sitting in the same seat as we roared down the narrow track. Of course we arrived safely, but I'd be lying if I denied that my palms sweated every inch of the way.

Roger had a large work force on his ranch, mostly of the Mashona tribe. The war had swollen their numbers as many black Rhodesians sought safety from the Terrs. The impala were beyond counting on the ranch, and a good thing, for part of the wages were paid in a meat ration. The next morning Roger asked us to go out and shoot several rams, since it was time for him to distribute meat. I had a lovely little Mexican Mauser in .250 Savage with me, and while we weren't really hunting—shooting was a more apt term—we took care to pick only older rams with badly worn horns. I've never been a fan of the neck shot, being primarily a trophy hunter. That day, though, I was concentrating on head and neck to avoid meat damage. We shot a number of rams, fairly close to the quota Roger had given us, but I clearly recall one old ram with badly worn horns. He went down to a neck shot, pole-axed in his tracks, and we moved on into the glade a bit farther to try to take another out of the herd. I think Barrie shot that one—he was quite deadly with his peep-sighted F.N. assault rifle set on single fire—and we were dragging it back to pick up the one I'd shot earlier. We rounded a thornbush just in time to see my "dead" impala jump up and run off as though nothing had happened. We never did recover him, nor did he leave a drop of blood. I'd just creased him, something that's surprisingly easy to do with the neck shot. It's one of the reasons why I stay away from that shot, concentrating instead on the much larger heart/lung region. And since I rarely try neck shots, I'm probably not good at them. I've never forgotten that impala, and I doubt if I've taken a half-dozen neck shots in all the years since.

When we got back to the ranch, much company had arrived. The Grey's Scouts, a mounted infantry unit, had set up camp just down the road from the ranch. Composed of men with much bush experience, they were highly mobile and changed areas often, patrolling one area for a time, then another to keep the terrorists off guard. In company strength, they would stay on Humani for a couple of weeks, then move to another ranch. I was glad to see them, but I have to admit that they didn't look like much at first glance. I had recently made captain in the Marine Corps Reserves, so had more than just a passing interest in this concept of mounted infantry. They were field troops, many with long hair and beards, and most wore nondescript bush shorts and soft floppy hats—none of the banging helmets and clattering cartridge belts of an American unit. In that war parade-deck appearance meant nothing, but performance in the bush was everything. The Grey's Scouts held an enviable record on that score. Their tactics were to patrol for fresh tracks, then use the horses to overtake their quarry. Up close, they would dismount and use conventional infantry tactics. They didn't look good to my Marine Corps-trained eyes, but in the things that counted they were magnificent.

We had a grand *brie* (barbecue) that night to welcome them to the ranch—kudu steaks, warthog, impala, and Boerworst, the thick, spicy sausage traditional in southern Africa. Those were the days of Jimmy

45

Carter and his hated emissary, Andrew Young, and as the only Americans present we took a fierce, although friendly, verbal beating. America played a strong hand in the transition from Ian Smith's government to the short-lived administration of Bishop Muzorewa; one has to speculate if the ultimate outcome would have been different under a Republican administration.

The days passed all too swiftly. Several times we tracked a big buffalo bull in the dense riverine growth by the Sabi River, but he had been hunted before and proved too smart for us. We never laid eyes on him or the smaller bull he was running with. Nearly a year later a hunter would finally take him, and he was indeed as large as his tracks indicated, with a great spread and an 18-inch boss.

There was a cattle-killing lion on the ranch as well, and we built two different *machans* and sat up for him several nights. Tony Dyer, the great Kenya professional hunter, retired from hunting years ago to his cattle ranch near Mount Kenya. Though sport hunting is closed, he is still able to hunt the occasional cattle killer. Years later he told me that hunting these beasts remained his greatest thrill. It seems that a lion that takes to killing domestic cattle knows that it's doing so at great risk and knows that it will be hunted in turn. According to Tony, such a lion becomes nocturnal and hangs out in the most dense thornbush imaginable. It tends to be solitary, a wanderer that avoids its own kind and rarely returns to a kill, and like a hard-hunted bull elk that ceases bugling, it never roars.

This was such a lion, big and old and very smart. He had been working over Roger's cattle for some time, but no one had ever gotten a shot at him. We waited over his kills for several evenings—first a young steer, then several days later a half-grown heifer. He never came, but one night two serval cats fought on the carcass, hissing and screaming like two tomcats in the back alley. We stayed 'til well after midnight, then returned the next morning to check for tracks. The lion hadn't passed nearby, but the booted tracks of 20 terrorists coming in from Mozambique had. We got on the radio—always monitored at the ranch house in case of emergency—and alerted the Scouts. Later they would catch this band crossing the river, killing several and taking no casualties in a short, sharp contact.

It seemed absurd to be hunting in a war zone, but Rhodesia's terrorist war had gone on so long that it had become just another facet of life. The end was in sight, theoretically; Muzorewa was taking the reins of government, and the future was uncertain. The Rhodesians we met

The klipspringer is a beautiful little buck with multi-colored stiff hairs that are almost tiny quills. Although common nowhere, they are widely distributed throughout Africa. This one was taken on a rocky kopje near the Sabi River—a classic klipspringer haunt.

hated to give up. Militarily they were still winning, but they were tired. Their children had grown up knowing nothing but bush warfare, and they could stand against the world no longer. Most would be glad when it was all over, and most planned to stay for better or worse. Barrie and Roger were among the many who stayed, and today they have developed an excellent safari business. In the years that followed the Zambezi Valley would reopen to hunting, and along with other good outfitters they would secure concessions there for fine elephant, buffalo, and lion. Areas they could hunt the way such game should be hunted,

47

without worry about terrorism or nagging doubts about staying out hunting 'til sundown.

But all that was in the future. Right now there was just this cattle-killing lion that proved too smart for us, a few buffalo along the river, and an awesome influx of booted man-tracks crossing the ranch. We were never to see that lion, but I saw a photo of him sometime later. Roger has defended his cattle against lions and leopards his entire adult life, and he finally outsmarted this one. I wish the luck had been with us—he was a huge old male with a full black mane, incredibly rare in the Rhodesian thornbush.

We didn't have much luck with the big stuff, but there were other triumphs. The thornbush in that region is studded with rocky *kopjes*, perfect hideaways for leopards, mambas, troops of baboons, and, occasionally, a few klipspringer. These small straight-horned antelope re-

Boddington's beautiful southern greater kudu came as a consolation prize after a long, fruitless stalk on a herd of sable. Although one of the most prized of all African trophies, kudu are actually quite common across much of southern Africa; a good bull can be reasonably expected on even a relatively short hunt—in the right area.

mind you of chamois as they leap from rock to rock, and their hollow, multicolored hairs are really more like tiny quills and giving them a grizzled appearance. We climbed several *kopjes* and looked hard before we finally found a fine male, and I saved him for a life-size mount.

We spent several evenings down by the river searching for bushbuck in the densest bush. We had jumped several only to hear the bark and the crashing, but we had seen no good males. Then, just as the sun touched the horizon, we eased through some thick, tangled vines and overlooked the river. A hundred yards up and on the opposite bank a beautiful male bushbuck was drinking. He dropped in his tracks without a twitch, and at the shot a small crocodile splashed into the water below us. Barrie's men had no fear of terrorists, nor of buffalo and lion. But they feared the crocodile, so Barrie and I waded the shallow river and carried the bushbuck across. We didn't get eaten.

The day before we were to fly back to Bulawayo we cut the tracks of the big sable herd one last time. They were passing through unusually open mopane, and this time the wind was right. We caught up to them quickly and worked carefully around towards the front of the herd, then allowed them to pass us. There were several bulls, but we had eyes for just the one. In later years I was to see many sable, and perhaps this one, as often happens, has grown in my memory. But I still feel he was the largest I have ever seen. His horns didn't curve sharply but angled back forever and seemed to touch his rump when he lifted his neck. He was passing through an open grove with yellow grass brushing his belly, and he was screened by brownish cows. Then they parted and he was in the clear, just walking slowly ahead. He was all mine, and the Ruger .30-06 that had been so dependable was steady behind his shoulder.

The shot crashed in the silent grove, and he stood, bewildered. "You're high. Shoot again, quickly!" The hold was right, and I couldn't believe what I had just seen. I shot again, even more carefully, and then he was off running with his herd. Over the years I've had more than my share of luck; it was the first time a professional hunter or hunting companion had been given due cause to be angry with my performance. Barrie was livid, and rightfully so. He swept off his hat, threw it to the ground, and glared at me. "What the bloody hell is wrong with you?" And just as quickly he cooled off.

We backed off a good distance and fired the rifle at a tree. The day before it had cleanly taken an impala for the pot at 150 yards. Today it shot three feet high at half that distance. I sighted it in again as carefully as I could, bringing it back down so that I could hit the center of a four-inch blaze. Angry and frustrated—a bad combination in hunting—we set off to circle the herd.

We found them again all too easily. Barrie knew this section of woods, and we circled them perfectly using the quartering wind. They had calmed down by now, and we were waiting for them on a brushy slope when they started filtering down the opposite hillside.

We picked out the big bull easily, and I got ready as he stepped behind a bush. This time there could be no mistake. Once again we had him, and we knew the gun was back on. I held on his shoulder as he stepped into the clear, and I shot him exactly where I intended to. But I had shot the wrong sable, and as this one made his last heart-shot run the big bull cantered off to the right, mighty horns sweeping his rump as he ran.

CHAPTER IV
THE MATOPO HILLS

Cecil John Rhodes is buried there, in those imposing mystery-shrouded hills southwest of Bulawayo. He tamed the land, claiming it for England but intending it to be a personal legacy for all time. Rhodes, a giant of a man encased in a sickly body that was never meant to withstand the labors his will demanded. For just 89 years, from 1890 until 1979, the land he created and loved bore his name. But perhaps he was the victor after all, for although the land has changed names again, Cecil John Rhodes still rests in the forbidding Matopos, sacred ground of the Matabele nation.

The Matopos are a low hill mass, but cut with deep ravines and seams of black rock. The deepest superstitions and religious beliefs of the Matabeles are centered here, and it was here, too, that the great American scout Frederick Russell Burnham is said to have sought out and killed the Matabele *Umlimo,* high priest, during the 1896 Matabele war.

The hills rise quickly from the thornbush and farmland below, and their rocky slopes are unlikely to see the plow. They're stark, yet ruggedly beautiful in their way. Rhodes chose his resting place well, for in all the land that was once called Rhodesia, the Matopos might well prove the region most resistant to change.

There is little game in the hills, but also little hunting; those species that do occur grow to excellent size, and that was what we sought. We had come into the lower reaches of the Matopos to find a really fine southern impala, not a meat animal such as we had taken all too many of in the lowveld, but a really fine one that would place in the records. A little higher up we would search for a good common reedbuck, a mid-size antelope preferring open grasslands with plentiful water. Abundant in many areas, the reedbuck is like a number of other common

51

The Matopo Hills are lonely, rugged country, home to few species but producing fine trophy quality in those that are present. The "hedgehogs" atop this Land Rover hold buckshot-loaded 12 gauge shells; a yank on a lever and the pipes drop down and fire—extra insurance against terrorist ambush.

species—whitetail and wildebeeste, to name two—average specimens are fairly easy to come by, but record class trophies are the very devil to find.

We had flown into Bulawayo—professional hunter Barrie Duckworth, my wife, Sharon, and I—then had driven south to Barrie's family farm at Balla Balla. We had just a few days left, but we hoped to find reedbuck, really good impala, and tsessebe, plus spend some time shooting birds around the grainfields.

In comparison with the lowveld, there is little game in that part of the country. It's well-settled and much more open, and the great herds that Selous must have found are long gone. Good kudu still hold out in the brushy pockets, likewise the cover-loving bushbuck and duikers, and the hilly country holds some monstrous leopards. But it isn't really safari country; it is a beautiful area and a fine place to look for a few specific trophies.

The first evening was spent in the lower country looking for reedbuck, and we saw just a couple of young males and a few females. The next morning we went much higher up, seeing several fine kudu bulls on the way. But although the hills were beautiful, that was all the game we saw until midmorning. Then I witnessed some true witchcraft that would have made the *Umlimo* proud.

The ability of the best African trackers to spot game is legendary, and I hesitate to argue with legend. But in truth, I've seen few who were better than most hunters—of any race—with adequate experience. Tracking skill is, of course, another matter, and there no one can touch them. But spotting game is different, and I've seen few Africans that were true wizards at it. This day I saw a feat that I've never seen approached, let alone equaled.

The sun was high, and we had long since given up deadly serious hunting. Instead we were enjoying the cool breeze and warm sunshine of the Matopos, simply driving and seeing some country. Suddenly Barrie's Matabele tracker tapped on the roof, signaling us to stop. We did so, and backed up so that we could look into a grassy swale that extended 200 yards or so off the dirt track. There was quick conversation in

Professional hunter Barrie Duckworth and Boddington with a superb common reedbuck taken in Zimbabwe's Matopo Hills. Actually, neither Boddington nor Duckworth deserve much credit—the tracker spotted just one horntip sticking up out of some long grass as an impossible distance.

Sindebele, accompanied by pointing into the grass. Barrie scanned the grass with his binoculars, then turned to me. "He says he sees something; he thinks it's the horn of a bedded reedbuck, but I can't see anything." He pointed out the area, about 125 yards off the road, and I put my Zeiss glasses on the spot. I could see nothing but gently waving yellow grass.

"He seems quite sure, and he has remarkable eyes. Let's walk out there and see what's what."

We closed in a bit, and Barrie's tracker pointed once more. "Jesus,"Barrie whispered, "there's a horn. I don't know how he saw it, but it's a good one." He pointed me in the right direction, and I scanned the grass with the binoculars once more. I could still see nothing. With the rifle now at port arms with a round up the spout, we moved closer.

At 30 yards I could finally make out a single black pencil protruding from a particularly thick clump of grass. It was simply impossible for this to be a reedbuck, and even more impossible for anyone to have seen it from the back of a bouncing Land Rover at 20 miles per hour. We moved in closer yet and finally could see the horn with our naked eyes. It never moved, and I had decided once again that it must be a blackened stick.

At 10 feet the reedbuck flushed like a bobwhite quail, and like a wild-flushing quail always does, he took me completely by surprise. It wasn't the first shot that connected, but he went down, and he was indeed a magnificent reedbuck with long, well-shaped horns. The reedbuck has soft pads at the horn bases, the pedicel, that greatly exaggerate the basal circumference. This one was particularly massive, a great trophy. But I would have taken any reedbuck that jumped from that grass and hung him on my wall gladly to commemorate such a feat in game spotting!

We had expected the reedbuck to be the most difficult trophy in that area, so we took a break that afternoon and hunted birds around the cornfields on the Duckworths' farm. Shotshells—or any kind of ammunition—came dear in wartime Rhodesia, but in preparation for the occasion I'd managed to find a few boxes of German shells in Bulawayo. Only once have I taken the trouble to carry a shotgun to Africa, though I've wished for one any number of times. This wasn't the occasion that I brought my own, but Barrie had two—a lovely Franchi skeet gun, which he loaned to me, and an old English Osborne side-by-side, which he carried.

Late in the afternoon we would try to catch guinea fowl and francolin along the edges of the cultivation, but first Barrie suggested that I warm up on some doves. I took a quick count of our shells and decided I could allocate three boxes of 10. If these doves were like all other doves I've seen, that wouldn't put much meat on the table—but I was more interested in the unfamiliar species.

About four o'clock I took a position along a treeline bordering a huge field of corn—locally called maize. It could have been Kansas, or California, or Mexico, or anywhere else in the world that doves are hunted. As if on cue, the birds started winging over, first in singles, doubles and triples, then in larger flocks. I shot carefully and slowly, not to aid in my shooting, but to husband the shells. These birds looked only slightly different from mourning doves, with pretty bluish bars on neck and head, and they flew like doves fly everywhere, twisting and turning and presenting every imaginable angle. A small pile of birds grew beside the meager heap of hulls, and I was sorely tempted to stay right there until all the shells were gone. But I resisted and, after just a half hour or so, hiked out to the corner to join Barrie.

"Right. If you've got your shooting eye in shape, now we'll go have some real sport!" he said.

It would have to be really spectacular to be better than that, but I was game. The only guinea fowl I had seen were the barnyard variety in the States, so I wasn't altogether certain they could even *fly*, let alone offer good wingshooting. The first covey rise was a real revelation, and I've never again missed a chance to hunt guinea fowl with a shotgun!

We hunted them as you might hunt sharptails or sage grouse, first glassing for a feeding flock. As is their custom, towards evening they'll come out to the grainfields to feed. We had spotted the first flock at considerable distance, then stalked them by staying in the brushline along the field's edge. When we felt we were adjacent to them, we cut to the right quickly and stepped into the field with shotguns ready. Or at least at the ready. I simply wasn't prepared for 50 chicken-size birds taking to wing as nimbly as bobwhites, and the Franchi's twin tubes punched nothing but air.

Barrie had one down, and he watched carefully as the birds fanned out and settled into a treeline a quarter mile away. "Perfect. They're spread out well, and if we hurry we'll get some good shooting."

We hurried, swinging wide to come in behind the birds so we could push them back towards the open field instead of deeper into the brush where, like pheasants, they would run rather than flush. It worked perfectly.

Guinea fowl are occasionally seen in American farmyards, and they seem quite stupid. The wild African birds are a bit different. They're great runners and strong flyers, and offer outstanding shotgunning sport.

First I heard wingbeats as Barrie flushed one off to the left, then the crash of the Osborne. I was ready this time. Four black-and-white speckled rockets came up underfoot, and the Franchi came up smoothly. Two birds folded, and as I broke the gun open several more flushed behind me, passing directly overhead. I got two shells in the gun, snapped it closed, and dropped two more as they passed, the first hitting with a thud right beside me. That was more like it, I thought to myself, and I couldn't help but think that this was, after all, much more fun than hunting sable . . . .

We chased that flock a little while longer and picked up a couple more birds, but the bulk of them had simply vanished. Later we got into more coveys, and just at dark flushed several francolin, a lovely partridge known for its all-white meat, from the edges of the fields.

It was a beautiful day, the only off note sounding at last light when Barrie's mother met us at the huge gate to the barbwire-topped fence encircling the house. She was a lovely lady, past middle age with white hair and rosy cheeks, perhaps five feet two and a touch on the stout side. She reminded me of my grandmother and seemed the type that would be much more at home serving tea in the English countryside. But she seemed perfectly at ease with the massive Sten gun slung over her

The tsessebe is a close relative to the hartebeeste clan. Said to be the most fleet-footed of Africa's antelope, he is found in just a few scattered locales in southern Africa. This one was taken near Bulawayo in Zimbabwe.

shoulder, and I wouldn't doubt for a moment that she knew exactly how to use it.

The next morning we drove to a nearby ranch to look for a good tsessebe. A close relative to the hartebeeste clan, the tsessebe has shorter horns without the absurd back, forward, and back again twist typical of true hartebeeste. It has an unusual—and very attractive—purple pelage and is said to be the fleetest of foot of all the African antelope. This speed is deceptive, for the tsessebe has an odd pogo-stick gait that eats up the ground at an alarming, effortless rate. Its distribution is very spotty; the tsessebe is locally plentiful in Botswana's Okavango region, Zambia's Bangweulu Swamp, and central Rhodesia—and darned few places in between. Though hardly a highly prized antelope, it's one of those local rarities that a hunter shouldn't pass while he's in the right spot.

We saw relatively few of them, and in truth they aren't overly abundant in that region. We glassed for them in open grasslands interspersed with stands of hardwood, and turned down just a couple. Then we saw a fine specimen, a lone bull easing along a treeline. We worked him for a short time, trying to get a shot in the heavy cover, and finally he offered a clear shot at his shoulder for just an instant. I shot quickly, and although he was off as if nothing had happened, he was down and dead within a few yards. He was truly a beautiful tsessebe, and although he doesn't place high in the listings, he's one of the largest to come out of Rhodesia.

Oddly, the impala came the hardest. Now that we wanted a really good one and were in the area that should produce one, we just couldn't find them. We looked high and we looked low, seeing very few animals and no good ones. Finally, on the last day, we found a herd with a lovely ram, the back portion of his horns rising dead parallel as a good, mature ram's should, and rising plenty far enough.

He was with a dozen females and stayed screened by them seemingly forever. We moved with them, not pushing them but moving slowly and quietly and waiting for the shot. Finally it came, with no females in front or behind, and we had the trophy we had been looking for.

There have been many changes in Rhodesia—now called Zimbabwe—since this safari ended, and many changes for Barrie Duckworth and Roger Whittal and their families. The F.N.'s, Stens, and grenades are long gone, along with the armor plating under the vehicles and huge fences around their homes. They still worry about the future, but the safari business has been good for them, and the endless bush war is now a memory. Change is inevitable, and it's really neither bad nor good, just ongoing. I'm not sure Cecil John Rhodes would agree, but his was a time that has long since passed, and I'd like to think that he's content resting there in the Matopos. Perhaps one of these days I'll visit him there, for in his hills Africa goes on as it always has in spite of man's folly. For the empire-builder—and for the hunter—few things are as painful as change, and rapid change is a fact of life in the hunter's Africa.

CHAPTER V
GERMAN SOUTH WEST

I took another sip of the strong local beer, then leaned back in my chair and peered down the dry riverbed in the gathering twilight. I was seated on a wide veranda overlooking the sandy bottom, and two kudu had already come to the seep a couple hundred yards downstream. If the light held, soon zebra and warthog would surely step out, and just maybe a couple of shy eland. This really was the life, I thought as I breathed deeply of the cool, clean evening air.

I had plenty of reason to be pleased, both with myself and with the surroundings. I had spent the day in some of the prettiest game country I had ever seen, a day that had brought into sight virtually every animal present in South West, and towards evening I had taken a fine bull kudu.

The sun had shone on his lovely gray coat as he trotted up a sidehill away from us, and the old .30-06 and its trusted Nosler bullet had done their work perfectly. Now the bull was hung in the meat shed, and it was time to enjoy the last few moments of twilight, my favorite part of any hunting day.

It was odd, I thought, how gladly one might trade all the hours of bright midday sun for just a few moments more of lingering twilight and graying dawn. Of the two, the dawn unquestionably holds the most promise for the hunter, at least with most types of game, but I prefer the evening. In the morning, once it's light enough to see crosshairs the chances of seeing game diminish with each passing moment. But in the evening, the tension builds as night gets closer, and the odds are the very best at the very last, when you must peer into the gathering gloom and wish away the night for just a few moments longer. It was that time of night now, those last few instants when you know there's something out there worth seeing if you could only pierce the deepening gray. But the hunt was over for the day; I was just looking now and enjoying the cool night air.

I was at Ben Nolte's Epako Farm, north of the little hamlet of Omaruru in South West Africa. We had combed Epako all day looking for kudu and especially for a big gemsbok, the giant oryx of Africa's southwestern deserts. We had seen gemsbok, but the big bulls had eluded us. The kudu had come as a last-light gift as we made our way back to camp, a fine ending to a perfect day.

South West Africa was colonized by the Germans, but after World War I became a protectorate of South Africa. German remains the common language in many districts, while in others Afrikaans—the South African dialect that developed during the Boers' four centuries in southern Africa—is heard more frequently. English is spoken by many, particularly in the larger towns, but in outlying areas Afrikaans is a more sure bet. Ben Nolte, my host and professional hunter, was raised in the southern part of South West near the South African border and had only come north to Omaruru as an adult. Like many in South West, he was fluent in all three languages, though Afrikaans was his native tongue.

He had been a sheep farmer, but a few years before had sold all his sheep and had developed his land for game. The fact that he took visiting sportsmen hunting wasn't unusual; most ranches in South West have kudu and gemsbok, and, depending on the habitat, perhaps hartebeeste, zebra, and springbok. Many ranchers take the occasional hunter, particularly visiting Germans, and the proper licensing enabling them to do so on their own property is easily obtained.

Ben had gone the whole route, though. His own farm—we would call it a ranch—was devoted entirely to game management. He had also qualified himself as a full-fledged professional hunter, one of just a handful so licensed in his country. To obtain the license he had been required to undergo both practical and written exams in his choice of two of the three common languages, and to demonstrate his skills at tracking, spotting, shooting, judging of trophies, and trophy care. With the full license he could guide foreign sportsmen anywhere in South West, and he had secured nearly a half-million acres of hunting leases and concessions on which to hunt.

Except for a few large tribal homelands, virtually all of South West is private land, homesteaded in years gone by. The typical ranch in good grazing country is some 15,000 acres, and only a few ranches in the entire country have actively attempted to develop their game. Instead, the

Giant termite mounds are a common feature in much of Africa, but this one in South West is a real record-breaker. Anthills are superb to use for glassing game, but only with caution—they're a favorite home for mambas and cobras.

Hunting in South West Africa is a game of glassing—climbing the rocky ridges and knolls to peer into the thornbush below, then planning a stalk if anything looks interesting. The country is similar to Arizona's desert ranges, with just a bit more brush in the valleys.

game is present just as it is in so much of the American West. The only fencing being three-strand barbed wire.

All through the day I had been struck by how similar this hunting was to American hunting. The country was much like the rugged Arizona mountains where I've enjoyed hunting Coues whitetail—rough and rocky, with just a bit more brush in the low areas between the hills.

We had hunted it the same way, too, climbing up a steep *kopje* to a vantage point, then glassing the flats below and the opposite hillsides. That day I had fully expected to see javelina or the telltale flag of a whitetail. Since then, in Arizona, I've often let my mind wander and imagined I was glassing for greater kudu.

The springbok, a lovely gazellelike antelope, is easily South West's most common game animal. To the south and east, on the fringes of the Kalahari Desert, and to the west, along the edges of the Namib Desert, huge herds of springbok numbering into the thousand aren't uncommon. But we were in the hilly north-central region, 200 kilometers northwest of the capital of Windhoek, and here the southern greater kudu, largest of the kudu clan, was unquestionably the most common animal. It was country where one could glass, and in a day's time a number of shootable bulls would likely be seen. In a week of careful looking, a hunter just might find the kudu of his dreams.

The gemsbok or giant oryx is a huge, stoutly-constructed antelope. They use their rapier horns to good effect against lions, and are among the few truly fierce antelope. A wounded oryx is simply nothing to mess around with!

63

But I hadn't come to hunt kudu. I had come primarily to hunt the gemsbok, largest of the African oryx, and also to hunt the springbok, one of the most attractive of Africa's smaller antelopes. Ben's gemsbok herd was building, and he hadn't expected us to find what we were looking for on Epako. Instead, he wanted to take things slowly the first day and show me a bit of the country, perhaps take a kudu—which we had done—and if we saw a good gemsbok, fine. If not, the next day we would start hunting areas where the chances were better.

I was to learn that South West is not the place to find the very best gemsbok. Out on the deserts, both the Namib and Kalahari, there are some very fine bulls. But in the hilly regions where most hunting is con-

The springbok is a beautiful little relative of the gazelle clan, found in the deserts and plains of South Africa, South West, and Botswana. Hunting them is quite similar to hunting America's pronghorn antelope.

ducted today, the gemsbok bulls tend to have short, massive horns. As with all oryx, both males and females have horns; the females often have much more length but always thinner bases. The Holy Grail for the gemsbok hunter is 40 inches, but most of the 40-inch gemsbok in the record book are females. A bull that reaches that magical figure is the ultimate gemsbok trophy, but very few bulls reach that length. In the Omaruru district, such bulls are practically unheard of. It's theorized that in the rocky hills the bulls wear down their horns fighting; they do have wonderful mass, and it's mass as much as length that makes a gemsbok trophy. Ben had been honest; I knew what I could reasonably expect—a heavy horned bull somewhere between 33 and 37 inches—and now we would look for the very best we could find.

Over the next few days we hunted hard, mostly on foot. It was winter in South West, with cool nights and pleasant middays but a nagging wind that kept the animals spooky. We saw many gemsbok—thickset, powerful animals, gray in color with striking black-and-white markings on face and knees. A big bull may weigh 450 pounds, and we saw several such bulls. But, as Ben had warned, their horns were short.

After a few days we rose extra early and left Epako hours before dawn, headed for a ranch deep in the Orongo Mountains. This spine of steep, rocky mountains rises northwest from Omaruru, fine kudu coun-

Springbok in South West are larger in both body and horn than their South African counterparts. This one was taken on the edge of the Namib Desert, one of the best places for true trophy springbok.

try and the home of the beautifully striped Mrs. Hartmann's zebra. Ben knew an old German farmer up there, Carl Hinterholzer, who had good numbers of gemsbok on his land.

Again it was so much like hunting the American West. We had coffee in Hinterholzer's kitchen while he and Ben discussed what areas might hold the best gemsbok, a scene that would be familiar in Wyoming, Montana, Colorado, and so many other places. The only difference was that the conversation was in German, too fast for my high-school German to follow well. With coffee cups empty and game plans laid, we started off in the graying dawn.

Early on we saw a fine kudu, one of the best I've ever seen, and just as the sun broke through the cold dawn we rounded a bend and surprised a small herd of Hartmann's zebra. They were indeed beautiful, and I was sorely tempted, but I had set my sights on a gemsbok. Besides, I had taken a tremendous liking to the country; the mountain zebra would give me something to come back for. We also saw a pair of Damaraland dik dik, a beautiful blue antelope little bigger than a Chihuahua, fully protected in South West.

We saw gemsbok, too; there were indeed many on this farm. First a big herd down on the flat, a herd that vanished into the thorn long before we could pick out any good ones. Then a dozen that wound single file out of a draw while we were glassing, and then several more bunches. But, as on Epako, there were no really big bulls.

The country was beautiful, skies the clearest blue possible and the mountains starkly attractive. At one point Hinterholzer took us to a cave to see some fine examples of ancient bushman paintings, well preserved on the cool rock. The paintings depicted many things, including some early-day pornography, but the main theme was the hunt. In those days many elephant, rhino, buffalo, lion and leopard roamed this land, but today only the leopards remain—hunter-educated leopards that almost never come to bait and, although fairly common, are almost never taken by hunters.

It was shortly after lunch—a fine farmer's lunch at the ranch house—that we finally saw the kind of bull we had been looking for. He was alone, skylined on a ridge, and we were just driving up a long incline to get into some new country. Ben and Carl studied him, then spoke rapid-fire German. Ben and I bailed out of the truck as the bull began to run, and we ran as well, cutting across the angle to try to head him off. We moved around the ridge, and we had made it in time. The bull was standing in the brush, and he was clearly the best we had seen.

I was carrying my .375; gemsbok are exceptionally tough, and I wasn't certain the .30-06 would be enough gun. The bull was past 300 yards, and this time I couldn't stretch the big gun quite far enough. One shot and he was gone forever.

Now, though, it seemed as if we were in a pocket containing several good bulls. Only a few minutes later we found a beauty in a large herd, and we stalked him in heavy brush until late afternoon. There were just too many pairs of sharp eyes, and we never got a shot.

As the sun sank lower, we climbed yet another ridge to glass, and far down in the valley were three bulls. It was too far to shoot, especially after already having blown one chance, but they were feeding towards us. We waited them out for a precious half hour, then moved ahead along the ridge when then they went out of sight in some brush.

With the sun just touching the distant hills, we got above them and I laid my hat across a boulder for a rest. Ben hissed softly, placing a hand on my arm. Just below us were a half-dozen zebra, much closer than the oryx. If they spooked—and zebra *always* spook—the game was over. They didn't; instead they fed off to the left quietly. We waited; the oryx had to be in the brush below us. They were. A few minutes passed, then a horn tip and a flash of gray showed in the brush. More minutes, then the flick of an ear much closer. They were feeding to the base of the hill and would be in the open in another dozen yards.

One bull showed himself, then another, finally the third. Ben whispered, "The one in the middle. He's a very good bull, not long but with tremendous bases." Then, in his careful English, "I think he will go no less than 35, but I do not think he's 36. His bases are *vvvery* good."

He stepped behind an acacia, but not before I had made up my mind. Time was growing short now, and he was a lovely bull. I settled in behind the big Mauser and put the crosshairs on the acacia. The bull was steeply downhill, but the range was close this time, perhaps 150 yards. When he stepped out I put the crosshairs well up on his shoulder to put the bullet down through his lungs, then finished the trigger squeeze.

Even after the awesome impact from the .375 he went 20 yards, then piled up in some brush. I walked up to him quickly, but Ben pulled me back. Wounded oryx can be extremely dangerous, and they're not an animal you take chances with. He was finished, though, and he was truly a fine bull, big bodied and old with unusually heavy bases, and Ben had called his length exactly right.

I had a couple of days left to hunt springbok, and for that we would go to altogether different country. It was a long drive to the edge of the Namib Desert, and after a late arrival back at Epako we hadn't gotten an early start. Dawn had long since come and gone before we arrived at the springbok farm, but these animals are creatures of the sun and may be readily hunted throughout the day.

This was a piece of ground owned by a small village; the springbok harvested there helped to support the town. The mayor himself accompanied us, a fine gentleman whose English was about on a par with my German. The country was wide open grassland, dead flat with just a few scattered trees. We saw one herd of kudu and crossed gemsbok tracks, but springbok were clearly the only common game. Of them there were literally hundreds—big herds, small herds, pairs and singles. They reminded me much of Wyoming pronghorns—in their numbers, in the country they inhabited, and in their habits. They were spooky and seemed to have the pronghorn's keen eyesight, but it was clear that finding a shootable buck would not be a problem.

In this area, Ben was assured that we could find a spectacular springbok head. We looked over very many, but he was determined not to shoot until we found the right one. Although the springbok's horns bear no relation to those of a pronghorn—they rise up, then curve outwards and back in again—in terms of inches they are judged the same way as Wyoming pronghorn. A 12-inch buck is common, 13 inches is respectable, and over 14 very good indeed.

We passed many in the 13-inch category, but anything bigger seemed impossible to find in spite of the great numbers. With gemsbok, Ben had known exactly what we could find and what we likely couldn't find. With springbok, Ben also knew, and towards midafternoon we found him. He had amazingly thick bases, bases so thick that we underestimated his length. He was spooky, like all of his kind had been all day, but at 200 yards he finally gave me a standing shot. He was indeed what we had been looking for, and although I've been in springbok country several times since, I've never seen his better.

With the little time remaining we made a halfhearted effort to find a better gemsbok, and I looked over a few more kudu and some warthog. But I was content to just enjoy those rocky hills for one more day and to pass the last evening on Ben's veranda watching shy, graceful kudu come out to water.

CHAPTER VI
ZULULAND

The Natal countryside appears peaceful and prosperous, with large acreage under cultivation and many cattle. The western part of the province was brown from lack of rain, but as we drove through the hills towards the ocean the more dense—and better-watered—coastal vegetation took over.

Nowhere are there visible signs of how bitterly—or how often—this land has been contested, but a quick look at the roadmap of Natal is like a synopsis of warfare in southern Africa. Ladysmith, site of the endless siege during the Boer War. A bit farther north and east, Blood River, where the trekking Boers met and withstood the full might of the Zulu Nation. Just to the south, Isandhlwana, where a generation later and just a century ago those same Zulus wiped out Lord Chelmsford's column, inflicting the greatest military defeat Great Britain would suffer until the fall of Singapore. Nearby, Rorke's Drift, where a small garrison held the victorious Zulus at bay as they swarmed off the bloody field at Isandhlwana—there was no snatching of a victory from a defeat so total, but the men of Rorke's Drift, a single company of the 2nd/24th Foot, saved the honor of the British nation and gathered the largest number of Victoria Crosses ever awarded in a single action.

No one with even the slightest imagination could help but dawdle along a route studded with so much history, but in truth the few monuments are Spartan, and perhaps that's fitting; the peoples of southern Africa are aware that they're commemorating battles only and their centuries of conflict are far from over.

But there are no signs of conflict in the lush countryside of Natal, nor in Zululand proper, south of Swaziland and encompassing much of the prime coastal bush country. In fact, Sharon and I felt perfectly at home motoring through Natal and on into Zululand in a rented car, rolling into the little hamlet of Mkuze shortly before dark. We found a room at a lovely little place called the Ghost Mountain Inn, just in time to watch the sun set on Ghost Mountain itself, a high sugarloaf of a mountain believed to be haunted by the spirits of Zulu warriors of old.

We had a short hunt arranged nearby but had come out of Johannesburg earlier than anticipated. Our schedule had deposited us in Jo'burg on a Friday night, and little did we know that Sunday blue laws essentially started at one o'clock Saturday afternoon! It appeared that, for foreign travelers, a Sunday in Johannesburg would be as exciting as watching paint dry, so we had quickly canceled plane reservations and rented a car. That had been a good decision; the countryside had been beautiful and the driving easy, but once again I was struck by the paucity of game that one saw from the road. In fact, we were within 50 kilometers of Mkuze before the country even started to look gamey.

That makes sense, when you think about it logically. But Americans don't think about Africa logically; they expect to find game literally everywhere—and it just isn't there unless there's a good reason for it to be there. South Africa's vast and varied game populations suffered the same ravages of her pioneer days as our own game. The Cape was set-

Camp in Zululand was permanent rondavels, set in a grove of trees with blooming bougainvillea. Close by the Indian Ocean, this part of South Africa is hot and steamy in the summer, but during the winter—the prime hunting season—the weather is extremely pleasant.

tled long before the Pilgrims landed, but much of South Africa wasn't fully settled until long after the buffalo were gone from the American West. In the last few decades the South Africans have worked miracles bringing their game back, but in general they're a good 20 to 30 years behind American game management.

The exception to that, of course, is the game ranching concept, and here South Africa has no equal. Farmers—we would call them ranchers—in numerous parts of the country have learned that game is more profitable than cattle, and the laws are such that game may be harvested on private land essentially at the landowner's discretion, although not without some central regulation. The South African government was farsighted in its establishment of parks and game reserves, of which there are many. Surplus animals live-trapped in the numerous parks and made available to landowners have reestablished significant game populations on private land in South Africa and have saved a number of unique species that could easily have been lost.

We had come to Zululand specifically to hunt one of these unique species, the spiral-horned nyala. First identified at St. Lucia Bay in 1847, less than a hundred miles to the south of us, its primary home is limited to the southeastern Indian Ocean coast of Africa. A wary creature of the dense, lush, coastal bush country, the nyala has never been substantially depleted in numbers, unlike some of South Africa's plains species that were more vulnerable to hunters. However, its actual range in South Africa is limited primarily to Zululand. Formerly the nyala was commonly hunted in Mozambique, with its range extending into Malawi. But Mozambique and Malawi offered no hunting, so in the late 1970's Zululand offered virtually the only chance to take a nyala.

As these lines are being written there still seems little chance for hunting to reopen in either Mozambique or Malawi, but it's worth mentioning that the nyala is extending its range significantly, both naturally and through live-trapping and release programs. Ranchers in the eastern Cape, the northern Cape, and the Transvaal have released nyala, and the animals seem to adapt well. As their numbers have increased in the heart of their range, they have also moved westward along some of the major river systems. They're increasingly common in Zimbabwe along the Limpopo and its tributaries, and far to the north are now seen along the Zambezi Valley as far as Kariba—country where nyala were unknown just a few years ago. But back then, in the late Seventies, Zululand was the only place to secure a nyala, and it was this beast that

In the Zulu language, inyala means "the shifty one," a good name for this cover-loving cousin to the bushbuck. Though not a rarity, it's a beautiful animal, and its shy nature makes it interesting to hunt.

had brought us here.

The Zulu word, variously spelled *inyala* and *nyala*, means "the shifty one," and it's apt. The nyala is actually quite common in those coastal hills and valleys, but it's very shy and prefers the most dense cover available, much like the bushbuck with which it shares its habitat. The nyala ia a large antelope, with a big bull weighing perhaps 300 to 350 pounds and strikingly beautiful. Chocolate brown, he has the kudu's vertical white stripes from the shoulders back and the nose chevron so common to the spiral-horned clan. His neck and chest have a long, silky ruff which often extends back along the body. His legs are surprisingly yellow—truly a striking animal. His horns more closely resemble those of a bushbuck rather than the radical twists of the greater and lesser kudu. As they spiral they turn outwards, then in again. The very best bulls conclude in a last outward turn with tips of polished ivory.

In my travels in Africa I've spent little time within the parks, generally preferring to use what precious little time there was in hunting areas. But this trip we spent some time in the Hluhluwe and Mkuze game reserves, choice tracts of dense bush that are literally full of nyala and a few other species. I have previously admitted to a fondness for the spiral horns, and I must further admit to a special fondness for the nyala. They're plentiful enough that finding even an exceptional bull is far from Africa's greatest challenge, but they're a remarkably beautiful antelope, surely one of the prettiest—and no pushover to hunt, as we were soon to find out.

I had arranged to hunt with Garry Kelly, then of Nyalaveld Safaris. At the time Garry was in his late twenties and had been hunting professionally for a dozen years. As a youngster he had apprenticed to the late Norman Deane, the great hunter who literally opened the safari business in South Africa, and by the late seventies Kelly was rated one of the top hunters in the country. He's still in business today, and has grown as the hunting opportunities in his country have grown. Today he's even better, easily one of the best-known outfitters on the continent.

At the time I hunted with him his headquarters was Tshaneni Game Ranch, close to Mkuze. The ranch had been carefully developed for hunting and contained a variety of animals that had largely disappeared from the surrounding area—wildebeeste, zebra, and white rhino, along with impala, nyala, bushbuck, duiker, reedbuck, and a few greater kudu. These last were still resident on the neighboring sisal plantations and surrounding hills, so we were able to hunt a sizable chunk of country exclusive of the fenced game ranch.

That was my first exposure to game fencing in Africa. I didn't like the idea of it, but the reality of the fencing had no impact whatsoever on the hunting. Tshaneni was a magnificent example of a well-kept game ranch—several thousand acres of ideal game habitat, with dense cover ideally suited for the species found there. In the clearings and grassy meadows one would see the plains species—zebra, wildebeeste, impala—and in the heavy cover that predominated, nyala and bushbuck and kudu lived as they always had, unaware that they were held by a fence.

The hunter could easily be unaware, too. Those bush-dwelling species simply had to be hunted on foot, and the animals had all the advantage, fence or no fence. In later years I was to see game-fenced ranches where the open cover precluded the opportunity for a truly satisfying hunting experience, but not there. Garry's camp, too, was a shining example of what is possible in southern Africa. Comfortable thatched *rondavels*, the traditional circular hut, were joined by common bathroom facilities with running water, and blooming bougainvillea climbed the sides. Dining tables were outside with thatched cover, and of course there was a *boma* for the evening's campfire. It was lovely setting, and Sharon and I enjoyed it very much.

Our guide was Ed Hannon, a Rhodesian who had come south during the war when concern for his family's safety became too great. He was a good hunter, and his Zulu trackers, Magilwane and Four-Feet, were extremely competent. Like so many of the bush-dwelling antelope, the nyala are most active in the early mornings and late evenings, with chances for success virtually nil at midday. We planned our hunt accordingly, intending to take life easy through the middle part of the day and hunt hard early and late.

That first evening we hunted Tshaneni itself, seeing numerous truly exceptional impala and great numbers of wildebeeste, but no nyala at all until the last few minutes of daylight. We saw them across a clearing to

Boddington and guide Ed Hannon with a fine Zululand nyala. These beautiful antelope are confined to South Africa, Mozambique, and a few drainages in Malawi and Zimbabwe. In Zululand they're exceedingly common, but nonetheless a fine trophy.

the left, four dark forms fading into the trees. They were bulls, all of them, and we circled quickly into the wind hoping to catch them before it got too dark. At the edge of a larger clearing we felt we had gotten in front of them, so we waited, I with the .30-06 rested over the fork of a tree.

They came slowly and silently, picking their way cautiously like the big bushbuck that they are. These were all mature, but none had the outward turn that marks an exceptional trophy. We watched them walk by and I marvelled at their incredible beauty.

The next day we left Tshaneni to hunt a large sisal plantation nearby, part of the huge Mkuze Estates. This was much bigger country, huge fields of impenetrable sisal with brush-covered hills and thick, dark brushlines. There had been little attempt to manage the game, and Ed admitted that the overall populations weren't high. Yet we were to see many of the small, reddish nyala females, and I saw a magnificent bushbuck that tempted me severely. In fact, in spite of relatively few animals spotted, my ability to withstand temptation was tested to the limit. We saw a fine reedbuck on the edge of a sisal field and later, on a brushy hillside, jumped a beautiful greater kudu bull. He was in full rut and was surrounded by his harem, and had we been hunting kudu he would have been just fine. It was one of those days when you see everything except that which you seek—we never saw a nyala bull that morning. That evening we did find one, a real dandy that crashed off through the sisal, tantalizing us with only the occasional glimpse of ivory tips as he made his way through the dense growth.

We worked at it for several days and eventually saw a great number of nyala bulls. Only once was I fully prepared to shoot—it was a beautiful bull with horns approaching 30 inches—but in the gathering gloom we were too slow to make up our minds, and once we had decided the opportunity was gone. The rest of the bulls were small, perhaps in the borderline 24-inch class but not what we were looking for. Still, it was one of those hunts where there's lots of time and little pressure, and the ultimate outcome seemed assured if we stayed with it.

We alternated hunts between Tshaneni and the Mkuze Estates, and I lost track completely of the fact that the former was game-fenced. In fact, it made no difference at all as we ghosted through the thickets at gray dawn and last light. One evening, with just a half hour of daylight left, we slipped through a lovely open glade. Magilwane stopped us, pointing to the brush on the far side. Reddish-brown forms moved silently through the brush—nyala females. I couldn't see horns, but Ed whispered, "I think there's a good bull with them." I still don't know if he saw him or just felt he was there with that sixth sense that good hunters have. I wish I'd asked, but like most good guides, he might not have given me a truthful answer.

The wind was right, and we stayed behind them, moving as slowly and quietly as we could. The bull was there; I saw just his horns in the brush a few minutes later, and he was better than anything we'd passed up, perhaps as good as the one we didn't quite shoot. We had drifted out to the right of the herd now, trying to get ahead to set up a shot in the few minutes of light remaining. We were close to them, almost too close, but the brush was too thick for a shot.

Finally the nyala stopped. We had pushed them as hard as we could, and now they were doing exactly what we were doing—straining into the gloom trying to determine what was out there. The bull was just 25 yards away, a black blob screened by thin brush, and we were out of time and out of options. I had the scope cranked all the way down to 3X, but the bull was still just a dark mass.

I finally made out what had to be the front leg, followed it up, and tried to recall exactly how long the hair was—at that distance it would be all too easy to try for the heart shot and shoot too low. The .30-06 crashed in the silent glade, and the nyala were gone.

Ed put a hand on my arm. "Let's wait a moment. I think he's well hit." He lit up a cigarette, and I watched the last of the light trickle away as moments ticked by slowly. Cigarette finally finished, we moved into the dark brush. He had been well hit and was down 20 yards into the brush, nearly invisible in the gloom. He was beautiful, with the perfect out-and-in-and-out-again lyre shape of a mature, record-class nyala. He was what we had come to Zululand to find, and he had provided what still ranks as one of my most *enjoyable*—if not most exciting, most productive, or most challenging—African hunts.

CHAPTER VII
ON THE BUBYE RIVER

W e picked up the tracks in the dense thornbush close by the river, cloven-hoofed spoor the size of soup plates and the strangely familiar stockyard smell where still-warm dung dotted the track. We followed, as we had for so many days, but this time the wind was right and the tracks were fresh. During the night the buffalo had come out of the dense riverine growth to feed, and maybe, just maybe, we could catch them before they returned to the nightmare thorn.

This herd knew many things about man. They knew that men followed their tracks and sought the biggest bull in their midst, so they shifted their path with the wind. During the time when all buffalo in southeastern Zimbabwe were being eradicated to remove the threat of hoof-and-mouth—within the memory of living buffalo—they had learned that all buffalo were in danger. Modern technology had brought aerial shooting; they had learned that terror also comes from above, and they had learned to spend their daylight hours in the darkest, thickest, most impenetrable thornbush they could find. Over the course of a dozen bovine generations they had been speared, snared, shot with balls from big-bore muzzleloaders and, later, bullets from modern express rifles, machine-gunned, and even darted from low-flying helicopters. They knew men, and they knew how to avoid them. They were southern Cape buffalo, in many ways the closest thing Africa has to the American elk.

The beautiful greater kudu has been likened to the wapiti, and in carriage and size the simile is apt. But the kudu—and in truth all the spiral-horned tribe—are much more akin to the whitetail deer. They're totally adaptable, living well in tiny patches of thorn between cultivated fields, living by their wits literally within the city limits of many southern African cities. When civilization comes, the wary kudu are often the last

77

Professional hunter Ray Torr, Boddington, and trackers with a good warthog. Though common in many areas, trophy warthog can be hard to find. The Bubye River produces excellent specimens. There is a lot of local differences in warthogs' color and coat; this one has unusually long hair.

to leave, sometimes followed only by the leopard.

Not so the Cape buffalo—or the American elk. They haven't learned to adapt to man and his ways, and have been pushed into the kind of habitat that thin-skinned, weak-legged man avoids the most. The elk was once a plains animal, found in great plenty on the Kansas and Nebraska prairies. Likewise the Cape buffalo, in days gone by a creature of the open savannas. No more. The wapiti has retreated to the high mountains, where it can use its keen senses and its ability to traverse the roughest terrain to elude its enemies. The Cape buffalo, in spirit a close cousin to the wapiti, has given up the open plains in favor of the nastiest, thickest thornbush it can find. Where there are mountains, the Cape buffalo has gone to them—Mount Kenya, Mount Kilimanjaro, the highlands of Uganda, the plateaus of Zambia. Where there are no mountains, it has taken to the brush, and like the elk, it has learned to survive.

In later years I would meet buffalo that had seen little hunting pressure, and I would find herds that stood in the open and stared. But the buffalo of southern Africa—Zimbabwe and South Africa—have been subjected to the worst that man can dish out. They've learned the tricks, and like the elk in the public hunting grounds of the Rockies, they have survived. Today the threat of hoof-and-mouth is far from forgotten, but the revenue that can be extracted from a buffalo bull so far exceeds the price of cattle that the danger is forgiven. The buffalo are rebuilding, but they're not the same buffalo that Selous found.

They've learned to use their excellent ears and keen sense of smell, and they can see a good deal better than legend would have it. A herd such as the one we now began trailing could offer a real hunt, and the odds were all on the side of those being trailed.

We were on the Bubye River in southeastern Zimbabwe, true lowveld country that has changed but little in this century. It was private land, where some cattle ranching had been attempted, but it was basically untouched thornbush, a million acres of it in one great chunk. The war was over now, and Rhodesia was officially Zimbabwe. Game that had been left to its own devices over the years—save to provide the occasional *brie* or piece of *biltong*, the jerky that passes for money in so much of Africa—had built back up, and now with the cattle market a disaster and the area free of terrorists for the first time in many years, the safari business had become singularly attractive.

My host was Ray Torr, a jovial, dark-haired Rhodesian whose quick step belied his 50-odd years. He had ranched in the area for many years, and was the proprietor of the Lion & Elephant Motel, a whistle-stop on the Bubye River between Beitbridge on the South African border and Nyanda, closest town to the Great Zimbabwe ruins. At war's end he had secured a hunting concession that ran clear from the Bubye River north to the Nuanetsi. In years to come he would sell the motel—a scenic collection of well-kept *rondavels*—and turn to hunting as his sole profession, but at that time he was just getting started.

I had come to see the country, to find out what it had to offer, and most particularly to hunt buffalo. Ken Cloete, a South African pilot who would later become Ray's partner in the hunting venture, had met me in Johannesburg and had whisked me up to Ray's dirt strip just north of the Bubye River.

We had departed Jo'burg too late to clear Zimbabwe customs at Beitbridge that evening, so had flown over the rugged Soutpansbergs and put in for the night at a lovely game ranch in the northern Transvaal, hilly country with perfect leopard *kopjes* and fine herds of hartebeeste, impala, and zebra, with kudu and bushbuck vanishing into the bush at every turn. In the morning we flew to Beitbridge, where I had the mild panic of an African border crossing with firearms. There was no problem. A smiling 'Shona in pressed khakis issued the needed permits, and shortly we buzzed the Lion & Elephant Motel, then circled for a landing.

Not only had I never laid eyes on Ray Torr, but I also had never corresponded with him nor heard of his new hunting company. The circumstances that brought me to him were too convoluted to relate, but his reaction on our first meeting is worth recording.

After formalities, and after lunch was served and a cold beer was well in hand, he eventually asked me what I would like to hunt. "Buffalo" was my immediate reply, and the look on his face told me that the outcome others had assured me of was in grave doubt.

There were buffalo, he told me, but the Parks Department had done their best—or worst—to get rid of them. He had a few, perhaps quite a few, living along both the Bubye and the Nuanetsi, but the hunting would be extremely difficult. It seems to me that he suggested that I might like to hunt for a magnificent kudu or a huge waterbuck instead—or perhaps I only recall being aware that he was *thinking* those words quite clearly.

But buffalo it was, and buffalo we hunted. Not exclusively, of course. I did not shoot a kudu there, but I rate that area as one of the best I have ever seen for monstrous kudu bulls—tough to hunt, but plenty of good ones. I *should have* shot a waterbuck there. The country hasn't many, but those that are present grow to magnificent proportions, and I was a hair too slow on the best waterbuck I've ever seen. Along the river there were fine Limpopo bushbuck, and a few nyala were coming into the area from Mozambique. There were blue wildebeeste, too, but like the buffalo they had been harried because of the hoof-and-mouth threat and were more wild than any wildebeeste has a right to be. Once, still-hunting through dense thorn, we came eyeball-to-eyeball with a fine Livingstone's eland bull, and a few sable tracks were occasionally crossed.

The country was unbroken thornbush, virtually no openings at all, and just the occasional *kopje*. Lions still frequent the country, although the cattle ranchers shoot them at will, and of course it's fine leopard

Cape buffalo were nearly eradicated in many parts of Zimbabwe due to fear of their carrying the dread hoof and mouth cattle disease. The survivors learned to spend their daylight hours in the most dense thornbush available, and are like phantoms to hunt.

After tracking from dawn, Boddington shot this Cape buffalo near midday along the Bubye River. For some reason this herd made a mistake and failed to reach the security of the riverine jungles before resting—and it's mistakes like that that hunters pray for and rarely get.

country. Even the odd elephant still passes through occasionally. It's impressive country, and given enough time one might see virtually anything there. But time is the key, for this is time-consuming country to hunt. It simply must be still-hunted into the wind, and game that is sighted will be seen at bayonet range.

Oddly, one of the finest trophies I took there was a warthog. So common in so many areas, a really fine boar is a surprisingly tough trophy to locate, and for some odd reason this particular corner of Zimbabwe consistently produces exceptional tuskers. We were ghosting through a patch of heavy thorn when we saw him, head down rooting for a choice tuber. Even with his head thrust into the underbrush I could see teeth, and the big bullet from the .338 seemed to lift him into the air and throw him to the ground.

But buffalo was the main quarry, and it was buffalo that we spent our time hunting. These buffalo didn't really know they were being hunted; the government-sponsored slaughter was long since over, and there had been no sport hunting to speak of. Even so, these buffalo were the survivors, and they knew what survival required. Several times we followed their tracks, but always they made the riverine growth before we could catch them. In that stuff, there was simply no chance. On hands and knees a man could get into them, but he could never judge horns before he shot.

Just maybe, though, we could catch this herd. This time we were on them earlier than we had been on previous days, and their tracks took them farther than usual out into the nighttime feeding grounds. Even these buffalo just might have made a mistake.

We followed until the sun was well up and the heat was building, and by then it seemed unlikely we could catch them. And yet, the tracks were still wandering aimlessly as the animals fed, a small herd of perhaps a dozen but with several outsize tracks in their midst.

It was hot now, and the big .470 that I had carried at port arms since daybreak was getting heavy. I wished for some water, and then wished for the tracks to do something—anything—even it meant a beeline for the cover that signaled the end of the hunt, one way or the other. The sweat ran freely, and I kept wiping my palms so they mightn't slip if the chance came.

Ray, more than twice my age, stepped along gaily. He was good in the bush, and unlike all too many African professionals, hunting dense cover on foot was his game. Perhaps he sensed we would catch them, or perhaps just the act of following them was his kind of tonic, but he never lost the tiny smile that played across his weathered features.

We did catch them, not in the most dense thorn, but in a belt of dry brush where a few yards of visibility was possible. The tracker saw them first, stooping slowly and pointing ahead like a staunch English setter. Ray and I came up behind him slowly, and I dropped to my knees. There was nothing there, and then I could make out a black form through the thorns about 50 yards ahead. And that was all it was, just a black form.

Ray mouthed, "Bull," and I looked some more. The animal was feeding slowly from right to left, quartering strongly away from us, and I finally saw a well-curved horn tip through a tiny opening. "Big bull," formed Ray's mouth.

I had no concept where to shoot, but the big Wilkes double settled into my shoulder and I nestled the ivory bead into the shallow V. There were no openings, but there were spots with less brush than others. I waited for such a spot, and when it came the big rifle rocked me back onto my heels. Mechanically, from long practice against just this occasion, I extracted the case and fed in another, and only then realized that I had seen the buffalo go down without a twitch.

From somewhere far off Ray was slapping my back, and then we were carefully advancing on the animal I had walked so many miles to bring down.

CHAPTER VIII
THE NORTHERN CAPE

South Africa's Cape Province is a vast piece of real estate encompassing nearly half of South Africa's land mass. Obviously it's the largest of South Africa's four provinces and contains the widest diversity of terrain. From the lush coastal hills of the south north through high mountains, fertile wine country, the wind-swept Great Karoo, to the edges of the Kalahari exist virtually every type of habitat imaginable save tropical rain forest. It should come as no great surprise, then, that South Africa's Cape Province is home to one of the greatest diversities of game species on the African continent, and hence in the world.

In the days of Roualeyn Gordon-Cumming and Cornwallis Harris the game of the Cape must have been truly something to see—elephant, white rhino, lion, endless herds of blesbok, seas of Cape buffalo, and so many animals that were hitherto unknown in Europe. One striking black antelope with white face mask and backswept horns—today called the sable—was first described by Harris in the northern Cape in 1837 and is still called the Harris buck by many. There were quagga, a long-gone relative of the zebra; roan antelope; bontebok; black and blue wildebeeste by the legion, greater kudu (then spelled "koodoo"); hartebeeste; oryx; Cape mountain zebra and Burchell's zebra; waterbuck; springbok beyond counting; impala and more—the full range of southern African species. In his 1838 book *A Narrative Of An Expedition into Southern Africa*—a "must read" for anyone interested in Africa—he writes thus of the shy eland: "Inhabits the open plains of the interior in vast herds."

But such plenty is no longer the case in the Cape, nor has it been for many years. As the Nineteenth Century progressed the Cape was settled, and as happened in the American West, little thought was given to the future and no thought to game conservation. Even in Selous' day one had to venture much farther north to find concentrations of game.

Fortunately, the country was vast enough and enough inhospitable places remained that few species were lost, although several came perilously close to extinction. The blue buck, a relative of the roan and sable, became extinct before Harris' and Gordon-Cumming's time. The unique quagga went soon after, and as time passed the great game—elephant, buffalo, rhino and lion became ever more scarce. The bontebok were reduced to a few individuals, likewise the Cape zebra and the black wildebeeste or white-tailed gnu. But the quagga and the blue buck were the only total casualties. In the early days of the Twentieth Century last-minute measures saved what remained of the Cape's once-limitless game populations, and the long road back began—much similar to what happened in the United States.

Today, thanks to game ranching and an increasingly active and astute Nature Conservancy department, the Cape offers a truly incredible variety of game and has growing populations and ever-increasing opportunities for the hunter. It is said that as much as 27 percent of the total land mass is devoted to game today!

Of course, the large and dangerous game is forever gone to the well-settled Cape. A few elephant and buffalo remain in the various parks, including Addo Elephant Sanctuary in the Eastern Cape, just north of Port Elizabeth. White rhino survived in a few parks, and surplus animals are occasionally taken by hunters for a trophy fee of enormous proportions. Lions are virtually gone from the Cape, excepting a fine population in the Kalahari Gemsbok National Park in the northwest. Leopards have fared better and still occur wherever sufficient cover exists—but the Cape leopard is smart and is only rarely taken by a hunter.

The antelope species, large and small, have fared better still. The Cape isn't a place for the hunter in search of dangerous game, but it is place that offers varied hunting for a full range of plains game, including several species not found elsewhere.

Springbok and greater kudu remain common in numerous areas, and gemsbok, red Cape hartebeeste, waterbuck, blesbok eland, impala and blue wildebeeste have been reintroduced on a large scale. The rarities are there, too—bontebok, southern mountain reedbuck, Vaal rhebok, black wildebeest, black and white color phases of the springbok, white blesbok, Cape grysbok and blue duiker.

It was the promise of this variety, plus the lure of big gemsbok, that drew me to the northern Cape. Headquarters was to be the little town of Douglas, just south of Kimberley from whence so many of the world's diamonds emanate. But, unlike so many safaris, "headquarters" is an apt term. While some ranches do have a variety of species, the trophy hunter in search of the oddities—and good trophies at that—will find himself travelling vast distances in the Cape in search of one specific animal. It was a kaleidoscopic hunt—one day 200 miles to the south in the fringes of the Great Karoo hunting black springbok, the next off to Orange Free State for a black wildebeeste, and still the next climbing rugged hills to the southeast following the rumor of big Vaal rhebok.

As the days passed I lost all sense of time and direction, and could no more retrace our course on a roadmap than chart the topography of Mars. Most of it was not difficult hunting, but it was hard hunting in that we pushed ourselves hard and tried to cover too much ground. There *is* such a thing as too much of a good thing, and the Cape's game is far too varied to do it all on one safari. I know that now, but Lord how we tried!

My professional hunter was Raymond Theron, very young and full of nervous energy and, in his first full season, determined to make a name for himself. We started by hunting gemsbok on Jimmy De Smidt's huge estate out of Douglas. After my initial trip to South West a couple of years before I still wanted a really large bull in the worst way, and Raymond thought we could find one on Jimmy's place.

This was big, open country, with some dense thickets along the river but mostly scrub thorn and grassland, not unlike the true Kalahari region just a couple hundred miles to the north. This was historic home to the gemsbok, but those that are present today have mostly been reintroduced and have been nurtured carefully.

They were in fair-sized herds, and the country was open enough to glass them at long range. As before, they all appeared to have long horns, and there was no way I could tell a truly large one from an average trophy. Nor, in all cases, could I tell the bulls from the cows by their headgear. Raymond could, and he could do it quickly.

We passed up several herds, but at length Raymond found a bull in a mixed herd of 20 that rated another look. They were spooky and it took much time, but finally we got close enough for that look. Several cows had horns that exceeded his in length—not unusual—but this was clearly a fine bull, with massive bases and the most length I had ever seen on a bull. It took more time to get a shot, much more time. Not only did he have to stand clear from the herd, but we had to count carefully from right to left or left to right and agree that we had the right one.

Finally, at about 200 yards he stood clear long enough, and we could clearly hear the big 250-grain slug from my .338 strike home. He was off with the herd, immediately mixing with the cows and lesser bulls and offering no second shot. We waited, then followed over the rise. He was there, down and alone; the bullet had punched clear through just behind the shoulders. Raymond had judged him at a bit more than 38 inches. He was, just on 39 with evenly matched horns and huge bases. Not quite up to the magic 40-inch mark, he was still the finest gemsbok bull I had ever seen, and he made a great start to the safari.

My memory fails me as to where we went next or what we hunted; we were covering too much ground, unfamiliar ground at that. I suspect there are whole days that I have no recollection of, but some I remember with tremendous clarity. One of those is the day of the mountain reedbuck.

We left Douglas well ahead of dawn, as seemed to be standard procedure by then, and drove endlessly through the dark in what direction I know not. Dawn caught us well up into a range of rough, rocky hills—perfect country for the little Vaal rhebok and his cousin, the mountain reedbuck. The Vaal rhebok is a unique little antelope,

The northern Cape Province of South Africa borders on the Kalahari Desert, and open scrub brush country such as this produces the best gemsbok trophies. The gemsbok hunter's Holy Grail is a bull that reaches 40 inches; females often grow to such length, males only rarely. This bull is 39 inches, short of the goal but still a fine trophy.

weighing no more than 40 pounds and with sharp spears of horns. A good one with horns of eight inches or better has headgear that looks all out of proportion to his tiny size. His coat is woolly, and he inhabits only rugged mountains, one of Africa's true mountain species. Whereas so many of South Africa's game species have been ranched successfully, attempts to ranch him have failed miserably. The males are too territorial, and they use their wicked little horns to fight to the death. They exist only in their natural state in their native habitat and just may be one of Africa's most challenging species to hunt. The mountain reedbuck is found over much of the same country, plus a lot more, and is generally much more plentiful and easier to find and shoot. This was an area that could produce either and, if we were very lucky, just might produce both.

We hiked into a wide canyon, sidehilling upwards and glassing the opposite side as we went. Far across we saw two rhebok, a small male and a female, leaping away over the far rim. They had spooked at 500 yards, and it occurred to me that this could get very interesting.

Another female flushed far ahead of us, and then nothing more. We worked our way around the top, then climbed back down across a valley and pulled ourselves up the next range of hills. It was lovely country, and the hunting was familiar again; we could have been hunting mule deer in a dozen different states. And for all the game we saw, we might as well have been.

This went on for some time, down one hill and up another, glassing as we went. Towards midday, when the game should have been long since bedded, we switched tactics. We had hiked across a broad flat to a long, rocky ridge. Raymond and I would climb up near the top and sidehill along, while his two trackers would follow lower down; they just might push something past us and offer a shot. They did, not more than 10 minutes after we started the drive.

Raymond and I were perched on a rock, watching some dense underbrush below while our trackers came up a hundred yards behind. I saw him first, just a flash of gray, but Raymond picked him out as a Vaal rhebok. Another followed, and they stopped just below us, a good male on the left and a female on the right. I had a steady hold from the sitting position and a clear sight picture, but I somehow slipped either high or low. The rhebok vanished, and there was no sound of a bullet hitting and no blood or hair at the spot. I just plain blew it. As the days passed we would hunt hard for Vaal rhebok in several different areas, but I was not to see another shootable male that trip.

Having made sure the shot was a miss, we continued on. The ridge ran for another 600 yards or more, so the potential was far from gone. As we reached the end, though, it seemed that one chance had been the whole story. Raymond and I were resting on a flat rock. The ridge dropped steeply away in front of us, and far to our left we could see the two trackers making their way out towards the flat and the track where we would meet. Then, in front of them, Raymond saw movement. We both got our glasses on the distant form, hoping for Vaal rhebok. It wasn't, but it was a superb mountain reedbuck walking well ahead of our drivers.

Raymond urged me to try a shot, but I resisted. It was too far to describe, and after all, I had just missed a much easier shot that by all rights I should have made. The reedbuck was unconcerned, walking in an arc in front of us, not overly concerned, stopping occasionally to look back over his shoulder.

Raymond persisted. Finally he said, "There's no way we can get closer in time to do any good. That buck is gone anyway, and if you get one of those big bullets into him, we'll get him." I couldn't argue with logic, so I gave in and lay down on the rock, adjusting into a tight sling and getting into the steadiest prone position I could.

It was really terribly far; even with the variable turned up to 9X the reedbuck was tiny in the crosshairs. The angle was steep enough downhill to make a difference, but I still held well high and into the wind and, with a bit of a prayer, squeezed the trigger as carefully as I knew how.

The odd thing was that he went down. I had hit a little far back, and he was up again quickly, but he didn't go far. We found him quickly—and a superb trophy he was. As unlucky as he was, I can't imagine how he lived long enough to grow good horns . . .

Another fine day was when we drove down into the Great Karoo to hunt black springbok. The Great Karoo is a vast expanse of low, rocky hills and arid grassland, ranching country of big spreads, little water and few people. It's beautiful in its way, and calls to mind the stark sagebrush country of eastern Wyoming. There is little variety of game there, but the springbok are incredibly plentiful.

This black variety that we sought is a bit of a mystery. They weren't known historically, but as legend has it the first one was seen in a herd in the Cape around the turn of the century. The rancher apparently bred them carefully as a curiosity, and it's possible the trait is somewhat dominant, if not widespread. Today black springbok are found on many farms, and on this farm there was a large herd of all-black springbok. The white springbok is much the same situation, but for some reason I don't find them attractive; they seem merely anemic next to a common springbok, while the black phase is strikingly beautiful. Although up close their coats are more of a dusky charcoal, at a distance they indeed appear glossy black. Both black and white springbok tend to have small horns, so finding a good trophy that happens to be black is a difficult trick.

They're also extremely spooky. In fact, all springbok are spooky, but it's possible that the black springbok, lacking the natural camouflage of his kind, is spookier yet. This herd had several nice rams, and we made innumerable approaches that fizzled out. Just as we closed to long rifle range, they would run a few hundred yards, then mill nervously. Either we could wait a while for them to settle down, then continue, or we could back off and try from another direction. We tried both tactics and neither worked. Eventually we decided that one man alone might have a better chance, so Raymond sat back and chuckled while I belly-crawled endlessy through the short grass.

Very late in the day, with the sun just touching a distant range of hills, I finally had them where I wanted them, more or less. I had circled around and come in from a new angle, and the herd was moving slowly in my direction. I lay across an anthill and waited them out, picking out a good buck a half-dozen deep in the long file of black animals. They came on, and I shot him when he stood quartered to me, still a long ways off but much closer than I'd been all day. He was truly beautiful, one of those animals that I hadn't really intended to hunt but have been very glad that I did.

Some of the hunt was shared with Jack Hollimon from Texas, a fine gentleman who I hadn't met before but has remained a good friend. Some days we hunted together, and other days went different directions with our own guides. We hunted together for black wildebeeste and both took unusually fine trophies. Another memorable day was when Jack shot his lion.

He had come to hunt lion, and after a few days of hunting the Cape species it became obvious that this wasn't lion country. Raymond explained that he knew a farmer up north who baited lions across the border from Botswana and that as soon as he had one on bait we would go. Finally the call came—there was indeed a lion on bait, and we must leave in the middle of the night to hunt him in the morning.

In retrospect Jack and I have long suspected this was not a wild lion, especially since the shameful practice of releasing lions for the gun has come to light in South Africa—and been largely stopped by an increasingly aggressive South African Professional Hunters Association. The area was indeed on the Botswana border, and it was remote enough that a wild lion was possible—if only remotely so. I was there as an observer, and I don't know the truth of it. I'm not sure I want to know, and I wish the question didn't nag at my mind.

We tracked the lion in the Kalahari sand, fair and square for several hours. We pushed him as far as he would be pushed, and Jack shot him fair and square at 15 feet when he finally turned to charge. He was a nice lion with the thornbush mane of a wild lion, not the impossibly-maned lion that the put-up jobs usually are. I will never forget the anger in those cold yellow eyes in that last second before he sprang, the very second that Jack's bullet caught him. I want very much to believe it was all as real as that endless moment when every part of me was willing Jack's rifle to go off—and that moment, regardless of the truth of the whole situation, was very real indeed.

Jack was with me when I shot a fine blue wildebeeste, my first, and I learned that all I'd heard about the toughness of these creatures was true. Pound for pound, they can soak up lead better than a buffalo, and yet on other occasions go down readily to a small-caliber rifle. This wasn't one of those occasions. It took four big Silvertips from the .338, all solid chest shots, and all hits were several minutes of shooting, waiting and tracking apart.

I had a few days left to hunt when we put Jack on a plane for Texas, and Raymond and I continued to try for a Vaal rhebok. We followed several leads on new areas and hunted favored hotspots as well, but the big males eluded us altogether. I picked up a blesbok somewhere in there and declined on a bontebok. While the purple-hued backskin of the much more rare bontebok is quite distinctive, few people can distinguish the mounted heads. For a trophy fee six times that of the blesbok, I couldn't see enough difference to matter!

Late in the hunt we tried one last spot for Vaal rhebok. There were indeed many on that mountain, and this time, for a change, we saw numerous females and several young males. But the big ones stayed hidden. On the way back to the truck Raymond spied a small herd of springbok and asked if I would mind taking one for camp meat.

We circled to get the wind, then used the cover of a pond dike to get close. We eased up the low embankment and peered over the top, me sliding the .338 into position in front of me. It was a small herd, fewer

The white-tailed gnu or black wildebeeste is another unique South African species. Nearly eradicated during South Africa's pioneer era, they have been brought back by careful management. It would be difficult to call them pretty, but they're an extremely interesting trophy.

than a dozen, but there was one quite nice male. Exactly behind him was another ram, and we were far too close to wait too long.

When the larger ram's head came up, I put the crosshairs high on his neck and finished the squeeze. The recoil rolled me up and back, but I came down in time to see both springbok roll like rabbits. The smaller ram had lifted his head just as I fired, and the bullet took them both through the neck. Raymond was happy with the meat and the blacks were elated, believing I'd done it on purpose. I was happy to have the skins, but chagrined as well. Once again I resolved to stay away from the neck shot—it just doesn't agree with me . . .

In between forays after Vaal rhebok—those "little woolly bastards," as I came to call them—we made several short hunts for two of my favorites, the greater kudu and the bushbuck. In neither case did we find what we were looking for, but those are two animals that are always rewarding to seek; no hunt for a truly great game animal is really unsuccessful.

Kudu are quite common in the hills near the confluence of the Vaal and Orange Rivers, and while real trophy bulls are rare, once in a while a monster is taken. Just two years later Bob Petersen, our Chairman of

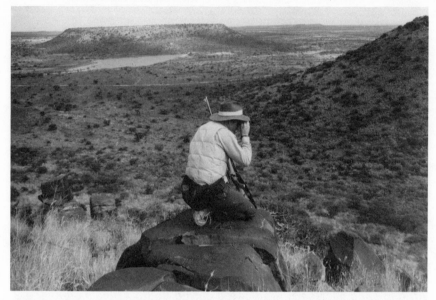

These rocky kopjes near the Vaal River in South Africa are ideal habitat for mountain reedbuck and their elusive cousin, the Vaal rhebok.

the Board at Petersen Publishing Company, took a 60-incher out of that area. We didn't see such a bull, but it was fun hunting, glassing in the thornbush hills. The only big bull we saw crossed the road in our headlights late one night as we returned from God-knows-where, and he was huge.

The bushbuck there were dark, nearly black animals of the Cape bushbuck variety. Like with the kudu, the big males stayed out of sight. But the hunting was in stark contrast, strictly still-hunting in the dense riverine growth along the tributaries to the Vaal. It's exciting hunting, especially in Africa where you don't know what you might see next. Take a few steps, scan the dense cover, then take a few more. You will see game in African cover like that, but it may not be the game you're looking for. In our case it wasn't, but we bumped eland bulls, the occasional impala, shy duiker, and every once in a while a bushbuck female or young male. There were alarm barks from an unknown source, too—the short sharp harsh bark of a bushbuck. And when you hear it you just *know* the big black male you're seeking has bid you good bye.

In retrospect, the northern Cape offered some of the most varied

The little mountain reedbuck is a fascinating and often difficult animal to hunt. Although apparently insignificant when compared with a common reedbuck, this ram easily makes the record book. But the author is grinning mainly because his best, longest, and probably luckiest shot was required to bring it down.

hunting I've ever seen, much of it in scenic country more than worth the trip to see. But for the man in search of good trophies, it's hectic hunting. Never have I covered so much ground in so short a time. And that's the kind of hunting it is, for the opportunities are excellent and growing annually—but few areas can offer exceptional quality in more than a couple of species. A well-rounded bag of good specimens simply requires mobility and flexibility, and plenty of each. In retrospect, too, it was a very fine hunt—but I had to get home and rest up a bit before I could begin to enjoy the memories!

CHAPTER IX
THE ORONGO MOUNTAINS

It felt like coming home to be driving back to Epako, and it felt like I had waited too long to return. The skies were just as blue, and the rocky ridges and *kopjes* were just as familiar. It's actually a fair distance from the capital of Windhoek northwest to the little town of Omaruru, but it goes quickly. The road is well paved but little-traveled, and every few miles a kudu or sounder of warthogs will cross ahead of you. The country had changed very little since 1979, when I last had hunted there. Though the decade had changed this was still South West Africa, although the tagline "Namibia" was seeing ever more frequent use. *Namibia*, of course, is the name preferred by the black Africans who inhabit this arid land, while *South West* is a holdover from colonial days. The country itself is a bit of a holdover, still a protectorate of the Republic of South Africa in spite of increasing international pressure for complete independence. In all of Africa, South West is one of the last vestiges of the colonial era, and in time—perhaps before these lines see the light of day—it, too, will become an independent state.

For South West, that may not be a bad thing. With one of the world's smallest populations per square mile—a million people in a country nearly a quarter larger than Texas—and a stable economy based jointly on agriculture and mining, South West has a chance to develop into a successful multiracial state. Provided, of course, the Communists will allow it to happen. And that only time will tell.

For the present, though, South West offers some of Africa's most scenic, most easily arranged and conducted, and most inexpensive hunting. It's pleasant country with few species, but what there is is good. And even if it weren't, it's a place that one needs little encouragement to return to.

The goals of this trip were modest but very specific. First, I wanted to take a good Cape hartebeeste, largest of the damaliscs. Second, I wanted to hunt on foot for a Hartmann's zebra and see a bit more of the rugged Orongo Mountains. And last, I just wanted to enjoy a bit more of the company of Ben Nolte, one of the finest professional hunters I had been with, and a good friend besides.

Epako had changed but little, but there were signs of prosperity. A swimming pool had been added next to the guest quarters, and trophies now hung in the big common room. Good trophies, but not the very best available—Ben wanted his new clients to see what they could reasonably expect, and then hope to pleasantly surprise them instead of showing them animals they might not be able to equal. The hunting business had been good for Ben. He still complained of not enough clients—what outfitter doesn't? But his English was smooth and self-assured now, his manner expressing confidence and satisfaction. He complained about the drought, of course—more than a year had passed without rain, and soon he would start losing some of the game he had so carefully built up. He complained, too, about the constant call-ups, which took him away from business to patrol the Angolan border against the Soviet- and Cuban-trained guerrillas. But overall he was confident and content—the rains would come, the guerrilla activity would be contained, and the hunting clients would arrive in increasing numbers.

In the years since then, Ben's confidence has proven well founded. The rains have been good, and they've arrived on schedule. The call-ups have diminished, and the guerrilla activity has indeed been contained and virtually stopped. And the clients have come, too. Never enough, perhaps, but more than in years gone by. When Ben first sold off all his livestock and devoted Epako's acreage to game, the word in the district was that Ben Nolte had gone mad, and he was laughed at behind his back. There's little laughter today; instead there are others who have followed his example.

Ben was just finishing with another client, so for the first couple of days I would hunt with Joof Lamprecht, a pleasant, competent guide who was then working with Ben. The hartebeeste would come first, and we would hunt for him on Epako—a fact that pleased me, since I had nothing but pleasant memories of the place and was anxious to see how it looked. As I write these lines I realize that far too much time has passed again since I've seen Epako—more than five years now. Sometimes one gets caught up with the wrong goals in hunting—and in life—and there have been too many new horizons and too many different challenges. But of all the places I've seen in Africa, South West—or Namibia if it must be—is a place that I've promised myself I'll return to. I think it's time to see Epako again; I'd like to see it much greener than it was in that year of drought.

The bush was frightfully dry then, but deep wells were still supplying plenty of water. The game was generally in good shape, so far, but continued drought would be a disaster. Already the warthogs—the first to go in a drought—were beginning to suffer. But the kudu were in good shape, and the gemsbok had multiplied significantly since I was there last. The great eland, too—only recently introduced when I was there before—had taken hold well and produced many calves. Nolte had experimented with black-faced Angolan impala, very rare in South West, but they alone had not taken to Epako. Too many cheetahs was Ben's theory; his painstakingly acquired breeding stock had simply vanished.

The hartebeeste, also recently introduced on my first visit, had done exceedingly well, and while the overall herd wasn't large, Ben felt he had

South West Africa produces some of the best red Cape hartebeeste. Although an ungainly animal, this large member of the hartebeeste group grows spectacular twisted horns. At 24 inches, this is a fine specimen.

99

several superb bulls. We hunted for them by glassing from the *kopjes* and by hunting on foot along likely canyons and hillsides.

Early in the hunt we walked carefully up a narrow, steep-sided canyon, following the squarish tracks of a small herd of hartebeeste. The hartebeeste had gone on, but up ahead we saw movement on a brushy hillside. We put our glasses on them and saw four of the beautifully striped mountain zebra pick their way along a narrow game trail. We followed for a while, watching, and there was indeed one fine stallion in the herd. But we broke off after a time and let them go their way. Ben wanted to hunt them much deeper in the Orongos, and so did I.

That afternoon we caught a good herd of hartebeeste, oxblood red with black nose blaze and gnarled horns mounted on a ridiculously high pedicel. They're an ungainly creature, seemingly clumsy with their pogo-stick gait and deceptively fast. This herd was in some dense brush, and there was a very fine bull. But with hartebeeste, only a couple of inches separates very fine from mediocre, and we didn't want to make any mistakes. We watched them for a time, stalking closer as they milled in the dappled shade, but we were never sure enough to risk a shot. Finally the wind shifted and that deceptive gait—accompanied by a cloud of red dust—carried them safely away.

The next couple of days produced more of the same. Just getting a hartebeeste was no problem, nor was putting one in the record book—even the Rowland Ward minimum is surprisingly low for this species. But we had time, and I had interest in few animals; we were determined to find the best bull we could.

We finally found him, feeding along a brushy hillside with a small herd. The cover there was much like the miserable chaparral that plagues our California deer hunting. From a distance, you might glass game in it, but up close you can't see through it or walk through it. We worked the edges into the wind, knowing the herd was in there and knowing we would see them if we were careful enough and quiet enough. We fought our way up a little knoll, and the herd was angling up the far slope just 80 yards away. Joof picked out the big bull more quickly than I did, but I got the dot reticle on him and fired just as he began to run. The bullet, a big 350-grain Barnes softnose from the .375, passed through his heart without expanding, and he ran through a low saddle with his herd. We found him just on the other side, and Joof had called him correctly—just the kind of hartebeeste we had set out to find.

Ben was free now, so he took over and we began our search for a mountain zebra. As is his custom, we hunted a different area each day, driving deep into the Orongos to an isolated ranch, hunting the day, then returning to Epako just after dark.

We hunted them by tracking, checking water sources at daybreak until we found the fresh horselike spoor, then following up into the hills. There are unquestionably easier ways to take a zebra, but few as rewarding. Nor is there a better way to see game country.

These zebras are extremely wary. Hunted hard for generations, they had been hammered unmercifully by the farmers in recent months. With the drought, they were viewed as offering too much competition for domestic cattle and sheep, and the tolerance for them was at a low ebb. There seemed to be no shortage of them; finding tracks to follow was no great trick. Finding the zebra standing in those tracks was another matter.

We closed in several times only to have the wind shift or a rolling rock give us away. Sometimes we were in sight but were unable to pick out a stallion—and sometimes we never sighted our quarry at all. But we saw a good deal of those rugged, rocky mountains—and most of the animals that dwell there.

Fine kudu were sighted every day, and large herds of gemsbok. One morning we watched a big troop of baboons far up a steep face, and several times we glimpsed the tiny blue Damaraland dik dik dashing off into the brush. The mountains felt much like home; they were virtually identical to the Chiricahuas, Peloncillos, Catalinas, and Galiuros in far-off Arizona, favored hunting grounds of mine for many years. We could have shot trophy kudu on any day, and while we saw no huge gemsbok, above-average bulls would have posed no problem. But it seemed we simply couldn't catch up with Mrs. Hartmann's zebra—although I've heard so many say that there's no sport to shooting a zebra.

It was about this time that I came down with a nagging intestinal ailment, unusual for me and my normally cast-iron stomach. It wasn't serious, but it was painful and sapped my strength, and I had to stop often and dash into the bushes. The mountains were getting steeper then, and I had to carry water to avoid dehydration.

It was on the day when I wasn't sure I could hunt at all that we finally got a break. We had driven ever deeper into the Orongos, and the sun was just breaking over the eastern ridges when we drove onto the ranch we were to hunt. I was dozing after a long, mostly sleepless night when Ben jammed on the brakes. There, far up the ridge with the morning sun glinting on their striped hides, was a big herd of mountain zebra,

After an endless wait, professional hunter Ben Nolte finally determined which of the Hartmann's zebra was the stallion. All zebra are surprisingly wary, but in the rugged Orongo Mountains stalking Mrs. Hartmann's mountain zebra is challenging and exciting—a great hunt!

just going up from water. We trained our binoculars on them. It was almost close enough for a shot, but they were shifting and moving as they headed higher into the mountains. I had stated that I wanted a big stallion, and purist that he is, Ben had determined that a stallion it would be. He couldn't be sure, and I think that, after the days of hard hunting, neither of us wanted to shoot this beast from a road. We last saw them topping out a thousand yards above us.

Although Ben had secured the hunting rights on this land, we still observed the formalities, stopping by the farmhouse for a cup of coffee and the friendly conversation much prized on lonely farms. (There's that word *farm* again, much preferred in southern Africa. To me this was a *ranch*, some 50,000 acres of rough-and-tumble mountains, with a few bedraggled three-strand barbwire fences here and there.) Then, with me more pale than the background color between a zebra's stripes, we drove back down the road, parked the truck, and trekked up the steep ridge to pick up tracks.

It was far too rocky here. South West, and to a great degree South Africa, offers hunting much unlike that in other parts of the continent.

There are a few great black trackers in this country, but those arts have mostly been lost. The game in South West is better now than at any other time in this century, and except in the most remote tribal areas, the traditional hunting skills have long since given way to herdsmen's skills. In South West, the professional hunter is very much *the* professional hunter, relying on his own hunting skills as outfitters do the world over, not on the bushcraft wizardry of a black African. It's possible there are black Africans who could have followed on that rocky ground. But I couldn't have, nor could Ben—who is as good as most black Africans—nor could any white man regardless of experience. We had no choice but to circle and cast ahead.

The wind was fickle in those mountains, but for the moment it was on our side. We had seen the zebra pass through a high saddle, so we climbed to that point and glassed. There were gemsbok on the very top, but we could see no other game. To keep the wind right we backed off, coming back through the saddle, then beginning a long circle to the right to look into some deep canyons with grassy benches.

The Hartmann's zebra is a very large zebra with unique stripe patterns that end short of the belly rather than joinging on the centerline as do common zebras' stripes. This zebra is found only in South West Africa's Orongo Mountains, and is an under-rated trophy well worth having.

I was sweating heavily and having trouble breathing. Ben moved slowly, stopping often to glass—and it was a good thing. We completed a half-circle around the highest peak, and now looked down a series of fingers and canyons that simply had to hold this herd and probably several more. Ben picked out a distant herd, far off across a deep canyon well over a mile away. They were on a small bench, feeding peacefully, and we marked them as a worst-case stalk: It might take half a day to reach them, so broken was the ground in between.

Then we started working down the ridges, moving and glassing. Four hours after we started we were still moving and glassing, and I was light-headed and lead-footed. I climbed up onto a little rockpile beside Ben and put my head between my knees, wincing as a pain shot through my belly.

"Listen!" Ben grabbed my arm, then pointed down into a winding streambed several hundred yards below us. "I heard a stallion scream."

It came again, a high-pitched whinny that, once heard, is never forgotten. It echoed through the canyons, but it had surely started somewhere below us. I gathered what strength remained, and we started down off the ridge. We had to circle to the right, cross a canyon, then climb a knife-edge ridge to look into the canyon from which we thought the stallion had screamed. It wasn't a difficult stalk, but I kept thinking that, win or lose, we would have to climb back up to get out—and I wasn't altogether sure it was in me.

There was other game in those canyons. We skirted wide around a big bull kudu, then worked our way carefully between two herds of gemsbok. Finally we started up the steep ridge, aiming for a rocky pinnacle that we'd seen from above.

We moved carefully now, one step at a time, easing ourselves up and testing each rock. There was a wide, flat boulder on top. We crawled onto it, then crept forward and peered over. Nothing. Then the stallion screamed again just below us, hidden by the overhang of the very boulder we were on. We were overlooking a sandy wash with a few scattered thorn trees, and we waited. Soon one zebra moved into view, then another. Finally there were six, straight below us at about 80 yards. One of them was surely the vociferous stallion—but which one? From straight overhead there is no chance to view the biological evidence.

A half hour later Ben was almost certain which one—but almost wasn't good enough for him. "I think we wait," he whispered. "We must be *vvvery* sure."

Another quarter hour, while the zebra milled in and out of sight below us. "Yes, I think it is this one. But I must be sure. We wait," he said.

Another quarter hour, and by now I wasn't sure how much the zebra's sex really mattered to me. "Yes, I am sure it is this one. Shoot him very carefully."

He had fed out from the cliff and was at a slightly less severe angle. Still, I needed to place the bullet well above the top of the shoulder blade to angle down into the vitals. This was the kind of shot the long, heavy Barnes bullet was made for. It entered right on target, drove down through, and exited beneath the off foreleg. Its force slammed the big stallion into the rocky ground, and he remained exactly as he had fallen.

It's odd, but the trip out wasn't as bad as I had expected. In fact, I recall fairly skipping out of that canyon, and whatever had been ailing me, I must have sweated it out that morning. By the next day I was ready for anything.

I had been intrigued by the Namib Desert, so a day or two later we headed out that way. Ben had heard of a place where there were some really large springbok, and I had a strange desire to take an ostrich for a pair of boots. The ostrich is farmed in many parts of southern Africa and is often used on game ranches as a sort of feathered antipoaching patrol. What makes them do it I can't say, but on many South African game ranches I've seen ostrich strutting up and down a fenceline for hours on end. Perhaps they don't like fences, or perhaps they have a natural desire to see what's on the other side. But it's for sure they don't like people very much, and woe to him who crosses a fence guarded by such a creature!

In the Namib, though, we could hunt a truly wild ostrich—and a wild hunt it turned out to be. The birds were tremendously spooky, and those outrageously long legs carry them in excess of 40 miles per hour. The males are quite beautiful, with striking black-and-white plumage as opposed to the drab brown of the hens. I finally got one, dropping him in full stride with a 7mm bullet to the base of the wing. His momentum carried him 20 yards, cartwheeling and leaving dust and feathers. It proved a worthwhile hunt, although a bit offbeat, and the boots are beautiful. A word of caution, though. By the time one shoots an ostrich, pays the trophy fee, ships the hide home, has it tanned and then dyed, and cons a bootmaker into working with it, one has paid the equivalent of a great deal of hunting. Or a whole closet full of perfectly acceptable boots!

We hunted hard for a really fine springbok, better than I had taken previously, but it wasn't in the cards. The wind blew constantly and the animals, indeed quite plentiful, were wild and spooky. We saw several acceptable males but nothing spectacular. At midday we stopped in a shady grove sheltered from the biting wind. We built a small fire, let it build into glowing coals, then threw on a small grill and cooked sausage and cubes of ostrich. Later we slept for a bit, then continued looking for the quality of springbok that didn't seem to be there. It was lovely country, and I was much saddened to have to leave it once again.

But I had one more day, and there was nothing that I wanted badly to shoot. I talked Ben into loaning me a Land Rover, and with a lunch, a book, a camera, and a rifle, I drove within a mile of a particularly good waterhole on Epako, then slipped carefully into one of the hides that Ben leaves at strategic points year-round.

I spent the entire last day watching that waterhole, alternately reading—occasionally dozing—and enjoying the sights and sounds of an African day.

Nothing much happened. A troop of baboons came down at mid-morning, drank greedily, then got into a terrible argument and screamed at one another as they retreated into the bush. Towards midday the thirsty warthogs slipped in, and a fine boar rooted around briefly, then dove into the brush when my camera clicked. That was the last photo I took, for I didn't want to disturb anything.

Cheetah might have come to this waterhole, perhaps even a leopard, but not this day. The kudu did come, though, as I knew they must. They came towards evening—first a lone cow, then a bull, then by twos and threes. Perfectly camouflaged in the gray twilight, they came like ghosts, looking and listening and scenting—for even in South West, no place is as dangerous as the waterhole. I watched them until dusk turned to dark, then gathered my gear and headed back to the Land Rover. The hunt was indeed over.

CHAPTER X
THE LUANGWA VALLEY

Our pilot circled low over the strip at Chibembe, taking a hard look at the state of the dirt runway before coming around for a landing. During the two-hour flight from Lusaka we had seen the patchwork of cultivation below us and occasionally the circular roofs of a village—but we mostly saw miles and miles of unbroken thornbush and mopane woodland. We had been too high to even attempt to sight game, but now we were plenty low enough and all eyes scanned the ground below. Our circle took us back over the sluggish Luangwa River, and we could see several hippo partially submerged in mid-channel. Then we were over the thornbush, and I saw the tan flash of impala running. Someone else called out, "Look, zebra," and then another voice drew our eyes to three elephants, great lumbering shapes moving away from the path of the plane. I had heard that Zambia's Luangwa Valley held one of the greatest remaining concentrations of game in Africa, and at first glance I couldn't dispute that.

Zambia—Northern Rhodesia in colonial days—is a latecomer to the safari business. Prior to independence a small amount of hunting was conducted, but there was no safari industry as such. That began in the early 1970s when the government began allocating hunting concessions on parcels of land around the various parks. While the country does indeed offer an excellent variety of fine game animals, it has very few local rarities and, although overall trophy quality is good, in very few cases does Zambia offer horn size that can't be excelled elsewhere. It's perhaps an accident of history that Zambia has become the popular hunting country that it is. Rosemary van Dyk, wife of my Kenya professional hunter, summed it up thusly even before Kenya closed hunting: "When East Africa was at its height, there was no reason for anyone to hunt in Zambia." But Kenya did close, following Tanzania, Mozambique, and Uganda. Tanzania reopened, but that country had lost its professional hunting industry during the closure and even at this writing is still rebuilding its lost reputation.

In the late 1970s and early 1980s, there were very few options for a traditional full-mixed-bag safari. Zimbabwe was still recovering from the disastrous war years. Botswana remained good, but its species list was limited and the illegality of baiting for cats reduced its potential. Zambia stepped into the gap. With a varied menu of plains game—including such desirables as sable, roan, kudu, eland, and sitatunga—and good populations of the entire Big Five, by the early 1980s Zambia had become the place to go for a general-bag safari. President Kaunda's government wisely saw hunting as a viable means of attracting tourism dollars and over the years has remained active in its support for the hunting industry. And of course, the government was stable, the road network was very good for Africa, and commodities were available. Zambia was not only a good place for the sport hunter but also a good place for the professional hunter to ply his trade.

Of course, nothing is constant in Africa. As poaching increased—and pressure from conservation groups escalated—Zambia was forced to close first black rhino hunting and then elephant hunting. The poaching did not diminish, of course. Instead it escalated now that it no longer paid the outfitters to maintain year-round game guards in their camps. But Zambia remained—and is today—a premier area to hunt the great cats along with a goodly variety of other game. I wanted to see it very badly and began to make plans.

There were drawbacks. Since the inception of safari hunting there Zambia has been one of Africa's most expensive countries to hunt, expensive in terms of both daily rate and trophy fees. It's worse today, and while the hunting is unquestionably worth whatever it costs, it's a moot point if you can't afford it. For the first time I became a part of a "group hunt," several hunters sharing a camp and hunting "2x1"—two clients with one professional hunter. The trip was planned for late May, very early in the season and a much less desirable time than the peak hunting months of July through October. These compromises made the hunt affordable, but only time would tell if the results would justify the savings.

There were other decisions as well, but the most agonizing was which area to choose. Each year Zambia opens a bit more of its vast hinterlands to sport hunting. Today there are a couple of other choices, but in the early 1980s there were only two general-bag areas—the Kafue highlands west of Lusaka and the great Luangwa Valley to the northeast. Distances are such that, unless you have ready access to an airplane or are willing to pay high charter fees, it's feasible to hunt just one area on a safari of normal duration. The two areas, Kafue and Luangwa, are vastly different, and like any hunters planning to hunt unfamiliar country, we were planning in a vacuum. There were some things we should have known, such as the differences between the two areas in May as compared with the differences later in the season. But we were ignorant, and out of ignorance—and blind luck—we chose the Luangwa Valley. We had been told the game was more concentrated in Luangwa, and that was true. We were also told that there were more lions, although at their best the manes weren't quite as good as in the Kafue. Having now been to both areas at vastly different times of year, I think that is also true. But a couple of us wanted sable antelope, present in the Kafue but absent in Luangwa, and we were sorely tempted. Ultimately better odds on the cats won out, and we decided on the Luangwa. It was a good choice, though perhaps made for the wrong reasons.

There were four hunters in our immediate group, all bound for the Luangwa. But the total group consisted of some 12 hunters, and four of them opted to hunt the Kafue because of the sable. All of us found May a difficult time to hunt Zambia. The grass was high and much of the game was scattered in the hills. But in Luangwa it was just difficult, and in the final analysis all eight hunters who chose that area had successful safaris. In the Kafue, May proved a disastrous time to hunt, with days passing between sightings of individual animals. The intent of this book is to provide enjoyable reading about African hunting, not to serve as a guide in the planning of a safari. However, careful planning—based on the most accurate knowledge available—is terribly important, and the lessons learned from planning this hunt are worth recounting.

We knew we would be hunting a bit too early; that consideration was part of this particular hunt. In the Luangwa, we arrived to find the hunting camps still under construction; all eight of us were based in the same camp, a large facility normally used for photographic safaris. Although the concessions were very large, that's far too many hunters operating from one camp, especially if cats are desired and more especially with the high grass and scattered game. And yet our party of eight—really seven hunters since two were a couple with only the husband hunting "1x1"—managed four cats and an impressive array of buffalo and plains game in the Luangwa. At the exact same time in the

Kafue, four hunters hunting 2x1 from one camp took no cats, two sable, a good kudu, and little else.

Of course, hunting success simply cannot be measured in terms of trophies taken, and in things that matter no African safari can be unsuccessful. But one has only so much time to hunt and so many dollars to do it with, so there is a finite limit on the number of hunts any of us will be allowed to make. Murphy was right—whatever can go wrong will, and the game will not always be brought to bag. That's part of the sport. However, planning properly is also part of the sport, and losing opportunities because of poor research or careless planning is an extravagance that the modern hunter on a limited budget simply cannot afford.

But we were committed now. The plane was touching down on the Chibembe strip, and now the chips would fall as they would. I was unusually tired for the start of a safari. The jet lag had hit me unmercifully on that trip, and although we'd stayed two days in Lusaka, I don't think I'd slept more than an hour a night. The delay in Lusaka, we would later learn, had been to give the camp staff extra time to

Lions on the bait early in the hunt is the best possible sign, and both the author and professional hunter Bill Illingworth were confident there was a big male in the pride. It took more than a week of stalking the bait and waiting up overnight in a machan to determine that the big boy had wandered off.

prepare for us. The annual flooding of the Luangwa had destroyed one of the camps, and ultimately it couldn't be finished in time, hence the decision to house us all at Chibembe.

It had been a boring stay in Lusaka—a little shopping, a lot of reading, and for most of us a chance to catch up on our sleep. Shortly after we arrived at our hotel there was just one piece of excitement. I was summoned to the lobby and directed to a tall, elderly African in black suit and bowler hat. With great dignity and a courtly bow he handed me a letter, which I still have.

It bore the elephant seal of the Barotse royal establishment, and it stated that the bearer was a senior *induna*—headman—of the Barotse tribe and had come to extend me a personal welcome to Zambia. The writer of the letter was unable to come himself because the Barotses were involved in their traditional move from summer to winter grounds, but he had sent his emissary to bid me hello. It was signed by His Royal Highness The Litunga of the Western Province, hereditary monarch of the Barotse tribe.

It had been about two years earlier that I had first seen that elephant seal. I had been working full-time for Petersen Publishing Company since 1979, and although I was with *HUNTING* Magazine at the time of this safari, that elephant seal had first appeared on my desk as part of some reader mail regarding the *GUNS & AMMO* Annuals that I had been editing. Through his secretary, the Litunga had written to my office to inquire about a magazine subscription and for some technical advice on .375 bullets. I questioned the authenticity of the letter at first but did some checking around. In colonial days Barotseland was administered separately, but when independence came it was incorporated as the Western Province of the new state of Zambia. The Barotse tribe has a hereditary monarchy with a lineage that outdates most of the European dynasties. The ruler of the tribe carries the title of Litunga, passed down from his father and his father before him. The current Litunga is far better educated than this scribe and has held a variety of positions in Dr. Kaunda's government. He's also a dedicated hunter, and over the years we have exchanged many letters. I had mentioned in a recent letter that I would be arriving in Lusaka on a certain date, and the Litunga had sent his emissary to greet me—an act that I will never forget.

The stay in Lusaka had also given time for our group to jell, and it looked as if all the diverse personalities would mesh well. From Los Angeles, paired together, were my good friends Bob Tatsch and Bill

Sims, with Dorothy Tatsch along as an observer. Sims, a genuine character, appointed himself official expedition historian—most of us still send him a monthly stipend to keep his version under wraps. As the trip progressed he decided that given names were too complex. Tatsch became Buffalo Bob, his wife Dynamite Dorothy. In a fit of modesty he decided his own name would be Super Hunter Sims, and since I had talked him into coming on the trip I became Karamojo Craig. My hunting partner, Kim Adamson from Salt Lake, became Calamity Kim—mainly because her luck was far too good to last! Dave Bernahl from Chicago, a gemstone dealer, became Trader Dave—he was wheeling and dealing every step of the way. Smokin' Bob Ellswick, his partner, was a quieter sort, but they made a good team and had hunted together many times before—unlike all the rest of us. It was to be Ellswick's last safari; he went down in a private plane just a year later. Rounding out the Luangwa group were Carl and Sharon Swanson from Colorado. They were fine people, and for the life of me I can't explain why Super Hunter Sims allowed them to keep their names intact.

It was midafternoon when we arrived at Chibembe, and it was blazing hot on the valley floor. The camp itself sat right on the banks of the Luangwa under a cool grove of huge missasso trees, and it was beautiful. Lodging was comfortable cabins with running water, and we all took time to get moved in and organized, then went down the road a piece *en masse* to sight in the rifles.

We had a good crew of professional hunters, competent and energetic. Sims and Tatsch drew Paddy Curtis, a redbearded young Rhodesian with quick wit and ready smile—and a burning desire to excel at his trade. Trader Dave and Smokin' Bob hunted with Alistair Gellatly, and from day one went their own direction. Other than the fact that they enjoyed themselves and had bad luck with the cats, I can't say much about their portion of the hunt. The Swansons hunted with Robin Voigt, another youngster but a competent professional. Around the campfire Robin was personable and told a good story, but he and the Swansons also went their own way; there was no rivalry amongst the professional hunters, as sometimes can happen in a large camp. Kim and I drew Bill Illingworth, the patriarch of the group and the resident professional hunter for this area. Past middle age and stout of build, Illingworth was past putting forth the kind of physical effort the youngsters would expend for their clients, but he knew his area well and hunted with his head first, then his heart and his legs.

In sheer knowledge and overall competence, Illingworth was the best of the bunch, and we were lucky to have him. But as the trip progressed I realized I was still (and perhaps still am!) in a stage where I often preferred to hunt with my heart and legs rather than my head—and I wished for a younger, less experienced, less methodical hunter so we could take one of those hopeless tracks and follow it wherever it might lead . . . .

The cats were the main thing, and Kim and I had decided that she would have the first crack at leopard while I would have the first go at lion. It was no great secret that pulling out two cats in two weeks' time would be a real trick, but the hunting of the two cats is different enough that lion and leopard make a nice combination for two hunters. First we would get some baits up; a big piece of meat or two along the river to catch a hunting pride of lions, and then some well-positioned impala or warthog in dense cover where leopards should wander. Then we would wait for something to happen, hunting buffalo and plains game as we checked the baits. Lion hunting over bait is primarily an early-morning activity, while hunting baited leopard is virtually always done in the evening; the two aren't mutually exclusive.

Our first morning in the Luangwa was one of those golden times when the air is cool, the breeze still, and every animal in the world is there to be seen. The Luangwa is indeed a vast repository of game—and that morning we saw it all. Impala, warthog, waterbuck, zebra, puku, wildebeeste—all were extremely common along the Luangwa. That morning we drove through a little fringe of trees and ran smack into a fine herd of buffalo, standing and staring as shafts of slanting sunlight drove through the hanging dust. Then they were off with a great thunder of hooves and more dust, billowing clouds of it sifting back down long after the hoofbeats had faded away.

Like all first days, that one served to acquaint us with the lay of the land and with our professional hunter—and vice versa. We were now hunting the valley floor of the Luangwa, a broad, flat plain as much as 50 miles across rising into high hills on the east and west. The Luangwa is actually the southernmost extension of the Rift Valley, a great fault line running from Egypt south through East Africa and into Zambia. Much of the Luangwa Valley is national park, but there's a break between Luangwa North and Luangwa South, and we were in that break. The common game was down on the valley floor—we had seen most of the species present in the first hour—but much game was still in the hills. Up there was where one might find roan, kudu, eland and hartebeeste—if one were very lucky. Down low, the common game

The Luangwa River and its tributaries are loaded with hippos, often in large herds. At night the hippos feed on land, and woe to the man who gets between a hippo and water. These seemingly ungainly beasts are very fast, and in some areas are a leading cause of death amongst Africans.

would fall into place, and with it the cats, following the biggest concentrations of buffalo and plains game.

The grass was indeed high, but on the valley floor it was dry and yellow and ready for the annual burning. The burning, I suspect, has gone on for tens of thousands of years, for the natives don't like to walk through tall grass—and I don't blame them. As soon as the grass dries enough to hold and carry a flame it is burned, and as soon as the ashes cool the new green pokes up through the charred soil. The locals had burned a few areas already, and they had an ally in Bill Illingworth—"Firebug Bill" in the lexicon of Super Hunter Sims. We started several good grass fires the first day, and as we passed those new burns as the hunt progressed I watched the magic of change that is Africa. The animals run from the fire, of course, but as soon as it cools you'll find the impala right there amidst the smoke, in the open where they feel safe from the hunting leopard. Warthog are next, rooting around for tubers or perhaps a charred carcass, and then the new green comes up and the herd animals—zebra and wildebeeste—search for the tender shoots amongst the ashes of last season's growth. The areas that we burned today would have impala and warthog tomorrow and new green within the week.

Part of the gameplan that first day was also to get some cat food hung, first a couple of leopard baits and then lion. Kim and I each shot an impala—her first head of African game, taken very nicely through the shoulders—and Bill hung them in dense riverine growth close by the Luangwa but a couple of miles apart.

Illingworth baited in the traditional manner, sometimes hanging a bait according to fresh tracks or previous success, but most often by feel. The tree had to be just so, and it had to offer a silhouette at sunset to allow a shot long after the sun had vanished and just a hint of pink remained in the western sky. He tended to bury his leopard baits quite deep in the riverine growth, commenting that the locals might take them otherwise. Much later I would remember his words.

With some leopard baits hung, the next step was to work on the lion situation. In the Luangwa very large prides of lions aren't uncommon, but where we were now the Park was on one side of the river and our concession on the other. To bring the cats across the river, and keep

The puku is a member of the kob family found only in eastern Zambia and adjacent southern Tanzania. In the Luangwa Valley this lovely reddish antelope is extremely common; a good trophy puku will come along in the normal course of the safari.

115

them on our side, a big chunk of meat was the preferred bait. Really big. So that first morning I shot a hippo, common in the Luangwa. In fact, the hippo are tremendously numerous and a bull with exceptional teeth is not a problem. But finding one where you can retrieve his three-ton carcass is another matter altogether. This hippo lived in a lagoon about a half mile from the river, a lagoon he shared with an amazing number of crocodiles. We shot him and got him out—not without difficulty—and dragged the huge carcass over to the Luangwa. We would retrieve the tusks later, when they had loosened in the great skull, but in the meantime we covered the carcass with branches to keep off the vultures and planned a couple of different approaches to the bait—just in case.

One more bait was in order, so Kim shot a fine zebra stallion with yet another good shoulder shot. We skinned him quickly, then dragged the carcass to the chosen bait tree. This was far from the Park, up a sandy tributary to the Luangwa called the Lukuzi River, no doubt a roaring stream during the rains but now just a dry streambed of shining white-hot sand with a few seeps and pools remaining here and there. Illingworth reckoned it was a favorite route for hunting prides, and certainly the bait tree was an oft-used spot, well scattered with bleached bones. It was a stout tree that looked much like an elm, and it stood right on the bank overlooking a lazy bend in the Lukuzi. Fifty yards away, along the narrow jeep track, was a wall of grass built the season before as a blind, and off to the right, in a much larger tree, was a platform machan 30 feet in the air. This place had produced for Firebug Bill, and he expected it to again.

The zebra was winched up high, then hung by the hindquarters with heavy chain. The hyenas could barely reach the front legs, and even the lions must strain to get to the choice cuts. If they found it, Illingworth wanted the bait to last long enough to give us a chance.

That evening we gathered 'round a beautiful fire, comparing notes and listening to the hippos calling. All the groups had done similarly, scattering to the four winds, checking the lay of the land, and getting a few cat baits hung. Now that was done, the hunt must begin to take its course. There was no hurry with the plains game, not yet; just take things slowly, checking each bait and waiting to see what happens. Just after we turned in lions roared across the river, in the Park—it was a tantalizing sound we were to hear often as the great cats hunted in their sanctuary.

We got a couple more leopard baits up the next day, one of them along a brushy streambed that bisected a grassy plain and another along the river, not far from where we had seen some good tracks. Just at dark Kim took a fine waterbuck, but when we got back to camp a celebration was already in progress. Buffalo Bob had just earned his nickname with a fine buffalo bull, taken with unusual ease out of a big herd. Later in the hunt he would learn much more about buffalo hunting, and a bit about himself, but for now he was happy to have a fine trophy.

We checked a couple of leopard baits early and then the hippo—nothing—and the sun was well up by the time we drove up the Lukuzi to check on our zebra bait. It was late enough that there was no reason for undue caution, and as we rounded the bend I was watching three elephant make their way across the sandy bottom—a lovely young bull and two grown cows. Mustard, our head tracker, had seen something else and he finally got my attention.

A hundred yards downstream, sauntering slowly away from the bait, was a tawny yellow form, golden in the morning sun. It was big lioness, and she turned to look back at us with disgust. She was the last of the pride; three more lionesses were in the shade of the overhanging bank, and on top of the bank, silhouetted by the morning sun, was a big lion. Was that a halo of blond mane, or was it just brush? There was no time to tell, for he gave us a quick look and was gone, followed one by one by his females.

There were indeed blond mane hairs on the bait, and with luck this lion would return. Certainly we would be there waiting for him in the chill of dawn.

With our next day's hunt planned and nothing on the leopard baits, we took the rest of the day and headed up into the eastern hills, picking up the Lukuzi again far upstream. Illingworth liked hunting the hills, and I liked what I saw up there. It was rugged country; not country that would hold a lot of game, but country that would hold good trophies. But the grass was very high in the hills and still green, and the tsetse flies attacked us in droves. We saw little game, just a few tracks, but we found the pugs of a huge leopard in the dry sand far, far up the Lukuzi, and we hung the one impala we had brought for the purpose.

The Southern Cross stood out in the star-studded sky when we parked the Land Cruiser the next morning. We were a good mile from the bait, an essential distance, and we must plan our approach so as to arrive just at the first hint of light—not too early but, above all, not too late. We would not follow the winding road to the bait, but would follow a trail through the brush that had been carefully chosen and marked the day before.

We had coffee from a Stanley thermos while we waited for the right moment to begin our approach, and I kept wiping my palms, sweating in spite of the dawn chill that had me in sweater and down vest. With great ceremony Mustard handed Illingworth a badly battered oak-and-leather guncase, and he carefully fitted together his big .470 double. Distant thunder rolled through the quiet brush and Illingworth grinned, twirling two huge cartridges in his thick, stubby fingers. "There's your lion on the bait. Hear him roar." The magic sound came again, then faded to a grunting cough. I wiped my palms once more.

Then it was time to begin. We walked slowly but steadily, and when we stopped we could still hear the grunting and roaring on the bait, much closer now. And then Illingworth stopped, raising his .470. In the black gloom ahead was movement, heavy footfalls and swishing of brush. "Damned elephants," came the whisper, and we backed away carefully, stymied. The elephants were feeding peacefully, and in the darkness we had no choice but to wait them out. When they had passed we moved on, but now there was a hint of gray, and when we reached our blind we could see two hyenas jumping and worrying the bait, a sure sign that the lions were gone. They were.

Of course they had been there, and they hadn't finished the bait. It was now a game of chess, and our next move was to bring half the hippo over to make sure they didn't finish all the meat in one sitting. Then we had done all we could do about the lions for now, and it was back to business as usual—and business was definitely picking up.

Two different leopards had hit two different baits, one in the streambed along the grassy meadow and the other in dense riverine growth. Both trees showed the broad scratches of a good cat, so we built a circular blind of woven grass at each bait, positioning them carefully to catch the best possible shot yet not disturb the leopard's most likely approach. The second blind was finished just as the heat of afternoon passed, so Bill left Mustard and me there while he and Kim went to wait alongside the stream.

I had waited for a leopard before and would do it again many times. It's an agonizing wait, and I'm not a patient person. Perhaps those accustomed to stand-hunting for whitetail would find it more familiar, but hunting with my feet and my binoculars is my strong suit. With leopard, all you can do is wait, without speaking, without moving, without slapping the incessant tsetses or mosquitoes. I had a good book, and in the

Just a few years ago elephants were an everyday sight in Zambia's Luangwa Valley. Poachers have taken a heavy toll, and today there are just remnants of a population that exceeded 100,000 in the mid-1970's.

early hours of the afternoon that helps pass the time. And for the first three hours or so in a leopard blind, all one does is pass time. Mustard, with the wonderful patience of the bush African, simply sat.

Mustard's village was here in the Luangwa; we'd passed through it on our way into the hills. He was a local headman, a well-respected elder although I doubt he was much past 40. His prestige had come from his skill as a hunter, and a hunter he was. He had an old trade musket, a frightful-looking affair with its stock repaired with wire. He made his own gunpowder for it, using charcoal and sulfur and saltpeter—or a suitable substitute—pounded from a local root. He cast his own bullets, too, pouring the molten lead into carefully shaped holes pushed into hard-baked clay before it dried. With this musket he had kept his family fed for many years, and on a couple of occasions had taken elephant with it. He had excellent eyes, and knowing what visiting sportsmen look for, he had become an exceptional judge of trophy quality. Illingworth had sought him out when he came to the Luangwa to hunt, and together they made a fine team. Illingworth was the professional hunter, but Mustard was more than a tracker; his role was more akin to that of a consultant, and Illingworth consulted with him often about game movement, where to place baits, or what area should be hunted on a given day at a given time. The discussions were held in Mustard's language, which I could not follow. But African language is usually accompanied by much talking with the hands, particularly when a white man converses in the unfamiliar tongue. It was apparent that most of

119

Mustard's suggestions were followed. He was one of the best hunters I've known—of any color—and I'd hunt with him again anytime, under any circumstances.

Now he sat quietly, waiting, as the heat of the afternoon passed and the evening cool began to seep in. The sun was getting very low now, and things could get interesting at any time. Our vision was limited from the blind, truly a blind in many ways with just the bait tree visible at the end of our narrow tunnel of sight. Through the afternoon a few impala had wandered past, and we could hear elephants feeding off to our right. I wondered if they would feed over the top of our blind—and how we would know if they were getting too close. The book had been put down long since and the rifle's muzzle rested in the shooting port. Still the wait was endless, and it would be broken only by darkness or the appearance of the leopard.

The light had turned golden, then red, and the last rays of sunlight were catching the bait tree, silhouetting the forlorn impala. A baboon barked in the deep bush to our left, then a troop of vervet monkeys chattered. Mustard inclined his head slightly and his mouth silently formed the word, "Leopard." I heard, or thought I heard, a light swish in the grass close by the blind, and then the elephants trumpeted just to our right and with a great crashing and breaking of branches passed just behind the blind. With disgust on his face, Mustard made a sign that it was finished.

Later Illingworth would explain, but no explanation was necessary. The light breeze had carried the leopard's scent to the resting elephants, and the great pachyderms won't tolerate the close presence of the predatory cats. We stayed in the blind, waiting, but now we were waiting to no purpose. Shortly after dark we heard the Land Cruiser's engine, then saw the lights approaching and gathered up our gear to meet Firebug Bill and Calamity Kim.

Their wait had been better than ours. In the back of the Toyota, stretched crosswise and occupying the full bed of the truck, was a magnificent tom leopard. He was a real brute, thick-chested and powerful even in death, the kind of cat the Luangwa is famed for. The 200-grain softpoint from Kim's .30-06 had gone in under one foreleg and ranged up through heart and lungs, and he had been lying dead exactly underneath the bait.

Back at camp, Super Hunter Sims also had reason to celebrate. He had taken a fine buffalo bull with his big .460 Weatherby, and he and Paddy had waded into the thick brush to get him. Super Hunter Sims

Cookson's wildebeeste is a variation of the common brindled gnu or blue wildebeeste. The Cookson's variety is found only in Zambia's Luangwa Valley, but is extremely common there. The skins of the wildebeeste are quite beautiful, while the mounted heads are much less attractive.

A heavy-horned Chobe bushbuck came purely by accident; for some reason he was feeding in an open glade at midday—most un-bushbucklike behavior. There are plenty of bushbuck along the Luangwa, but the riverine growth is so dense that few are taken.

121

reckoned he was a world record—at least in his personal record book—and I guess he was at that. Sims is a good hunter, and a tough hunter—but for him to hunt Cape buffalo in the thick stuff on foot takes a great deal more guts than most of us have. You see, some years back, as a motorcycle patrolman, he lost a leg above the knee . . . .

It seems that the elephants of the Luangwa had a conspiracy going to keep me from the cats. The next morning we heard lions on the bait again as we left the truck, but again the elephants loomed as dark mountains in the darker brush, and again the lions were gone when we reached the bait. At least they had been there; the leopard—"my" leopard—didn't return.

But there was another leopard on another bait, so I spent another agonizing, tail-breaking evening waiting. Nothing. Nor did we have better luck the next morning—elephants again, and now it was painfully obvious that our bait was right along their nightly feeding pattern. We had to break the pattern, so it was time to shore up the old tree platform and spend the night there, hoping to catch them just at gray dawn.

We moved into the *machan* a couple of hours before dark. It had been made comfortable with mattresses, and as soon as it was dark I had no trouble falling asleep. That didn't last long. The maniacal whoop of a hyena set me bolt upright, and I listened for many minutes to their wild music until I drifted off again.

The lions came at midnight. Bill's hand gripped my shoulder firmly, and I awoke silently, fully aware, eyes trying to pierce the darkness. The moon was up, but the bait was in deep shade. Barely I could make out a tawny form standing by the hippo, and another lying beside it making great ripping sounds. They were just pale shapes; there was no chance to see if it was a male or, if it was, how good. They moved off well before dawn, and we were never sure what we had seen.

The truck came for us just after dawn, Calamity Kim jumping down and hoping to see our lion and sharing our disappointment when she saw he wasn't there. Later that day I shot a zebra so we could hang fresh meat to keep the bait going. We rested a bit at midday, and I think it was that afternoon that Kim shot a fine puku.

The lions came again that night. I could see one standing on his hind legs tearing at the zebra carcass, a big animal—surely the male we had seen. Later he stood in the moonlight in the riverbed, dark against the white sand, and although, had it been legal, I could have shot him easily, I couldn't see his mane. He moved off about four a.m., just before the first hint of dawn, taking his females with him.

I had grown used to the whooping of the hyenas, and I was dead-tired, ears ringing from lack of sleep and too much caffeine. I was in a sound sleep when the lions came the next night. It was midnight, and the male roared directly underneath the *machan*. The sound lifted me two feet off the mattress, and when I came down I was wide awake, and there was no more sleep that night. We watched them circling below us, tearing at the bait, then going off to lie down for a while before eating again. We watched them all through the night, and in the gray dawn they were still there, lazing about the bait as they should have been nearly a week before.

There were two males. They had roared often in the night, and in the gray dawn one of them was making love to a lioness right underneath us. They were full-grown, but they were worse than the scruffy-maned lions common in the Luangwa—they were virtually maneless, and we had to let them go. There had been a well-maned lion; we had seen him, and even if our eyes had played tricks on us the blond mane hairs on the bait hadn't lied. But he was gone, and chances were he wouldn't come back. We had to come up with a new plan.

The primary plan was hippo again. We drove to another lagoon close by the Luangwa, with the Park on the opposite side. Kim and Bill stalked carefully along the reeds by water's edge, and she shot a big hippo just by the bank. We dragged it into a thick patch of bush and cut a clearing around it, then a shooting lane 30 yards across the wind. If the bait was taken, we would build a wall of grass to come up behind. Now, though, we would have to wait for a day or two and let the prevailing breeze waft the scent of rotting hippo across the Luangwa.

That afternoon we drove far up to the broad Lopita Plain to look for a good waterbuck for me. This was a true plain with sparse grass and little bush, and the zebra and wildebeeste were thick. Waterbuck were common, too, but we had seen no good ones as the sun sank lower.

Firebug Bill wanted another large animal for a lion bait to take to the hills the next day, so we picked a particularly fine Cookson's wildebeeste out of a herd. I was just squeezing the trigger on the .375 when Mustard touched my arm and pointed. Far off to the left, perhaps 250 yards, a big waterbuck—easily the best we'd seen—stepped out from behind a tree.

I swung onto him and shot quickly, holding well up on his shoulder. He dropped instantly and lay still, the solid "tunk" of the bullet drifting back to us. I hesitated a moment, but he was down hard. Why not? I swung the rifle back to the wildebeeste herd, just starting to trot off, found the bull we wanted at the rear of the herd, and swung the crosshairs with his shoulder. At the shot the herd was off, cantering wildly and mixing haphazardly. But we heard that bullet hit as well, and we found the bull down and dead in 100 yards. The waterbuck had stayed where he was, taken through both shoulders with the Speer Grand Slam bullet.

I felt better that night; the disappointment of the the lion had worn on me badly. But Super Hunter Sims and Buffalo Bob both had real cause to rejoice. The day before, when I had been in the treehouse, Tatsch had taken a truly superb waterbuck, well over 30 inches and thus very rare for the Luangwa. But when we arrived in camp with our waterbuck and wildebeeste, Super Hunter Sims had preceded us with a fine tom leopard. They had been late in checking this bait, and the afternoon was nearly gone when they glassed it from across a sandy streambed. It had been fed on the night before, but it was too late to build a blind and too late to drive away safely.

Paddy and Sims had merely crouched down in a patch of grass and waited. The leopard had come, crossing the open streambed 100 yards from them. He had sat down in midstream, and Bill had taken him there with a perfect shot.

The pace became frantic from there, and my memory of the rest of the hunt is jumbled. We hung the waterbuck well up in the hills and now had baits widely scattered that had to be checked. There were several failed stalks for buffalo, and endless waits for several leopards that never appeared. I distinctly remember that we had five different leopards hit five different baits after Kim shot her cat, but although we waited for several of them, for some reason they would hit the bait just once and never return. Or, worse, would hit at odd intervals—every other night or every third night. Had we concentrated, we could have taken one, but lion was still uppermost in my mind and time was running out.

Somewhere in there Kim took an exceptional warthog—the only really good tusker I saw in the Luangwa—and a fine Cookson's wildebeeste, and somewhere in there, too, a lion took the waterbuck bait. We had come in on foot to check the bait. It was high in the hills above a little waterhole, a perfect spot, and as we approached it we could see meat had been taken. It was midday so we proceeded, although cautiously. The lion was there, a lone lioness, and at close range she stood and sized us up; we were grateful that she slunk off into the tall grass. From the tracks, she was hunting alone.

Late in the afternoon we saw a herd of roan, the only roan anyone in the entire camp was to see. They had crossed the road in front of us well up in the hills, and I leaped off the truck and followed over a low rise. They had stopped on a sidehill in a fresh burn a couple hundred yards away, and Bill picked out the bull. I put the crosshairs behind his shoulder, fired, but nothing happened. Quickly I worked the bolt on the .300 and fired again holding on the shoulder, and this time the whole herd exploded. The bull ran with the herd, but we saw him go down just as they topped the ridge. We approached, and I tried to run up on him. But Illingworth, who seemed to have no fear of lions, pulled me up short. "Don't go near that damn thing. Roan will kill you more quickly than anything." I slowed down, but he stopped me again. "Come in from the rear, slowly, and be ready." Illingworth was right, of course. The roan is one of the few fierce antelope and is indeed deadly when wounded. But this one was finished; the two 200-grain Noslers from the .300 Weatherby had crisscrossed in his chest, and I'll never understand why there was no reaction to the first shot.

The roan antelope is a lighter-colored, shorter-horned, and bigger-bodied relative of the sable. He is becoming uncommon over much of his range, and today is hunted in few countries. Although not a particularly big bull, this Zambian roan has a beautiful cape, and is the only roan antelope Boddington ever had a chance to take.

We tried hard to get Kim a buffalo, but the high grass was against us. Several times we got close, but never quite close enough. Bushbuck, too, were a problem, especially in the lush riverine growth that they preferred. Kim had no luck with them, but I got an amazing stroke of good fortune. We were checking a leopard bait close by the river but in open thornbush. It was high noon, the heat of the day, and virtually all the game was resting in the shade. I was riding in the back of the truck, and as we bounced towards the bait I glanced to my left and saw a brownish animal in some thorn. It registered on me that it was a puku, and we rolled on past to the bait. We were just pulling up, perhaps 200 yards farther on, when it hit me that puku don't have a white throat patch. I jumped out and looked at Mustard. "Bushbuck?" I asked. He said, "Yes, boooshbook," and followed me into the bush. We circled around, and the bushbuck, a superb male of the Chobe bushbuck subspecies, was still standing watching the track. I shot him just as he turned to run.

Time was running out by now, but we got a last-minute reprieve. With just a few days left, we found mane hair, lion tracks, and much meat taken on Kim's hippo. We built a wall of grass, and the next morning, well ahead of dawn, wound our way carefully along the banks of the lagoon towards the bait.

It was just graying up, and off across the lagoon, on a broad meadow that led to the Luangwa itself, we could see the dark forms of hyenas coming to the bait. We walked a few more steps, and a flock of guinea fowl, roosted in a tree directly overhead, flushed with a great flapping

Common waterbuck with the distinctive white rump circle are plentiful in the Luangwa Valley, although good trophies are few and far between. These are young bulls; only the one on the far left walking away is getting close to shootable size.

Taken on the Lopita Plain near the Luangwa River, this is an average common waterbuck but exceptional for Zambia. Waterbuck have an odd greasy substance on their hides, said to ward off insects and also said to give their meat a foul flavor. The former may be true, but the latter is bunk—waterbuck, like almost all African game, is good eating!

and squawking. After my heart dropped back where it belonged we continued, but we were too close to the bait and I felt that surely the game was up.

There were peepholes cut in the wall of grass. Illingworth and I went to our designated spot and peered through carefully. There were hyenas in the background, standing off from the bait. And just visible in the gray light was a lion, just the hint of blond mane showing in the dimness. I carefully ducked back down and turned to Bill. He nodded, and I raised up again, this time lifting the .375. The lion was gone. Or had he really been there? A lioness lay in the same attitude just beyond where he had been—or had it been the lioness all along? The light was uncertain, and we wanted so badly to see the mane. She got up slowly, took three steps, and vanished into the tall grass. Then hyenas closed in, a great snapping, yapping crowd of them, and we backed off uncertain of what we had seen.

The next morning we left the truck at exactly the same time, and ex-

127

actly on schedule the guinea fowl burst from the same tree overhead. I was ready for them, but it scared me just as badly. I wiped my palms on my sweater for the twentieth time in as many minutes, and we crept on up to our wall of grass.

There was nothing there. No lions, no hyenas, no nothing save the gray mound of decaying hippo. Bill dropped back down, shaking his head and shrugging. I motioned with my hands as if to say, "Let's go up and see if anything has been there." We stood up slowly, totally defeated, rifles at a careless port arms just out of habit, and stepped to the right around the hide and walked towards the bait. We had covered most of the 30 yards and could now see past the hippo to the edge of the clearing. I was on the left and had the clearer view. I saw him first. He was lying down, sideways to us but head turned away from the bait.

He wasn't a great lion, but even in the gray dawn I could see the wisps of his thornbush-lion mane. Dimly I was aware of Bill nodding, but the rifle was already up and the sweating palms were long forgotten. At 10 yards the 350-grain Barnes softnose entered his skull, and he never moved. An eternity later, just as the realization was sinking in, the tail twitched, and a needless insurance shot was added.

The hunt was truly over for me, but there was this day remaining, and yet another full day. Just the day before we had hung a last-chance leopard bait in a lovely patch of dense bush, and after the lion had been safely skinned we went to check it. It had been taken by a monstrous leopard that left deep scratches in the tough bark of the tree, and now Illingworth smiled his broad smile. "Tonight we will *drrrill* 'im," he said, using his favorite expression.

But it was not to be. We had built a beautiful blind just so we could catch the leopard's silhouette at last light, but when we returned at 3:00 p.m. to sit in it bare footprints—man-tracks—had preceded us. Illingworth scowled and cursed, knowing what he would find. Locals had found the bait and taken it, and there was no point in waiting for this leopard.

The next day, the last day, we got into a big pride of lions far up in the hills. Kim had decided the lion would wait until another safari for her, but I saw the big male, a beautiful well-maned monster, resting under a tree far up the hill. We were in the vehicle and had surprised them as they rested, and they moved off into the heavy brush. Kim was unsure now, and we tried to circle around. We found the lionesses again but never got a glimpse of the big male.

That last day, too, was the day that Buffalo Bob really earned his

Boddington's first Zambian lion wasn't the kind of lion he's been looking for; it was nearly maneless, and as such was more typical of today's lion than the M.G.M. variety. But it came after an aggregate of more than 100 days of lion hunting, and was a welcome sight!

nickname. He had wounded a big buffalo at midday, and after hours of tracking in the heat he finally shot him at last light. He made the final stalk alone and shot him well when the great bull turned at long last to have it out with his pursuers.

The last day also brought a fine lion for Carl Swanson, and it was a tribute to his young professional hunter who simply wouldn't quit. Carl wanted a lion above all—like me—and they had exhausted all possibilities. They had baited, they had tried to track, and they had glassed in the hills, and had seen nothing but lionesses. On the next-to-last day Robin had pulled out all stops. With a fresh zebra carcass in tow, he had laid miles of drag spoor on the Lopita Plain, and he and the Swansons had slept out up there, waiting for the dawn just on the faint hope that lions might have found and followed the spoor in the night. They had, and Swanson had taken a lovely red-maned lion that last morning.

We ended our hunt far up in the hills, finding yet another of our baits that had been fully consumed in the 48 hours since we had checked it.

While we stood there wistfully, pondering the "what ifs," a lone elephant bull stepped into the sandy riverbed a hundred yards downstream. He stood for a moment, checking the wind, and his tusks stood out like great polished logs, well curved and massive. He carried 80 pounds of ivory on each side or more, making him one of a handful of truly great tuskers remaining in the whole of the vast Luangwa Valley. He never saw us or smelled us, but he was on the move, and with great swinging strides he crossed the riverbed and made his way into the mopane forest beyond, the red sunset tinting him in pink hues as he passed in and out of the slanting rays.

CHAPTER XI
THE KAFUE PLATEAU

The morning was clear and cool. It was humid even in the predawn blackness, but both a sweater and down vest felt good in the open Land Cruiser, and that was a blessing and a surprise. October is the hottest hunting month in southern Africa, the time just before the rains when both the heat and humidity build daily. The first European settlers in this region—later they would call themselves Rhodesians—termed it the "suicide month."

But we weren't in the sweltering hot lowlands, where the temperatures would exceed 100 degrees Fahrenheit as soon as the sun came up. Instead we were in the Kafue highlands, a vast plateau of 5,000 feet elevation stretching northwest from Lusaka, capital of what used to be Northern Rhodesia but has been Zambia since 1964. I hadn't been prepared for the morning chill; and while the down vest was mine, fetched along "just in case," the sweater was borrowed from my professional hunter, Russ Broom. The brisk air was just one of many surprises awaiting me.

To my mind it was a bit too late in the year to be hunting this part of Africa, and I felt, too, that we were in the wrong area. The lateness of the safari was my fault; I had been in Spain for the World Hunting Congress and had delayed the hunt until its conclusion to avoid two trans-Atlantic crossings close together. The area, however, wasn't of my choosing, and I wasn't too happy about it. I well recalled the disaster that had befallen the part of our group that had gone to the Kafue just the season before—when I had been in the Luangwa—and I didn't need an instant replay. Still, this was a trip with limited objectives, really just two: good sable and exceptional buffalo. The lateness of the year shouldn't matter with only those goals in mind, but I had expected to hunt buffalo in the Brooms' new area at the top of the Luangwa Valley

131

and sable in their old stomping grounds at Matetsi, in Zimbabwe.

So far, though, the trip had been a model of efficiency, vastly different from the start of my first Zambian safari. Just 18 hours before I had been on a British Caledonian jet making its final approach into Lusaka. Less than two hours after landing all the formalities had been handled and Rusty and I were on the road to our hunting blocks west of Mumbwa. Before dark we had been hunting our way to camp, and we had glassed, judged, and passed up a pretty decent sable bull. The decision to hunt the Kafue had been made while I was out of touch in Spain, and if I'd been asked I'd have flatly stated I didn't want to hunt there. I would have been very wrong.

Like all first days, this was a day to see some country, get acquainted with each other, and get a feel for the present game movement in our area. Much of that groundwork had been laid, for Rusty had been in the area just a week before, getting the camp organized and doing some scouting of his own. The camp was in the Namwala hunting block, and we would hunt both Namwala and Mumbwa East, the latter bordering the Kafue National Park to the north. It was a vast region of brachystegia woodland, the heart of the Kafue Plateau. Flat country it was, in the main, with a few scattered *kopjes* and broad open *dambos* (meadows) long since burned off and showing the new green from early rains. Mostly, though, it was unbroken hardwood forest, and those early rains had already brought the new leaves. Visibility would be limited in the trees, and it was in the trees that we would find the game.

Dawn caught us on the hard-surface road that formed the boundary with the Park. Rusty had scouted several good sable bulls along the northern edge of our concession and had noticed, too, that herds of buffalo seemed to wander both sides of the Park boundary in the early mornings. We found one of them well before sunup, a big herd just fading into the trees on the wrong side of the road. I gazed wistfully at a big bull, and then we drove on, eventually cutting south into the Mumbwa block.

Just at dawn we had glassed a few Lichtenstein's hartebeeste in open *dambos*, and a few warthogs had crossed the road in front of us. But the sun was well up now, the sweater and vest had been abandoned, and we had seen very little game. My fears about the Kafue region were returning in force, but I recalled one piece of advice that a dozen sources had given me on the Kafue: "You won't see very much game, but when you do see something it's likely to be good."

We stopped at the opening of a broad, green *dambo* and began glass-

The Toyota Land Cruiser—the real workhorse of a modern safari. A professional hunter must not only be a public relations wizard, a walking animal encyclopedia, and at least reasonably cool under pressure—he must also be an accomplished shade tree mechanic to keep that workhorse in order.

ing the treeline on the far side. As if on cue, three reedbuck stood from their beds in a tiny patch of brush just a hundred yards away. The male was clearly outstanding, as fine a common reedbuck as I had ever seen. Rusty was still glassing into distance; I tapped his shoulder and inclined my head towards the reedbuck, who so far seemed more perplexed than alarmed. The big male was behind a screen of brush now, but when he stepped out Rusty gave a low, admiring whistle. I shot the buck just behind the shoulder with the big .375. He was a bonus trophy, a good one, and seemed a fine beginning to the hunt.

133

I was concerned about our ability to find both sable and buffalo of satisfactory quality in this area. Rusty, on the other hand, was concerned about those two animals giving us enough hunting to keep us occupied. He had asked me the day before if I would mind putting up a few baits and hunting the cats as well—surely the strangest question any professional hunter has ever asked me. No, I didn't mind, though I suspected the effort and the cost in licenses for bait animals would be wasted. The reedbuck, cut in half and with a few choice cuts taken for camp meat, would serve for two leopard baits; a little later on we made a short stalk and took a hartebeeste bull for a lion bait.

By then it was midmorning, and although the day was warm and building storm clouds on the horizon made it muggy, it was far from unpleasantly hot. We had seen plenty of buffalo tracks, but we had lots of time to track buffalo. We had seen one more herd of sable, but the bull was young, beautiful and glossy and just coming on 40 inches. There was no rush to take such an animal. This was a day to get some baits up, if indeed we were going to hunt the cats, and just to look around. It was clear there were no great concentrations of game, but it was also clear that there was more than enough if we hunted hard. In the first hours my misgivings about the Kafue had faded completely, and I was happy to be there instead of in the low-lying Luangwa, where the temperatures must already be 30 degrees warmer.

Since it was to be an easy day, it was time to make our way back to camp, glassing as we went, and then get some baits hung in the afternoon. We stopped briefly to glass a long, narrow *dambo*. This one hadn't been burned, so Rusty and I climbed onto the roof of the Land Cruiser to better see over the gently waving yellow grass.

I don't recall if Rusty or Samson, our head tracker, saw them first. I know they were deep in the trees and I had trouble picking them out. They were just fawn-colored shadows, shadows as big as oxen with vertical white stripes and long, twisting horns. Livingstone's eland, six cows with long, thin horns and a great gray bull, a bull that fooled us at first since his horns were as long as those of his cows, impossibly long for a bull. It seemed a day for unexpected gifts; eland aren't common in Zambia, and good bulls less common still. They're great wanderers, here today and gone tomorrow, and those seven were the only eland I have ever seen in Zambia.

They were in the trees paralleling our *dambo*. We dropped off the Toyota when they were behind some brush and cut across the opening, making for a big anthill that they would pass close by. We made it just in time, and in moments they began stepping through some thick trees just 30 yards from our perch. The cows and bulls have similar horns, and indeed many of the top trophies listed in Rowland Ward—which uses simply length of horn—are cows. We had to be very careful now. Rusty picked out the bull, just a patch of fawn gray moving through the heavy cover. He paused with a bit of shoulder exposed and the .375 went off. The herd scattered in all directions, with the bull breaking back and circling around, heading straight towards our anthill at a dead run. He piled up literally at our feet, and as we admired his great bulk, beautiful markings, and perfect horns, I wondered if, though unexpected, he would turn out to be the very best trophy of the trip.

There's a lot of work involved in caping and butchering an eland bull. A monster like this could weigh up to three quarters of a ton, as large as a Cape buffalo or a big Alaska-Yukon moose, and every ounce excellent eating. By the time the chores were completed noon had come and gone, and it was past time to head for camp.

We moved quickly, not really hunting or even looking hard in the heat of the day. But Samson, our head tracker, was always looking, and he had a superb eye for game. He saw them as we sped down the hard-surface road, a herd of black scimitar-horned antelope drifting into the trees. His frantic tapping stopped us, and Rusty got the glasses on the sable just before they vanished. All I could see was curving horns, black bodies, and the flash of white underbellies, but Rusty got a good look at the herd bull, although I don't know how. We held a quick powwow.

The Kafue region of Zambia produces some of Africa's finest sable, and in his scouting a week before Rusty had seen a couple of bulls that he judged past the mid-forties. But the sable were moving a great deal at this time of year, and the brush was thick with new green. He judged this one at 44, perhaps 45 inches—a magnificent sable anywhere, but not the best the area was capable of producing. And he asked me if I wanted to go after him.

I hesitated a moment, but my mind was already made up. The sable had become a symbol for me, a symbol of failure and unacceptable mistakes. I could never erase the feelings of inadequacy that the Sabi River sable had given me, but just perhaps I could break a jinx of four years' standing and continue on with a slate, if not clear, at least even. I told Rusty that I'd like to have a closer look, but if the bull appeared anywhere near to the initial judgment, I knew I wouldn't hesitate.

But I also knew that the sable had become a special trophy, and I felt more fear than I feel in proximity to lions—and lions, quite frankly, terrify me. With palms sweating and hands shaking, I followed Rusty as he eased quietly into the heavy bush.

It was a big herd, and we caught sight of them quickly. They had seen the truck and were nervous, but the midday heat had made them lethargic and the wind was in our favor. We paralleled their course for quite a distance, unable to close in but able to watch through the trees and wait for an opening. We saw the bull several times, and although his cows screened him from a shot, he was clearly as good as Rusty had thought. In the trees it was impossible to judge his length perfectly, but the bases were exceptional and neither horn was worn or broken.

If I could get a shot, I knew I would take it—but I wasn't sure I could pull it off. My breathing was ragged, my hands were out of control, and my mind had wandered back to another time and place. I remember little of the stalk, which is unusual since that is the time of heightened sensitivities that I enjoy the most. I don't know how long it lasted—probably not long, though it seems we followed those sable for an eternity. Nor do I know how the sable was standing, and that's doubly unusual, for I can recall the exact placement of the sights on virtually every shot I've ever taken on game. But not this one. I was in a fog, and the last thing I remember is resting the old .375 across a log and waiting for the herd to step through a narrow opening in the trees.

My next image is of the sable going down and of my working the bolt as I ran towards him, hoping that I had shot the right one this time and knowing that I didn't have a clear picture of what had happened. There was no need for worry. Instincts must have taken over, for it was indeed the right animal, and he was shot well through the shoulders. Rusty's initial judgment had been on the money, and the bases were as heavy as we had guessed. At that moment I didn't care how many larger sable we ran across. This one was all I needed.

Had we hunted hard for sable, it is possible we would have found a better one. But it's also possible that we wouldn't have, for although we were to see many sable in the days to come, we never saw another that came close . . . .

It was pushing midafternoon by the time we reached camp, but it had been more than a full day and we were in no hurry. Amanda, Rusty's pretty girlfriend, arranged a sandwich for us and I lay down for an hour. But in spite of the jet lag—now just 24 hours old—sleep wouldn't come. Finally I wandered out to the skinning shed to look once more at those massive, curving horns and run my hands over the spirals of the beautiful eland.

Livingstone's eland are widely distributed in Zambia but not particularly plentiful. A superb bull like this one was an unexpected prize.

This was a lovely camp, the semipermanent type that has become most prevalent in Africa today, where labor and natural materials are far less expensive than canvas. A rectangular compound encircled by a high fence of tightly woven grass enclosed three sleeping huts and a dining hut at the four corners. Each hut sat on a slab of concrete, and the sleeping huts each had toilet and shower. The hot water was piped from a fire-heated drum, not in unlimited supply but terribly welcome after a long, dusty day. The dining hut opened to the open-air kitchen and staff quarters beyond, and the front entrance faced a huge open *dambo* where reedbuck and hartebeeste could be seen daily.

Just to the left was a low knoll, really a mound about 10 feet high,

137

and atop it perched the African equivalent of a gazebo, an open-sided, thatched *rondavel*. From it one could catch the slightest breeze in the heat of the afternoon and glass the *dambo* for game at first or last light. I took a book up there and read for a while, completely content. Presently Rusty and Amanda joined me, and Jeremiah, the old cook, brought the afternoon tea.

We had hunted the Mumbwa East block in the morning, but Rusty wanted to situate our baits in the Namwala block closer to camp. We saw little game that afternoon—the odd warthog and a few shy hartebeeste—but we covered a lot of country. The Namwala, though adjoining Mumbwa to the south, was slightly hillier country, with more relief and better-defined watercourses. We hung the hartebeeste from a stout tree along one of those streams overlooked by a cutbank where there was good cover and a good approach.

A couple of miles away we checked for leopard tracks in the soft mud of a streambed, no longer flowing but still holding stagnant pools in the low spots. The tracks were there, not fresh but the big pugs of a mature

Another gift while hunting for lion bait was this magnificent Lichtenstein's hartebeeste, at 22 3/4-inches one of the largest ever recorded. Bodington, left, and professional Russ Broom could hardly believe their good fortune.

With cat hunting, placement of the baits is everything. You always look for tracks along watercourses and in damp areas, but a good professional hunter places his baits by feel as much as by positive sign.

leopard. We put the hindquarters of the reedbuck close by, well up in a tree overlooking the streambed, a perfect route for a leopard on his nightly hunt. There were old wires in the tree—it had been used to bait leopards before—and while Samson, Shorty, and Sivembe arranged the bait Rusty took me for a walk.

A few months before, early in the season, a client had wounded a leopard in that same tree. Rusty showed me where the tracks had led, along the boulder-strewn streambed and past innumerable treacherous pockets of dark brush. Then we left the streambed, circling around a dense tangle, and made our way back to the undercut bank through vicious thorn. Rusty bent down and beckoned to me. I peered over the edge, into the mouth of a small rocky cave. "He was in here, waiting. I was just over there," Rusty said. And we climbed down and he took me to the spot, a small flat boulder on the edge of the watercourse. "I had gone past him, and Samson realized it and spoke to me. I turned and he was coming, bounding from boulder to boulder."

I looked, and shivered as I guessed three jumps from the cave mouth.

"I shot him there, and again there, and when it was over I was sick,"Rusty quietly explained. He had been carrying an Ithaca MAG-10, the short model they call the Roadblocker, purchased for just such use and loaded with 3 1/2-inch 10-gauge magnum buckshot. I shivered again, and wondered if he had shown me the spot to pass the time or to give me a subtle warning to be careful if we got a chance at a cat—or perhaps to remind himself that he had to be careful.

That evening as I drifted off to sleep the lions roared. The sound came like faint thunder or distant artillery, and the first time it was felt more than heard. It came again, and I tried to fix the location. It was a long ways off, perhaps toward our bait, and it was unmistakable. I listened as long as I could but finally gave in to the jet lag and fell into a sound and dreamless sleep, untroubled by phantom sable or charging leopards.

The next morning's hunt was uneventful, but I wasn't altogether certain my heart could handle another day like the previous one. And I was damned certain my pocketbook couldn't handle many days like that, considering Zambia's stout trophy fees. We hunted close to the Park boundary for buffalo again and followed one herd for a couple of miles until they turned towards sanctuary. We saw a few hartebeeste and fewer zebra, but got a good look at one fine elephant bull. He had crossed the track ahead of us with a small herd, and he had those incredibly thick, short tusks common on many southern bulls. Such ivory cannot be judged; perhaps 70 a side with luck, more likely in the low 60s, and still a superb bull today.

At midmorning we wound our way back to Namwala and found the baits untouched, but Rusty confirmed that this was the area where the lions had been roaring. We found tracks of a big buffalo herd, and he guessed that the lions were following them. Our first bait was in an ideal location, if those lions were in the area we guessed them to be, so he suggested that we sit and watch it for a couple of hours towards dusk. In the meantime, we must get another lion bait up in a spot he knew of, plus another leopard bait on the other side of camp.

Through the morning hartebeeste had been available several times, but now that we needed one we couldn't find any at all. We worked our way slowly towards the planned bait site, but no game was moving at all. We drove along a narrow track with a high hill mass on our left, a grassy meadow cut by a brush-lined stream on our right. "We'll put a bait at the end of this *kopje* if we can find something. It's a perfect lying-up spot for lions, and leopard love these hills as well. I have a tree that's ideal for a combined bait, and we'll see what hits."

As if on cue a small herd of hartebeeste broke from cover on the far side of the stream. I jumped out and picked a bull when they paused for a moment, but I waited a second too long. I got the crosshairs on him just an instant before he passed behind a big tree and made a quick snap shot. Rusty had the good manners to congratulate me on a superb shot, but I'm sure he knew as well as I did that it was pure luck. We had to follow up, but the big 300-grain Sierra had done its work; the bull was standing in some grass another hundred yards up the *dambo*, and I put in the finisher. The funny thing was that he was huge, the first try with the tape putting him over the world record. He wasn't quite that good, but he was close, an incredible hartebeeste.

We saved the horns and cape, of course, but the rest of him went into a perfect spot, a thick tree that leaned at a 45-degree angle so either a lion or leopard could get to the bait, and at this end of the hill the wooded slope gave way to a great mound of jumbled rock. Our other cat bait was down this same watercourse a few miles; if the lions were indeed working this area, we had the bases well covered.

Late that afternoon we headed west into a belt of dense bush. The Kafue River lay in that direction, and on this side the tsetse flies were fierce. A good insect repellent helps some but no chemical made will prevent a few of the hardier pests from sinking their red-hot needles into tender flesh. We found leopard tracks here, too, preceding us down the dusty track. We followed for a time, then lost the track when it turned into a small opening filled with high grass. The tracks were fresh, very fresh, so we backed off until we found a young warthog, then dragged him over the leopard's tracks to a bait tree.

We spent the last hours of daylight sitting in a patch of dense thorn watching our first lion bait. It was a long shot, perhaps absurdly long, but it seemed worth doing. We were thankful there were no tsetses there, but the mopane bems— tiny stingless bees that crave either the salt or moisture from sweat, maybe both—were a nuisance. The long shot didn't pay, but it was a quiet, pleasant evening without the tension of waiting on an active bait.

The roaring of the lions woke me sometime during the night. They were much closer this time, still a good distance away but close enough that the sound was crystal clear. I listened as long as I could, but the need for sleep was too great. It's odd how such a ferocious sound can be such an effective lullaby.

The morning hunt was again uneventful. We traveled north before daylight once again to hunt for buffalo along the Park boundary but this time picked up no tracks at all. The normal zebra, hartebeeste, and warthogs were moving through the scattered openings and hanging up at the edges of the trees, and we saw one small herd of impala, a surprisingly rare animal in the Kafue. But we saw little of interest, and since we had no reason to stop and look, we covered a lot of ground. The jackets and sweaters came off when the sun came up, and by midmorning the tsetses were out in force and the cool dawn had turned into a hot, clear day.

We had several baits that had to be be checked now, so the plan was to return to camp for an early lunch, rest for an hour, then check baits and hunt the Namwala for buffalo until dark. With the truck empty, we had left the Park far behind and were making maximum speed down the road towards the turnoff to camp.

It was Sivembe, our least experienced tracker, who tapped frantically on the cab roof. Rusty slewed to a stop and he and Sivembe spoke quickly in the native tongue. We must have been going 60 miles an hour, and I have no idea how anyone could have seen anything unless it was right on the road. And whatever it was, it couldn't have been on the road or Rusty or I would surely have seen it. I was fumbling with my binoculars, assuming that it must be a herd of sable or perhaps buffalo—something fairly visible and of great interest.

"Jesus Christ, he's seen a lion! Grab your rifle!"

I don't know if Sivembe really had seen the lion, or if he had seen just the lioness. In the excitement I never asked him, and I wish I had, for I would like to know exactly what he saw. I also don't know if I said anything or not, but I fell out of the truck after him with adrenaline surging and hands shaking at the simple two-syllable word. I do know what I saw when we dove into the brush.

Beyond the first fringe of thorn the trees opened, but there was thigh-high yellow grass. The lions were 50 yards in, and I saw the lioness first walking slowly away from us. I searched the grass, unable to believe there could really be a lion here. Then I found him, and I knew my eyes were playing tricks on me. He was still lying down, facing us, and his yellow eyes and tawny muzzle were framed by a great halo of golden mane. He wasn't the MGM lion; he was much better than that scraggly fellow. Dreams of that kind of lion had drawn me to Africa in the first place and had kept me coming back time and again. And if I could just get a grip on myself he was all mine.

142

I could see just his head in the tall grass, so I waited him out. When he stood he came up in one fluid motion, swapped ends casually, and trotted off at an oblique angle. I got the crosshairs on him, completed a short swing, and squeezed the trigger. He was a dead lion, drilled fairly behind the on shoulder and through the off, and it was all over—except that the safety was still on. Then he was gone, swallowed by the brush, and I'd blown the chance of a lifetime. Except that I hadn't, not completely. He turned to his right; I saw the movement and made out his outline behind a thin screen of grass. He was standing broadside, facing to the right, and this time the rifle went off when I intended it to.

Rusty lost sight of him after he first moved, and I did not catch sight of him after the shot. But Sivembe saw him go down hard, then lurch off into the grass. We waited—long nervous moments—then followed ever so slowly and carefully. He turned to face us when we approached and perhaps would have charged if he could have. But he couldn't. I shot him again in the chest, and he rolled over and lay still.

There were many pictures to take and much backslapping and celebrating, and finally we would have to take him back to camp for more celebrating, perhaps the traditional dancing that must be done when a lion is taken. But that would have to wait for a while. For now I could only look at him, admire his perfect blond mane, and try to hold back the tears.

In due time the celebrating did come, and Shorty—our tracker, skinner, and resident wizard—did the lion dance. Amanda broke out a bottle of champagne reserved for just such occasions, and we gave the lion his due in toasts.

In the late afternoon we headed out again, not to hunt seriously but to have a look at the leopard baits. We drove up to our combined bait casually. Amanda was with us, and we were still excited over the lion, jabbering away and enjoying a lovely warm afternoon. We drove closer than we usually would, and we should have noticed more quickly that much meat had been taken.

We jumped out, now speaking only in whispers, and Samson began examining the sign around the bait. It was confusing, for a leopard had indeed left its tracks, but the scratches on the tree were too deep. Then we found bigger pugs in a patch of soft earth, and it became clear that a leopard had come first, then a lion had followed. Rusty explained this to us quietly, and then we saw that Samson was carefully following an unseen spoor that led to the base of the rocky *kopje*.

We followed in turn, and eventually we looked up. The lion was there, in the rocks, a bit too close. He was watching us, the way a cat watches a caged bird, and he was in a perfect spot. Only his head showed over the top of the great flat boulder on which he lay, and overhead an overhanging slab gave him shade.

It looked like a place that he used often, and perhaps he still does. He was a big lion, perhaps much bigger than the one I had shot earlier that same day. He had a good mane, though not nearly so good, but I already had the lion I had wanted so badly, so we left him in peace. I like to think of him lying there, watching the hartebeeste work their way along the watercourse that his perch overlooks.

I don't know if the leopard ever came back to that bait. The lion had claimed it as his own, and we let him have it. But we had other leopards hit other baits, and we spent the usual tense, tsetse-bitten, mopane bee-pestered evenings waiting for them. Our warthog bait was hit the next day, and later another bait was hit. We waited in ground blinds, and we built a *machan* for the warthog. But the leopards hit once and never returned. Rusty wasn't surprised, and since he had given me the bad news, I wasn't surprised either. It was simply too late in the year for a good chance at leopard; the warthogs had dropped their young, and there was too much easy live prey available. Already we could see that most of the warthog females had only two or three young left of their litters—proof the leopards were working them over. But we tried, and I thought my luck might carry me through. Jeremiah, the old cook, thought so too; he felt I was traveling under a lucky star after the day of the lions, and indeed it seemed so.

But the luck left us after the day of the lions, and deep down I knew that we'd had more than our share. Not only were the leopards not cooperating, but we also couldn't find buffalo anywhere. We understood why the leopard business wasn't working, but the buffalo were a mystery. There were huge herds of several hundred each in this area, but wherever we went we found day-old tracks, nothing fresh enough to follow.

It was routine now. Buffalo in the morning, leopard in the evening, but nothing seemed to work. The weather was turning, too. The suicide month was over, and November had arrived. The rainy season was arriving with it, right on schedule. Already we'd had a few spatters, and the storm clouds built on the horizon every afternoon. The evening skies washed them clear and we had hot, sunny mornings—but we knew the coming of the rains was just a matter of days.

We rolled into camp about noon one day, with just a couple of days

Zambia's Kafue area doesn't have high concentrations of sable antelope—sometimes days may pass between sightings. But the area does produce some of Africa's best sable. Boddington had looked long and hard elsewhere before taking this 44-incher in the Kafue.

remaining in the Kafue. Amanda was excited, and when she told us why, we were excited, too. One of the camp staff had gone to the well to draw some water and in doing so had glanced up the *dambo* across from camp. A great buffalo herd was crossing the far end, apparently a herd beyond numbering. Amanda had climbed into the gazebo to watch them pass, and it had indeed been a huge herd. That was only two hours ago, and at this time of day our chances of catching them were outstanding.

We drove up the *dambo* from camp, stopping as soon as we hit the spoor and walking from there. The tracks were as plain as those of a freight train. We followed them through a belt of thick trees, then came out again onto another vast *dambo*. This opening hadn't been burned and was covered with long yellow grass. It rolled slightly, and several hundred yards to our left, almost hidden in the fold, was a mass of moving black worms shimmering in heat waves.

We had the wind, but just barely. The thing to do was cross this next opening and get on the far side of the herd, then approach them through the far treeline. The distance was great enough that it wasn't a

145

real problem, but we did it on hands and knees. Partway across, the meadow opened up, and for the first time we could see the whole herd. There must have been 500 buffalo, strung out across the meadow for a thousand yards and moving slowly away from us. There was water hidden away in a pocket, and the tail end of the herd still crowded around to drink. The front was strung out towards the end of the meadow, feeding along slowly. We waited, and finally all the great beasts had watered and they began to move with the rest of the herd. They fed along like well-contented cattle, and we waited until they moved into the far treeline.

We hurried then, moving up the opening quickly and picking up the spoor. You could track them by the cattle smell as well as by their tracks, but the bush was very thick here and the buffalo were on the move. The wind was fickle, too, and we had to keep shifting our approach as the wind shifted. Time and again we could see feet moving through the brush but could do nothing.

It was a long game of tag. I had never tried to work into a herd as large as this, and the difficulty became crystal clear as the afternoon passed. Several times the shifting wind did give us away, and we had to start over. Just ahead of dark we pulled it off. We had singled out a small bunch and had caught glimpes of monstrous sweeping horns several times. This was a true 50-inch buffalo, unheard of in the Kafue, and the wind was finally right. The twilight, too, was on our side—if we didn't run out of time. We belly-crawled to an anthill, then slowly climbed up its back side. We really had pulled it off; there were buffalo just 20 yards from us, standing in deep brush, and one of them had the magnificent spread we had caught a glimpse of. But for the first time we got a good look and saw it was a cow. There were bulls there in range, but they were very small. As we turned to go an eddy of breeze came from behind once again. The drumming of hooves echoed through the forest as our buffalo stampeded, then panicked the entire great herd and swept them all along.

Samson, who had done such a fine job of tracking, had come down with a bad eye infection. We had put off the inevitable trip to Iteshi Teshi, where an Italian mission had the nearest medical facility. Finally, with time running out in the area and Samson's eye getting worse, we could put off the trip no longer.

We left well ahead of dawn, reckoning that we could drop Samson at the hospital and be back by midmorning—and just maybe find buffalo tracks. Not a chance. The doctors kept us cooling our heels for two

Russ Broom supervises the completion of a machan, or tree blind. This one overlooks a leopard bait, but its location was such that the more commonly-used ground blind wouldn't work.

147

hours, then pronounced that they would indeed keep Samson. He could catch a bus back to camp in a couple of days, but in the meantime we would spend what time was left without his expertise.

It was past midday when we rolled back into the hunting area. We had given up on the leopard by now and were spending our time working strictly on buffalo—and there was simply no time left, not enough, anyway. We rolled on past camp to the Mumbwa block, then turned east and drove into the heart of that concession, country that we had not hunted before. There was a safari camp along the road, owned by the same company that had built the camp we were using. This one hadn't been used for several weeks, but there were game guards in residence. We stopped to ask them about buffalo and were told they hadn't seen any in several weeks. Rusty shrugged; we were committed now, so we drove on down the track.

We had seen virtually no elephant in the area—just the one herd with the big bull—but there are plenty of elephant in the Kafue. They had wiped out the road, pushing trees across it every which way. It was as if the elephant knew it was a road, and knew pushing trees into it would impede hunters' movements. You could look to the left and to the right and see no trees bulldozed over for as far as you could see into the brush, but right there in the road were a half dozen stout brachystegia trees uprooted and lying in the path.

Some of the roadblocks could be bypassed, others had to be cut through. It was slow, and when cutting had to be done it was noisy. By about two o'clock we were past the barricades and driving along the edge of a big *dambo*. The buffalo—those that the vigilant game guards hadn't seen for weeks—were right there, grazing peacefully on the far side like so many black Angus cattle. This was a good-sized herd, maybe a hundred or a bit more—not as easy to work as a lone bull, but more workable than a huge herd.

Had we seen them a bit sooner it would have been a perfect setup. The wind was ideal to circle the *dambo* and there was a lovely anthill within easy shooting distance of the entire herd. But we hadn't seen them in time, and the instant we stepped out of the truck, even though the distance was more than 500 yards, the entire herd was gone into the forest amid a cloud of dust.

Now the finding was over and the hunting could begin. The track was plain, and we were lucky; the buffalo had run just a few hundred yards and then slowed to a steady walk. We would catch them, but I was past believing we could do anything about it.

Boddington's second Zambian lion was the kind of trophy he'd been looking for, but had believed he would never find. Although lions aren't nearly as numerous in the Kafue as they are in the Luangwa, the high, cool country tends to produce outstanding manes.

It was an odd hunt. We did catch them quickly, and again there was just moving feet in the dense thorn. The buffalo were circling, as though they were loath to leave this patch of woods; several times we had to run crosswind to avoid giving them our scent. They were spooky in the manner of hard-hunted buffalo everywhere, but they were easy to stay with. A great flock of snowy egrets was traveling with them, birds that, like the rhino's tick bird, rode on their backs and picked parasites from the scabby folds of their hides. And often gave them early warning. A half dozen times the herd bolted, and when it did a great white cloud of egrets rose and we could run alongside the buffalo, ignoring them but keeping our eyes on the egrets as they hovered above the running herd. It just may have been the first time in history that these sentinel birds helped a hunter rather than ruining his stalk.

We had been making such a sprint, a long one this time—several hundred yards—and we were losing ground. Then we pulled up at the edge of the trees, on a narrow extension of the same *dambo* we had left a

149

Hunting in the woodlands of Zambia and Zimbabwe means tracking, often miles and miles of it—especially when buffalo is the quarry. All too often there won't be a good bull—or a shot at the good bull that is there—at the end of those tracks, but it's all part of the game.

couple of hours before. The buffalo were confused by the shifting breeze, or perhaps they really didn't want to leave that patch of forest. They were just across the clearing, milling in the open. I passed the open-sighted .458 back to Shorty and took the scoped .375 while Rusty located the herd bull. He was off to the right, completely clear, but the whole herd ran again before I could control my breathing enough for a shot. We ran too, ran like demons across the clearing. There was a straggler buffalo that had been left by the herd, a bull, and halfway across the meadow he broke from behind us. I got the scope on him, but we had seen the herd bull and this boy wasn't in the same class. We ran again, on across the clearing and into the trees.

The egrets were nowhere to be seen, and I believed we would have to start over and take the tracks. It wasn't necessary. The buffalo had run just a short distance this time, then stopped in a patch of the densest thorn. We got within about 60 yards, then started crawling to our right, looking for the bull.

We gained a few more yards and could see the buffalo clearly, not all of them, but many shifting black bodies and many others only partially seen in the thorns. The bull was there, too—the one we had seen or his twin. His vitals were screened by three trees, but his head was in plain view. We waited, and when he took a step I put the crosshairs well down on his shoulder and finished the squeeze.

He ran to the right and I got another one into his front half, then a 300-grain solid up his rear when he turned away, and then he was gone and the woods were still. Rusty sat down on an anthill, strained grin on his freckled features. "I think this calls for a smoke."

I don't smoke, but I joined him in one. It seemed the thing to do, and anything I could do to keep my hands busy might stop them from shaking.

When the requisite cigarette was finished, we moved ahead slowly. I had taken back the big .458, but I wasn't hoping that I'd need to use it. I didn't. The buffalo was dead in the lee of an elephant-bulldozed tree, a perfect hideout, and he had died facing us, waiting for us in an ideal ambush—but he had run out of time. He was a very fine buffalo, as Kafue buffalo go. He had about 41 inches of spread and nice bosses, an attractive buffalo and typical of what the area will produce. I was pleased with him and pleased with myself, and I was in the euphoria of success as Rusty and I strolled casually back to get the Land Cruiser. Sivembe had

Good buffalo are where you find them, but wide conformation like this is unusual in southern Africa. With a 45-inch spread and 17-inch boss, this is as fine a buffalo as anyone could ask for anywhere—and a real prize from Zambia's Kafue Plateau.

151

stayed behind to blaze a trail to the edge of the clearing, and Shorty led us in a straight line back across the narrow neck and into the woods once again.

We hadn't gone far when I heard Rusty's sharp intake of breath and saw him stop suddenly six feet ahead of me. It was ridiculous; we had just come through this patch of forest on the track of the herd, and much less than half a mile away there had been heavy gunfire. But it was true: Six bachelor buffalo bulls were feeding slowly through the trees just ahead of us; all were in the class of the one I'd shot and a couple were much better.

Rusty and I focused on the big one at the same time, a huge-bodied bull, and as he twisted his head to feed we could see the massive boss and the wide sweep of horns. "The second from right. Shoot him quickly," Rusty whispered. But this time I was a step ahead of him, and the crosshairs were already on his shoulder, waiting until he took one more step and was clear of some thorn.

It was an instant replay and seemed in slow motion. The shot, then another, then a solid up the rear as he turned, and then silence. Another cigarette, then move ahead slowly, climbing anthills to glass ahead.

And like the other, he was down a couple hundred yards ahead, and like the other he would have a hole through his heart where the first .375 bullet had passed. But this one was down in the open, facing away from us. He had gone down in full flight, and we had to approach from behind, slip in the insurance round, then circle him cautiously to see what we had done.

In East Africa he would have been more than shootable; in the Luangwa he would have been remarkable. In Botswana and Zimbabwe he would have been incredible. In the Kafue he was impossible, a monster of a buffalo with horns spreading a full 45 inches and bosses of more than 17 inches to match. He was an old buffalo, the kind of buffalo you could scour half of Africa to find, and he was the capstone to the greatest run of luck a hunter could have in a lifetime.

CHAPTER XII
LOCHINVAR

The Kafue River drops down out of the highlands west of Namwala, where the modern hydroelectric dam at Iteshi Teshi shackles most of its power. From there it flows to the southeast, eventually emptying into the mighty Zambezi River on its way to the Indian Ocean. Between Namwala and the Zambezi, about equidistant from each, the sluggish Kafue flows through a broad plain. During the rains the water level rises, forming vast floodplains and nurturing dense beds of papyrus reeds. During the dry months the water recedes, leaving wide-open flats dozens of miles across.

These floodplains of the Kafue River—the Kafue Flats—and the surrounding savanna grassland and thornbush have historically been, and remain, home to a wide variety of game—the great cats, buffalo, elephant, roan, eland, zebra, blue wildebeeste, and sitatunga. In colonial days much of it was private land; the best game country was on Lochinvar Ranch. Today the bulk of this country is national park, and the old ranch headquarters has been converted to a national tourist lodge.

Some of the Flats remain open for hunting, not as an exclusive concession, but as a common concession shared by all of Zambia's hunting companies and reserved on a first-come, first-served basis. Within the Park a wide variety of game may still be viewed, with a little luck, but today the Kafue Flats are not a general bag area at all.

Instead, the Flats have become a place for a very short and very specialized hunt for a very special animal—the Kafue Flats lechwe. To be sure, the hunter who goes there will see zebra, wildebeeste, and perhaps oribi and reedbuck. But chances are that he will ignore those animals, having eyes only for the largest of Africa's four lechwe, those odd aquatic antelope with lovely, heavily ridged horns.

Lechwe roam the Kafue Flats in thousands—here a group of a dozen, there fifty and over there more than a hundred. The Kafue lechwe tends to average several inches longer in the horn than the red lechwe of Botswana, and has been classified separately by both Rowland Ward and Safari Club.

The Kafue Flats lechwe is a contradiction; it is found nowhere else in Africa and thus is an unusual trophy—yet it can be viewed by the hundreds, even the thousands, on the vast flats and floodplains. This lechwe is a local rarity that is stunningly beautiful, and so lovely a trophy should be a hard-won prize—but it waits just a half-day's drive from Lusaka along good roads, and even the pickiest of hunters should find a good head in a day or two. If, that is, he can wade through the mud and muck, and if he is prepared for long shooting in the lechwe's wide-open domain.

I knew all these things about the lechwe and, knowing them, had decided they must be too easy to hunt and perhaps not worth the time, even if only a couple of days. Rusty had argued, with much conviction, that I must at least see the Kafue Flats at Lochinvar, and I had finally agreed. But I wasn't prepared to be impressed, either by the Flats or its lechwe.

From our camp far above Namwala, it would be possible to drive south to the dam at Iteshi Teshi, then follow the Kafue River eastward to the Flats. Such a journey would require traversing poor roads, and although it sounded like a beautiful drive, we opted to drive back east through Lusaka, then cut southwest, following Zambia's major highway from Lusaka to Livingstone. Our route took us through hilly country south of the capital, then across the Kafue River and through some of southern Africa's richest farmland. Finally we cut back north through open thornbush, ultimately arriving at Lochinvar Lodge in the early afternoon.

The country was savanna grassland, brown and dry at this time of

Lechwe are taken around reedbeds and on vast, open floodplains. The shooting is often very long, and there is nothing to rest a rifle on. A makeshift tripod is a tremendous assist.

year but virtually none of it burned. We saw just a few impala and the odd duiker on the way in, and so far it seemed only slightly more open than all the thornbush I'd seen in other parts of Zambia—hardly worth the effort. The lodge itself was a sprawling old ranch house, fairly well kept and comfortable but hardly an improvement over the typical safari camp in Zambia. The government would charge us a modest fee for the use of a room in the lodge and for the services provided, but we brought our own food. After unloading the truck, we took a short rest, then collected a game guard and headed towards the Flats.

We drove through sparse thornbush and dry, brown grass for quite a distance—far enough that I wondered if this was all there was. Then, as if we had reached an unseen wall, the vegetation petered out quickly and ended altogether. Ahead, shimmering with mirage, stretched the Kafue Flats—as far as the eye could see and well beyond. There was very short grass, almost more of a lichen, on the flats and no other vegetation at all. Over the horizon, on the river itself, would be reedbeds. But here, at the farthest extension of the floodwaters, there was nothing. I was raised on the Kansas prairies, and I've seen seas of unbroken grass and freshly plowed fields that reached the horizon. I've spent time in several deserts, from the Mojave to the Sahara, and I've seen the polar ice cap with its innumerable pressure ridges. Nowhere have I seen such featureless terrain. Dead flat, it stretched away towards the horizon until it was lost in the shimmering mirage.

We started across it, leaving a trail of fine dust hanging in the air. There was no game to be seen, nor even a low bush. The sun was dropping slightly, so west was clearly marked. At midday, or under an overcast, loss of direction would be virtually certain. We bounced on across the endless flats, heading towards the river that must be somewhere out there in the mirage. The Flats here were bone dry this time of the year, and the game would be concentrating nearer the water's edge.

We saw a couple of oribi first, a lovely reddish antelope about the size of a steinbok and just as pretty. They dashed away across the short

With its longest horn over 32 inches, Boddington's Kafue lechwe is a superb trophy placing high in the records. But he and Russ Broom looked over many fine lechwe before making their choice, and there's a nagging thought that the very first one spotted might have been larger.

grass, and we continued. Like most visitors to the Flats, we had eyes only for the lechwe. We would see them soon, but first we must see the Flats' other inhabitants. Zebra were next, first seen as shimmering black shadows on the horizon. The mirage magnified them, and as we drew nearer the zebra grew to 20 feet tall, then shrank back to their normal size as they pounded away across the dusty Flats.

Now there was game everywhere—huge herds of zebra and blue wildebeeste, the latter running along the horizon with their odd rocking-horse canter. And finally we saw lechwe, a small herd. Reddish brown in color with black highlights on the chest, they're a lovely antelope and their horns are totally out of proportion to their small body size. When they run they put their heads low to the ground, as if they want to hide those monstrous horns.

From here we were constantly in sight of lechwe, even though the river was still a couple of miles away. There we would find the big herds, but even here there were a dozen here, 20 there, and 50 off over there—lechwe wherever you looked. We saw a herd of bulls right off, just a dozen animals, and one was clearly magnificent. With so many good trophies to pick from, it's hard to call an extra inch or so of horn; by dark we would be weary of looking at lechwe, and we would have a superb specimen in the Land Cruiser—but we would never be certain if we had seen another as good as this first big bull.

Still, it was too early to think about shooting, and Rusty wanted to show me the "big" herds. We moved closer to the river, passing a Batonka fishing village. The mirage magnified their grass huts into tall towers, and their huge herds of sleek cattle seemed to reach the sky. These fishermen are amongst Zambia's wealthiest peoples, rich in cattle—the only true wealth to an African.

We were much closer to the river now, and there were pools of mud to avoid; it was a very long walk if we got careless. The bird life was incredible; shorebirds, waterfowl, flamingos, birds of every hue and description. The Flats were broken by papyrus beds here, and in the distance the mirage of the river shimmered. The big herds of lechwe were here, herds that started in the hundreds and ended somewhere in the thousands. These were impossible to hunt, just a mass of moving animals. It would be like trying to pick the biggest caribou out of a migrating herd—hopeless.

After maneuvering around one soft spot too many, we parked the truck and began working around the edges of the papyrus on foot. The reeds gave a little cover, and on each turning there seemed to be a new herd of lechwe to glass. Rusty had been right—it was worth seeing!

We worked around slowly, glassing innumerable nice bulls. The better bulls all seemed of a type, 26 to 29 inches and thus quite shootable. But the difference between the Kafue Flats lechwe and the more common red lechwe is about four to six more inches of horn on the Kafue variety, and we had set a goal of well over 30 inches. That first bull we had glassed far back on the open flats was in that class, but nothing else had been. Or so we guessed; when a herd may have a hundred bulls, not all will be seen. And those that are seen may or may not be seen clearly enough. Then, too, lechwe are difficult to judge, with some of the length coming from the degree of curve to the horn. Make no mistake—setting out to simply shoot a lechwe is all too easy. But setting out to shoot a good lechwe was proving extremely interesting.

We prowled in and out of the reedbeds on foot for a couple of hours, and the sun was dropping quickly when we finally found what looked to be a terrific bull. He was safely shielded in a big herd, seen for only an instant at a time as the herd shifted and then closed around him again. We followed for quite a time, trying to stay behind reedbeds and hoping for a shot. Rusty had wisely stopped before we left the brushline and had cut branches for a shooting tripod so I would have a good rest. It was clear that the shot would be long and also clear that I must get the chosen animal completely in the open; I was shooting a .375, and I had a horrible fear of that big bullet passing through half a dozen animals if we weren't careful.

At present that was the problem. We had the bull picked out, and I was resting carefully over the tripod at moderate distance, just 200 yards or so. But he wouldn't stand clear. He was in the center of the herd, and there was no shot at all.

We moved with them, setting up the tripod every time the herd seemed to line out a bit. Slowly we lost ground; the lechwe were getting nervous and were retreating ever closer to the river—and to the Park boundary, which we could not cross. It was starting to get dark, too; the game was pretty much over for the night.

Then, far out across the gooey mud flats, the herd lined out. We picked out the right bull, and I held well high and a little in front. We saw mud fly on the far side, so I moved the crosshairs higher yet and tried again. The bull lurched, then went a few yards and lay down while the rest of the herd ran on into the Park.

We had been standing on the last piece of dry ground; 400 yards of muck lay between us and the lechwe, and we must drag the animal back across that muck. Rusty had had the good sense to have injured his ankle just a couple of days before, so Shorty, our game guard, and I took turns carrying and sliding the heavy animal back through the mud while Rusty supervised. It was truly a killer of a job in the knee-deep mud, but the bull was well worth it. His beautifully shaped, nicely curved horns stretched past 32 inches, a lovely lechwe. He's mounted with his head down, the way they run, and he reminds me constantly of a perfect afternoon in the most unusual terrain I've seen.

As we drove off the Flats in deepening twilight there was a great thunderstorm on the horizon, with lightning flashes briefly illuminating the ghostly landscape. The rains were coming, and soon—and if the skies opened up before we got off the dusty Flats, we might stay until the next dry season. But just a few huge drops hit the windscreen, and during the night the clouds retreated once more. We had another clear, bright morning for the drive back to Lusaka.

CHAPTER XIII
MATETSI IN THE RAIN

We reached Geoff Broom's sprawling home just ahead of a brilliant African sunset, with the sun finally creeping beneath the cloud layer to bathe the thorn-covered hills. His main house sat high on a bluff overlooking a broad, well-watered valley and the hills beyond, and its exposure would catch the last pink rays of evening and, on the opposite side, the first rays of morning. Geoff Broom and his pretty wife, Sue, had built the house themselves. Its smooth cement floors and thatched roof were typical, but the design was unique in that it was planned to serve both as home for Geoff and his family and as headquarters and main camp for his safari business, and in both capacities it had served well for many years. There was a wing for the family and another with rooms for the clients, and there was a comfortable den with a much-used bar. The den was hung with a few good trophies but mainly decorated with photographs sent by clients over the course of 20 years of safari hunting. Passageways from the den led to the dining room behind, to Geoff Broom's office, and to the broad veranda.

The veranda was the very best part, especially in the last light of evening when the animals came out in the open to drink and feed. We sat by the bar just long enough to get a sundowner, then stepped out onto the veranda to watch the day end. The valley below was already shadowed, but slanting rays still caught the tops of the rugged hills beyond. Below us, in the valley, were a troop of baboons, several small groups of impala, and a herd of waterbuck with several young males. Using binoculars, we could glass other waterbuck on across the closest valley and through a grassy saddle into the next. Just at dark, when it was too late to distinguish trophy quality but not too late to get an impression of tremendous size, three great buffalo bulls stepped out into the valley to drink. They were still there when dark closed in around them—black,

Matetsi is famed for its fine sable antelope, and rightfully so—good bulls are a common sight in northwestern Zimbabwe, especially when they aren't what you're looking for at the moment!

mud-caked, ugly, and completely magnificent.

Matetsi. That hilly region of northwestern Rhodesia, now Zimbabwe, sits just to the southeast of Victoria Falls and just to the north of the great Wankie, now Hwange, National Park. For a quarter century and more it has been one of Africa's most famed hunting grounds, being a natural habitat for all that is most desirable of southern Africa's game and having the high, hilly country with good browse and good minerals that encourages exceptional horn growth. Synonymous with big herds of Cape buffalo, Matetsi's hills also hold well-maned lion, big leopard, and numerous elephant—including the occasional bull with good ivory. As regards the large and dangerous game, the area has little to offer over much of the Zambezi Valley or, in the days when elephant were still hunted, over most of Botswana and Zambia. But Matetsi is where the habitats of so many of the most desirable plains species come together—southern greater kudu, Livingstone's eland, waterbuck, and of course the sable. Matetsi has produced some of the finest recent heads of all these species—but the area's reputation rests on its fine sable antelope and on the consistent trophy quality that has existed over more than two decades of intensive safari hunting. Part of the reason for Matetsi's consistent quality—and its long-standing reputation—was the fact that, through happy accident, some of Rhodesia's best outfitters had developed there.

In the early days Ian Henderson and Brian Marsh had hunted there, when safari hunting in Rhodesia was in its infancy. Then Rosslyn Safaris' Peter Johnstone and Matetsi Safaris' Geoff Broom had settled in the area, acquired land, and become neighbors, competitors—and hunting legends.

Legends never die, but the realities that spawn them do. I didn't know it at the time, but I had come to Matetsi to witness the end of the game for Matetsi Safaris. The country would be hunted again, to be sure, but not by the people who carved it from true wilderness, built up its water sources, nurtured its game. In the future it would be hunted as a business, not as a continuation of a love affair.

I knew this was Geoff Broom's last season at Matetsi, and with the rains coming any day, it might have occurred to me that I was the last client. It hadn't, really, for we weren't there to hunt seriously. Rather, we were there to rest up for a few days, see some country, and perhaps hunt some of the buffalo that were overpopulating the concession.

We had arrived unplanned and unannounced, hiking across the border from Livingstone on the Zambia side into Vic Falls on the Zimbabwe side. Russ Broom and I had met Geoff Broom, Russ' dad, as planned at the airport in Lusaka. We were on our way to the Bangweulu Swamp, but the camp wasn't quite ready. Geoff suggested that Rusty head on up to Bangweulu, while we jumped in Geoff's plane and spent a few days at Matetsi.

So it was that we landed in Livingstone and crossed into Zimbabwe, a smooth border crossing made so by Geoff's fluent Sindebele. The bridge takes one literally over the falls, but it had been a dry year, too dry, and the great Victoria Falls—one of few landmarks in Zimbabwe to retain its English, and thus out-of-fashion, colonial name—was merely a trickle and a great disappointment.

A friendly Matabele cab driver picked us up on the Zimbabwe side and we commenced the search for Sue Broom, who just might still be in Vic Falls shopping or visiting with friends. She was. We caught her at a girlfriend's house, where she and her friend, Kathleen Williams, were just packing up for a weekend's retreat at Matetsi. We spoiled their plans—though I suspect, a professional hunter's life being as it is, that Sue was more than happy to have Geoff at home for an extra few days—and all four of us jammed into the front of the old Land Rover and headed for Matetsi.

During the short flight from Lusaka to Livingstone we had passed underneath high, billowing clouds—moisture-laden but far from

Francolin are lovely birds, in size similar to ruffed grouse and very strong flyers. They're great fun to shoot and lovely to eat—their meat is all white and very delicate in flavor.

threatening. But as we got farther south the clouds darkened, and there was no doubt that rain was due very soon. Just at sunset we had caught a few brave rays of sunlight, but during the night the rain commenced. In the morning it was a gray world, with the lovely hills shrouded in damp mist. We took our time with coffee, willing the weather to clear but knowing it wouldn't.

At length I followed Geoff into his office and he opened his gun closet. My own guns had gone on to Bangweulu with Russ, so I borrowed a .450 Ackley on an old Mauser action, and Geoff ceremoniously took his big .500 double from its case, checked it carefully, and then cased it again. We wouldn't be hunting seriously, we would be looking—but if we did any shooting, it would be at buffalo. Geoff Broom had made his reputation hunting the Cape buffalo, and he took them seriously. He knew how to find the vitals on a charging buffalo from any angle, but he used enough gun just in case.

Earlier in the season a client from Texas had been culling buffalo cows with great success and had gotten cocky. He ignored Geoff's advice and walked up too quickly on a downed cow. She got up and came, and the hunter—running towards Geoff with the buffalo gaining—blocked the shot. At the last Geoff got out to the side and put a .375 solid just under the curve of the right horn and into the neck. And then he watched with horror as an unquestionably dead buffalo overtook his hunter and collapsed on top of him. The hunter, shaken and bruised but generally unhurt, was said to be much quieter in camp that night . . . .

The rain was intermittent, but the clouds hung ever lower. We took a long swing through part of the concession, a series of hills broken by grassy meadows. There had been buffalo here, a big herd of 500 and more within a day or two, but they had moved out of the concession and onto a neighbor's. It was fine. I didn't really care if we shot anything or not; the buffalo were just an excuse to look, and I had begun to realize that Geoff wanted one last hunt on Matetsi.

In the beginning, when he had first arrived, he had owned the land, bought and paid for. He had developed the dams and cleared roads through the virgin bush. He had built the buildings, and he had seen the game through good years and bad. He had allowed his clients to take some of the best, but he had managed the land so that now, at the end, they could take trophies as good as at the start. Of course, the land was no longer his, nor had it been since the end of the war. It had been nationalized, and he had purchased the concession rights from the government on an annual basis.

Just before we left the house he had used the phone to speak to the local game warden, checking out the legality of my taking a few buffalo cows if the opportunity arose. The government had been given notice that he would not renew his concession; he and Russ were finished hunting in Zimbabwe and had decided that neighboring Zambia held more of a future for their profession. Although the land was no longer his, the buildings and improvements were, and he had expected that whatever outfitter tendered for the concession—arguably the choicest game country in all Zimbabwe—would purchase outright his house and other investments. The phone call dealt a real blow; the government, in its wisdom and with an unquestionable sense of fair play, had made the concession available to blacks only. To Geoff this meant that, considering the sums of money involved, he would not be recompensed in any way for the loss of his home and the equipment he could not take with him.

The gray skies were appropriate for the mood as we toured Matetsi that day. Geoff was acting a fine host, but it was a thin act; he was angry clear through, perhaps more angry than he had been since the war. We were checking for sign and viewing game, but he was planning where to put the explosive charges as we went. If his improvements couldn't be purchased, he had two options: He could donate them to the government, or he could return Matetsi to the state it was in when he arrived. As we drove, he calculated the dynamite the second option would require.

We found no buffalo that day, nor did it matter so much. We did see exceptional kudu bulls, several magnificent waterbuck, and of course the kind of sable bulls that Matetsi is famed for. One stood skylined on a low ridge leading up from a grassy meadow, coal-black and glossy from the rain, horns swept well back and silhouetted against the gray sky. It truly was the finest sable grounds in all Africa, country where a man could glass and evaluate and look for the very best—and, given enough time and patience, find the very best.

There were few elephant on Matetsi at this time, but we saw the occasional serving-platter track in the sodden earth. Once we saw two great forms, red from the damp red earth, disappearing into heavy bush. We bailed out, running alongside, just to see what kind of teeth they carried. They were bulls, youngsters, and they wanted no part of us at all.

As we drove, Geoff told stories, stories of two decades of hunting on Matetsi. Here was where Rusty took his first buffalo. There was where a particularly large leopard came to bait, and off there was where the biggest sable was taken. Here a good shot was made; there a charge stopped. Here was where Irvin Barnhart took his world-record buffalo; there is the house Peter Capstick stayed in when he worked for us. And here, just so, is where I will plant the charges to get rid of this dam . . . .

The rain came and went through the day, and towards late afternoon we called it a day and wound our way back to the great house on the bluff. A blazing fire was built in the fireplace; although early November, a hot month in southern Africa, it was cold in the Matetsi

During a short break in the incessant rain Geoff Broom stopped for the ritual of midafternoon tea. Much of Matetsi is true mopane woodland, a hardwood forest dominated by the sturdy mopane, a deciduous tree similar to the oak.

hills; a sweater and down vest had stayed on all day. With a warm fire, strong drink, and some good buffalo *biltong*, it turned into a fine afternoon after all.

The rain came again through the night, and in the morning it was cold and drizzling. By now we had decided that we weren't really mad at the buffalo, but I wanted to see a little more of Matetsi, and Kathleen came along to see some of it for the first time. We kept the big rifles just in case, but I don't think either Geoff or I had any intention of using them. We took along a shotgun as well, a much-battered Remington 870, and a single box of precious shells. In one fell swoop we had progressed—or digressed—from buffalo to birds, and before escalating rain showers drove us to the house that lonely box of shells had accounted for a fine mess of the lovely francolin partridge.

Before that happened, too, we had taken time between showers to stop in a grove alongside a beautiful meadow and brew tea, and glass a herd of sable on the opposite hillside while we sipped from steaming cups. We chattered away the day, listening to Geoff's stories and occa-

167

sionally taking turns with the shotgun when we saw francolin running ahead. We were extravagant with the hoarded shells, taking only honest-to-God flying shots, but as the Remington-Peters box emptied the pile of birds grew slowly. Towards dark we made our way back to the house, and for the first time that day the skies had lightened.

In the morning the overcast was present but very high. Kathleen, a nurse at the Vic Falls dispensary, had to be back at work, and Geoff and I felt we should take advantage of a break in the rain and get back to Zambia. If we were lucky, the rains might not have come yet at Bangweulu, but we wouldn't know until we got to Lusaka and could get Rusty on the radio.

So, as Matetsi Safaris' last client, a client who had shot nothing but a few birds after thousands of fine trophies had been taken, I packed up and prepared to head back across the border into Zambia. It had been a fine weekend, all told, and Geoff's mood had eased a bit. But as we stepped out the front door Geoff found his bull mastiff stretched peacefully across the front steps. He was a huge beast but had been gentle as a kitten, prone to invite himself into guests' rooms in the middle of the night. He was stiff, cold, and very dead, victim of a tick fever picked up from buffalo hides near the skinning shed. Or perhaps he simply didn't want to leave Matetsi and had chosen the only way he knew to stay.

CHAPTER XIV
LAKE BANGWEULU

Northbound out of Lusaka we took the little Cessna between tower-ing thunderheads and around beautiful—and dangerous—elec-trical storms. The storms ended well south of the Zaire border, though. We skirted that boundary for a distance, looking off to our left and wondering what one might find in that uncharted country. Then the arm of Zaire's Katanga Province that extends into northern Zambia was behind us and we were looking for our airfield. Geoff found it, right on course, and the dirt strip was dry.

Russ met us and we drove northwest to our tented camp along one of the tributaries to the Bangweulu. Lake Bangweulu is a huge lake in northern Zambia, and its surrounding swamps are bigger yet, extending as much as a hundred miles southeast from the true lake. The floodplains, islands, and brachystegia woodlands of the Bangweulu region hold a considerable variety of game—tsessebe, oribi, reedbuck, and lechwe on the floodplains themselves, sitatunga along the tributaries to the swamp, and buffalo, waterbuck, and elephant on some of the islands. In the surrounding woodlands one might find sable, roan, and eland, and the very occasional magnificent lion has been spotted at Bangweulu. But, like the Kafue Flats, Bangweulu isn't used for general-bag hunting; Zambia's other areas offer better quality and better odds for buffalo, cats, and most of the plains species.

Bangweulu is another specialized area and another common area available to all of Zambia's safari companies. Someday someone will penetrate deeply into the trackless marshes, too extensive to even con-template, and what might be found there will be interesting. Today, though, and for the immediate future, the hunting is conducted on the very southeast fringes of the Bangweulu Swamp—actually quite far from the lake itself. Tsessebe, reedbuck, and oribi are easily hunted along the floodplains, as are the black lechwe—found only in the Bangweulu area and thus one of Zambia's great prizes. The real quarry at Bangweulu, though, is the spiral-horned sitatunga, the semiaquatic swamp-dwelling antelope with absurdly elongated hooves to support its weight in the springy papyrus reedbeds it prefers. The sitatunga is what draws hunters to Bangweulu, for in its reedbeds and along its channels is one of Africa's best opportunities to bag a sitatunga of the large Zambezi race. But even the very best opportunity is far from a sure thing with this animal.

Camp was a tented affair, comfortable and well placed along one of the major waterways that flow into the Bangweulu basin. It had been sited by another safari company a few seasons back and, when it was first opened, fine sitatunga had been taken from treestands within a mile from camp. Like an aquatic whitetail, though, the swamp ghosts had learned quickly. Some time had passed since a good sitatunga had been seen nearby, and today the camp was just a base with the hunting conducted much deeper into the swamp. It was very late in the season, time to strike the camp and get the tents out before the long rains set in. We had arranged to borrow the camp for a few days, but just a few; time was running out.

Geoff and I put our gear in one of the empty sleeping tents, then drove towards the swamp for a little recon. It was obvious that the camp was situated much too far from the beginnings of the swamp; a couple of seasons ago it might have been fine, but now there was too much ground to cover to get to good sitatunga country. We drove endlessly along a narrow track, through fishing villages of barking dogs and waving children and along narrow dikes between flooded cassava plantations. Each cassava plant occupies a mound some two to three feet high and equally broad, so that a cassava field resembles the work of a huge and very well organized gopher. The fields are used for a few seasons, then abandoned and allowed to rest; the approaches to Bangweulu are filled with abandoned cassava fields.

Finally the last village was left behind and the brushline opened to true short-grass floodplain, reminiscent of the Kafue but not as infinite. Understand, the floodplains were vast, bare of trees, and completely flat—but one could see across these floodplains, at least in good light. Across the floodplains the papyrus beds started—first a few clumps, then, as the ground became soggier, more reedbed than opening, and finally no openings at all. The reedbeds of Bangweulu are such that the vast swamps remain uncharted and virtually untouched, a vast sea of channels, marsh, and papyrus that stretches away to the Zaire border.

We had no desire to explore the region; we merely wanted to penetrate deeply enough to find sitatunga. We drove along the edges for a ways, finding a few of the elongated V-shaped tracks and one skull with a single magnificent, though badly deteriorated, sitatunga horn attached. There was a plan, one that had worked for the Brooms earlier in the season.

On a nearby island, reachable only by canoe, was a small fishing village. The local game guard lived there, and the sitatunga lived there as well, often seen passing close by the village and crossing some openings in the papyrus that were within walking distance.

We drove along the edges of the swamp, following a faint track, and ultimately the track ended on the banks of a flowing channel. Geoff got on the roof of his truck and I followed suit. From that height we could look out across the papyrus to a small island dotted with palm trees and, underneath them, a few huts. The distance was perhaps a quarter mile, but it might as well have been the moon. We waved until a tiny figure by one of the huts waved back. Then we climbed back down and waited another 10 minutes or so. Silently a canoe glided into sight and its occupant pulled it into a muddy rut in front of us—his boat ramp—and jumped out.

Yes, he remembered Geoff, and yes, he knew where there were big sitatunga bulls. No, not very far. Close by the village, the same place the last big one was taken. He had no clock, but he would meet us right here before sunup and take us over to his village, and we would shoot a sitatunga. Very simple, no trouble at all.

The funny thing is that it almost worked. It could have worked, just as it had for the last client Geoff had brought into the Bangweulu, a lucky bastard who had shot a 27-inch sitatunga the first morning.

Our newfound friend was indeed right on time, and he poled us over to his village before it was quite light enough to see. The morning was cool, almost cold in the canoe, and the papyrus was dripping with heavy dew. He poled his dugout expertly and effortlessly; when I tried it, it wasn't as easy as he made it look!

We walked from his little village, following unseen low ridges between the papyrus. Just as the sun came up we were overlooking a broad, shallow pool ringed by papyrus, an ideal feeding ground for sitatunga. They were there, too; we lay atop an anthill, glassing, and we could hear one walking in the reeds alongside, a heavy animal that we never saw.

We did see two out in the pool, a female and an immature male, and

Black lechwe, found only in the Bangweulu, actually differ very little in markings from Kafue lechwe. Their horns are decidedly shorter, but only the occasional old male shows a truly black coat.

that in itself was a victory; many a sitatunga hunter never sees a single animal. These came cautiously into the open, a step at a time. The male appeared black, the female mousy brown, and they fed in front of us for a time, often mostly submerged. I called the male immature, but that's putting it a bit too strongly. He may have been as old as the hills, but his horns were simply too short. They made the right turns and seemed heavy at the base, but they were perhaps 20 inches long and made the bull appear like an oversize bushbuck. We tried very hard to get him to grow just a few more inches—I wasn't asking for the world—but he would not.

After those two faded back into the dense reeds we left that pool and went on, finding other anthills that would allow us to glass other pools. We saw a few more sitatunga, including another bull—this one decidedly immature—and then, when the sun heated up just a bit, we saw nothing more.

We walked back to the village and our friend took us back to his boat jetty. We arranged to hunt with him again that evening, just before dark, but we wanted to spend the midday hours with Bangweulu's other game.

Bangweulu—just before the rains came! This handy tree grew right from the summit of a sturdy ant heap, and from it local guide Isaac has just seen sitatunga and asked for binoculars for a better look. In moments waves of rain blotted out the sky—and just getting out of the swamp proved difficult.

173

We drove out over the floodplains, looking for and finding vast herds of tsessebe and plenty of black lechwe. The lechwe were close by the reedbeds, while the tsessebe hung towards the opposite side of the floodplains, working their way in and out of the fingers of trees extending into the edges of the featureless plain. I had no desire to shoot another tsessebe, though we saw several very good bulls. I had been ambivalent about the black lechwe, resolved to take one only if we saw a very, very good one.

In truth, the black lechwe isn't black at all. It tends to have a little more black along chest and flanks than a Kafue lechwe, which, in turn, has a little more dark coloration than a red lechwe. But only the very rare individual bull may actually be black, and he may or may not carry good horns. On a mounted head, virtually no one could tell the difference between a black lechwe and a Kafue lechwe. Except, of course, even the very best black lechwe will be six to eight inches shorter in the horn than a good Kafue lechwe. We saw some good bulls, particularly in one herd that was all bulls, and all shootable. But I didn't shoot one, and I regret it a little bit now. At the time, though, I couldn't see $1,100 worth of black lechwe—that was the trophy fee, justified by Bangweulu's being the only place to get one. It's probably just as well, because Bangweulu was truly beautiful in its unique way. There were virtually no insects, and in spite of the humidity caused by the coming rains, it was cool and pleasant. I'd like to see it again earlier in the season. Because we were so late in the season the tsessebe were congregated nicely and were just dropping their young—day-old calves suckled with every herd—but the bulk of the lechwe were across the river. That one herd of bulls was a stroke of luck, and they were all shootable in a pinch. But it was just as well I didn't want one, for earlier in the season the selection would have been much better.

The oribi was a different story; I wanted one of these little antelope very badly. Only slightly larger than a steinbok and much more reddish in color, the lovely oribi is a straight-horned pygmy antelope with a wide distribution across Africa. Over the years I had been in several areas where they were present, but I had never seen a big male.

In the Bangweulu they were common, and the trophy quality was superb. We found them in the abandoned cassava plantations, living amongst and between the mounds, and we had a marvelous time finding a good one. Just after we got him the skies opened up—just a shower, but a serious shower complete with much thunder and lightning. It was a harbinger of things to come, but that was no surprise. We were well

Good oribi are plentiful in the Bangweulu region, one of few places where this pretty little antelope can be hunted today. The oribi love the abandoned cassava plantations and can be stalked amongst the mounds.

into November now, and we were fortunate the rains had held off so long.

The sun shone for us nicely that afternoon, and a couple of shy sitatunga females came out to enjoy it—but the big males stayed hidden, if indeed there were any where we were hunting. But more rain caught us on the long trek back to camp, and still more came through the night. I woke up several times wondering if we were out of time, but when we arose there were stars in the predawn sky.

We gave our game guard friend a few more tries, but sightings of sitatunga dropped until ultimately we saw no more sitatunga at all. They're terribly sensitive to hunting pressure, it seems, and indeed they're a terribly secretive antelope. Apparently we had spent too much time in the one area and had made too much disturbance. Finally it came down to just one more day, and then we must fly back to Lusaka so I could catch a flight to the States. The afternoon and evening showers had been increasing in intensity, and the rutted track into the swamp was getting worse daily.

The next-to-last morning dawned bright and clear one more time, and

Geoff and I tried a new area where we had seen a number of tracks along the swamp's edges. Once again we saw no sitatunga at all. Even so, it was a beautiful morning, except for billowing clouds on the far horizon. The sun rose crimson that morning, and in spite of the beautiful day it seemed to promise I remembered the seagoing adage: "Red sun at night, sailor's delight; red sun in morning, sailor take warning."

We had to find a new plan now, and quickly. Our new plan took the form of Isaac, a fisherman, son of the village headman and a sturdy, steady young man in his mid-twenties. He knew the swamp, and he assured us that, if we would go with him, we would shoot a sitatunga that very afternoon. We believed him, and besides, it seemed about the only game in town. We looked him up shortly after noon and drove out across the floodplain towards a special patch of swamp that only he knew about.

We drove across the flat, open floodplains for quite a distance, then left the truck at the edge of the high grass. There were scattered anthills and a few trees, but mostly knee-deep water and elephant-high grass. We followed buffalo trails, winding our way deep into the swamp for about an hour. Elephant had been here, too, and the dung was far too fresh for comfort.

The grass began to give way to reedbeds. Isaac had some English, and he explained that we were walking towards the river, the same tributary we had been hunting but several miles downstream. The sun was behind the building clouds now and it had turned cool; my down vest would have felt good but it was far behind in the truck. There was no path except that of least resistance, but finally Isaac led us to a huge anthill with a stout tree growing from it. Gratefully we climbed up onto firm ground and looked out across a huge shallow pool ringed with papyrus. Isaac was right—it was a perfect sitatunga haunt, and it was a place no hunter had yet set foot.

Isaac climbed up into the tree and I handed my binoculars up to him. It was about three o'clock, and not 10 minutes passed before we saw the first sitatunga female venturing out to feed. A half hour later we had seen several more and were trying to size up a distant bull. It was about that time that the first raindrops hit us, big drops that fell heavily. No problem; water is part of the sitatunga's life, and any moment that bull would put his head up and give us the look we'd been waiting for.

And then we couldn't see him any more. The clouds had been closing in while we stared into the swamp, and with a fury the storm rolled right

Although everything was soaked, the skies had cleared somewhat on the last morning in the Bangweulu, enough for Geoff Broom, Boddington, and Russ Broom to have breakfast outside and dry out a bit.

over us. In seconds we were soaked to the skin, but long before that happened the skies had closed around us and the horizon had disappeared into a gray wall of wind-driven rain. Lightning cracked nearby and thunder rent the air; we all knew this was no shower.

Geoff knew how badly I wanted a sitatunga, but he understood the realities far better than I. We tried to stare past the rain for a time, but visibility had diminished to mere feet, and evening was falling much too early. In his polite way he suggested we might try to find our way back before it got dark, and only then did I recall how far away the truck was—and what lay between us and it.

We knew the floodplains lay to the west and the river was to our back, but after we stepped back into the grass we knew much less than that. Full dark caught us quickly, and full dark it was: no moon, no stars, no horizon—only drenching cold rain, sodden grass, and sucking mud. Isaac led the way, but he had never been in these swamps in the dark. Geoff and I suspected it for a time, but ultimately we knew we were going in circles.

Fear had crept in now; we had been walking for four hours and had no notion how far off course we were. We discussed crawling under a tree and waiting for daylight, but Geoff reckoned we were too wet and cold to chance it. He was right; the first soft kiss of hypothermia was already hovering nearby. We took a vote, the three of us. Geoff and I were close in our guesstimate of the right direction; Isaac was 90 degrees off. He shrugged and stepped in behind Geoff.

The lightning storm was still brilliant, so we sent Isaac up every large tree we could find, hoping the lightning flashes would show us the clear horizon of the floodplains. Several hours later one finally did, not clear-cut, but just a hint of a blackness that held no swaying branches. A few minutes later we stumbled out of the long grass and onto the mud-slick flats.

The truck could have been to the left or to the right. When we had been off course, we reckoned we had wandered to the south, so we struck off to the left following the contours of the high grass. Left it was; a half hour later a stroke of lightning glinted off the tan paint of the Toyota—and a welcome sight it was.

The road was nearly washed out; the safari was over now and this was our last trip in any case—but no vehicles would again traverse this road until after the rainy season. I couldn't have gotten the Toyota through it, but with a lifetime of experience, Geoff slipped and slid us back to camp. My unprecedented run of luck in the Kafue had well and truly run out, and yet it hadn't. We made it back to camp safely, and in the morning, just an hour to the south, we would find the dirt runway dry and sound. As we dodged thunderheads all the way back to Lusaka, I knew it didn't really matter—I'd had more than enough luck for one trip, and I could look ahead to a return engagement with the spiral-horned swamp fairies.

CHAPTER XV
THE OKAVANGO DELTA

They were just coming back from their night's hunt when we saw them on the dirt airstrip close by camp. African wild dogs, the first I'd seen since Kenya so many years before. In appearance so much like man's best friend, yet they're one of Africa's most effective—and most feared and hated—predators. It was our first morning, and we'd taken our time leaving camp; the hard hunting could come after the jet lag had dissipated. The sun was bright in a clear sky and its rays glistened on the animals' glossy, multicolored coats. There were a big dog and a grown bitch and five three-quarter-grown pups, a family group. "I've lived here all my life and I've never seen wild dogs before," said Ronnie Mac-Farlane, our professional hunter. "They showed up here a few weeks ago, and we decided to leave them alone. You'll see them around here nearly every day." And so it was to be. We watched and photographed them until we left, and they were happy to pose for us, realizing, perhaps, that we meant them no harm. But although part of my mind had a desire to reach out and scratch their ears, the more practical part kept me glued securely in the back of truck whenever the dogs were in sight . . . .

We were on Khurunxaragha Island deep in Botswana's Okavango Delta, although it becomes an island only during the rainy season. Right now it was July, the middle of the dry season, and Khurunxaragha was savanna woodland—broad expanses of waving yellow grass broken by patches of dense thornbush and mopane woodland. Close by our camp flowed the Xudum River, one of the Delta's countless channels, and like all the other permanent waterways in the Okavango, it had vast reedbeds and permanent marshes; its channel separated and flowed around sandy palm-studded islands.

The wild dogs were the first animals we saw from the ground in

Botswana, but when our charter plane had brought us in from Maun the evening before we had seen much more from the air. It had been just eight months since I had been rained out in the Bangweulu, and the sitatunga was my single purpose in the Okavango. I knew I would find the now-familiar reedbeds there, and I suppose I expected the floodplains I had come to associate with sitatunga country. The Okavango was different, vastly different. It isn't built around a lake, nor around the marshes of a single river. Instead it's a true river delta, an inland delta that ranks as one of the great natural wonders of the world. The Okavango River flows down out of Angola past the little town of Maun, and there it separates into a thousand flowing channels, clear-water channels free of bilharzia. The channels are kept clear by hippos and crocodiles, but the overflow of those channels has created vast papyrus beds and marshes, and among them are innumerable islands, some of postage-stamp size, others large enough to hold permanent populations of big game. The Delta stretches for a hundred miles,

From the air the Okavango Delta is a vast expanse of reedbeds, channels, and countless tiny islands. There is some animal life on almost all islands, and larger ones may have such diverse species as buffalo, impala, lechwe, giraffe, bushbuck, and even lion.

The sturdy makoro, or dugout canoe, is the primary hunting transportation for sitatunga safaris in the Okavango. Jack Atcheson, Jr., the author's hunting partner, looks a bit uncertain about his new craft, but he got better. Once you get used to it, the makoro is actually quite stable.

and then its waters flow out into the Kalahari and evaporate.

During the rainy season the Delta expands tenfold, but that was months away and now the surrounding country was dry. The contours are irregular, but from our light plane the demarcation was clear—on one side the emerald-green Okavango stretching away as far as the eye could see; on the other, yellow-grass savanna and dark thornbush. We flew over red lechwe and buffalo at the water's edge and impala and zebra resting in the shaded thorn. In the grassy openings were wildebeeste and tsessebe, and there were other animals in the woodlands and savannas that we did not see: greater kudu, warthog, eland, and the great cats that hunted them all. In the reedbeds, there would be sitatunga—the swamp fairy that I wanted so badly.

We were a party of four, two groups of two each with totally different objectives. Wayne Fletcher and Myron Blom had come on their first safari, and they would hunt mainly on the dry side of the demarcation line for a general bag: buffalo, kudu, and the common game. My partner, Jack Atcheson Jr., and I would hunt on the green side of the line for sitatunga and little else. Buffalo, of course, for one cannot be in

181

buffalo country without hunting buffalo, and if the time and circumstances allowed, I would try yet another time to hunt leopard. But the sitatunga was first and foremost. Jack and I would hunt with Ronnie MacFarlane while Wayne and Myron hunted with Alistair, Ronnie's younger brother. Together with their father, Ian MacFarlane, Ronnie and Alistair were collectively Vira Safaris, smallest of Botswana's three safari companies.

Ian, the patriarch, had another client in a separate camp about 20 miles away. Midway through the hunt he dropped in to visit. With close-cropped hair, bush shorts, khaki shirt and monstrous .475 No. 2 cartridges in his belt loops, Ian was every inch the professional hunter—and enjoyed his role immensely. I happened to ask him what the "Vira" in Vira Safaris meant, and in his soft, boarding-school-English he replied, "Well, Craig, when I went to the game department to register as a hunting company, they gave me the paperwork and told me there was a meeting that afternoon. I had just one hour to come up with a company name. Vira is my wife's Christian name, so it seemed appropriate." His father homesteaded the Tuli Block north of the Limpopo River, and his sons were born in Botswana, though it was called Bechuanaland then. I can't personally vouch for Ian as a hunter, but his sons are very good—and he taught them.

The first morning was to be more of a recon than anything else, and we left camp well past the prime dawn hours for sitatunga. It was in my mind that, while sitatunga was unlikely, we just might bump into buffalo. With that in mind, I fetched along the big .416. It was a wildcat cartridge designed by professional hunter George Hoffman, an American, and the cartridge was named after him. It used the .375 H&H case necked up to .416 and blown out, and I had Barnes 400-grain softpoints and solids for it. The gun, in fact, had been built for me by Randy Brooks of Barnes Bullets, and it wore a Chet Brown fiberglass stock—practical for the wet country I expected, but at seven pounds and change loaded it kicked like a beast.

After we left our wild dogs we traveled through a belt of thick woodland, spooking a number of impala from our path, and pulled up alongside the swift-flowing Xudum River. Ronnie had a motorboat here, but that was just the first step. We flew down the narrow channel, eased across a broad, shallow marsh, and poled our way through a reedbed to yet another channel. To our right was a big island called Xoronari, a true island surrounded by water year-round; as we passed we could see impala under the trees. On around its far end Ronnie had stashed our real hunting vehicles—two hand-hewn dugout canoes. Called makoros, they're long, heavy craft hollowed out from a single great log. But they're shallow of draft and surprisingly stable and agile. It would be another day or so before Jack and I tried our hand at poling; today we took just one canoe, and Jack and I sat very still and very carefully in the center while Ronnie poled in the prow and his head tracker, Baeti, poled in the stern.

Baeti was of a fishing tribe in the Okavango; the Delta was his home and he was a master boatman. Myron and Wayne, on the other hand, were hunting dry land, and their trackers were bushmen from the Kalahari region, trackers without peer. But the bushmen—fearless with the cats and proud of the scars each carried from leopard and lion—didn't hunt in the marshes; the water was a foreign environment to them and one they wanted nothing to do with. The marshes were indeed a dangerous place, too, no place for an outsider. The Okavango hippos are notorious for their dislike of humans, and the crocodiles grow huge in the uncharted channels. Baeti stated flatly that, in a hippo pool, an empty makoro could be pushed across safely—but a makoro with a man poling would be attacked as often as not. We didn't try it, but we would come to have reason to believe it. Every season in the Okavango makoros are found floating empty, perhaps with a blanket and a pot still aboard but no sign of their owner. Mambas, too, are common on the islands; one doesn't step from the marsh onto dry land without looking carefully.

We were in a different world as we poled along clear-water channels and through sparse reedbeds. Later we would learn that when you're standing and poling, the visibility is excellent. But right now we couldn't see over the reeds in many places, and in any case I was concentrating much too hard on not rocking the boat to worry about it. The sun was warm, and the sweaters and jackets that had felt so good earlier had long since come off. We passed a floating island, a dense mass of packed grass and thornbush, and many other genuine islands with tall palm trees and heavily leafed marula trees. Somewhere ahead in the reeds a herd of red lechwe splashed away, and several times small teal-like ducks took flight. A friend had told me that the Okavango was the most beautiful part of Africa, and I wasn't ready to argue the point.

Some sixth sense must have made me grab the .416 that morning, for indeed we did find buffalo. We had just poled out of a reedbed when Ronnie froze, grounding his pole deep into the mud. "Do you want a beautiful buffalo?" he asked. I could see nothing, but trying to move carefully I stood, and there on the bank of an island, partly shadowed by a stunted palm, stood one of Africa's most magnificent sights. He wasn't a huge bull, but he was a good bull for the Okavango, and he had his nose outstretched and his horns thrown back catching the sun as he tried to figure out what we were. I had the crosshairs on him, but I hesitated, fearing that the rifle would throw me into the water, and I didn't know what awaited me there.

When he turned to run the hesitation went away. The first shot looked solid behind his shoulder, but the second was too far back as he vanished into the brush. At the shots a great herd of buffalo jumped somewhere behind us with a tremendous splashing that receded and faded. And then all was silent.

We poled to the island and stepped around to the palm he had stood under. As we did, another buffalo jumped off to our left, giving just a glimpse of heavy horns and nice spread as he vanished into the thornbush. Jack and I grinned at each other, and then the grins vanished as Baeti took the track of my buffalo.

The bull hadn't gone far. He was in a patch of black thorn, very sick but still on his feet. The solid hit with a tremendous crack, and this time he went down to stay. It was strange; we had taken all our pictures and were halfway through the caping when the other bull, "Jack's bull," broke cover behind us. He ran crosswise to us, splashing through ankle-deep water, and Jack put three .375 bullets into an area you could cover with your hand as he ran past. He went down nose-first, sliding amidst great geysers of water, and came to rest about 75 yards from my bull.

That afternoon we got our first taste of what sitatunga hunting was really all about. With the buffalo taken care of and the meat covered up against vultures, we poled our way deeper into the swamp until Ronnie found the right kind of island, one with tall *marula* trees on the bank overlooking a likely reedbed. Then it was time to climb trees to glass.

I get scared on a stepladder. I gave up a perfectly good guaranteed-aviation contract in the Marine Corps and became an infantry officer—a grunt—simply because I don't like heights. Over the years, both on active duty and as a reservist, I found ways to evade the jump school quotas that other officers would have killed to get. I'm not a sheep hunter. I don't even like to look out a second-story window. And now I had to climb trees to glass for sitatunga.

I even got pretty good at it. In fact, after 10 days of it, you could even say I'm an expert. But I never got over being scared of it. The problem was the canopy. You had to climb over the canopy to see. But once I got over the canopy, I often found it was hard to glass with my eyes closed.

That first afternoon I had it easy. The tree was dead, and all I had to do was wedge myself in a nice fork and pass a sunny afternoon. Baeti was in the tree next to me, while Ronnie and Jack went on down the island. I envied Baeti his cool nerves—he found a fork not nearly as good as mine and promptly went to sleep, not waking up until about three o'clock, just when things might get interesting. I eventually learned to climb trees and be happy about it, but I never learned to sleep in them! Ronnie, I would find, was just as good at it as Baeti.

I was glassing a big reedbed that afternoon. It had been burned a couple of months before, and this was second growth—not impossible to glass into, but difficult. While Baeti slept I watched three lechwe about 200 yards out, and they kept disappearing and then reappearing elsewhere. The lechwe are downright outgoing compared to the secretive sitatunga, and I knew from that moment it wouldn't be easy. The papyrus was too high, even the areas that had been burned, and finding a good bull in the open would be a real trick.

We saw sitatunga, though. I saw some that very afternoon, and I was pleased with myself. One was a bull, a young one just starting into the second spiral. I watched him creep along a little finger of brush a long ways out in the reeds, and then I watched him step through an opening, pass behind a bush—and vanish altogether. When we compared notes, Jack had seen more sitatunga than I, including three other small bulls. It seemed a great start to the hunt.

From there on we learned a good deal more about climbing trees. We learned that although the *marula* tree has a thick canopy that you can't see through, its countless tiny branches are very strong. We learned that it was possible to work your way to the very top, then lie on the uppermost branches like a great spider, allowing a hundred branches, each smaller than your little finger, to support you while you glassed—if you could open your eyes, that is.

We traveled to numerous small islands on the far side of Xoronari (named in the odd clicking tongue of the bushmen and thus impossible to pronounce with utmost accuracy). Each island was different, each beautiful in its own way. Most were too small for resident game, but all had lechwe and buffalo tracks and, often, the absurdly elongated Martian-like tracks of sitatunga. Huge monitor lizards scurried through the brush while we glassed, and vervet monkeys played below us; they had sense enough not to climb so high. Once in a while a black African otter would pass underneath our trees and the monkeys would scream and hurl abuse at it. And every now and then a hippo would blow or a crocodile would cruise down a channel like a great green submarine.

But mostly we sat in our trees and glassed, usually coming down at midday and sleeping for an hour or two, but often staying aloft for 10 hours a day. That first day we all saw sitatunga, but from that point we might see one or two a day amongst the four of us. Once, on about the third day, Ronnie saw a shootable bull. But we were scattered like the points of a compass, and by the time he could get Jack into the tree the bull had vanished.

We tried poling close to an island, then stepping ashore. We tried wading in from some distance, moving as slowly and quietly as we could. We knew from the tracks that we were spooking sitatunga when we approached, but there seemed nothing we could do about it.

One morning we poled up a channel on beyond where we had taken the buffalo, a new channel we hadn't tried. As the channel opened out into a fair-sized pool Ronnie saw some mud floating along the bottom underneath us. He slowed the boat, and as we came into the open a hippo submerged about 80 yards away from us. He had surely seen us, and must be going the other way. The boat, caught by the current, had slewed around and was crossways in the channel. Ronnie put down his pole and out of habit grabbed his battered .458 Ruger bolt action.

Along the bank, 20 yards in front of us, a few reeds poking up out of the water shook violently. Then others a little closer, then closer yet. Jack and I were caught in the center of the boat, as if on the bridge of a tanker watching the torpedo wake close in and unable to do anything about it. Two seconds, maybe three, and the water boiled at Ronnie's feet and I saw the pink of a huge open mouth start up out of the water. The .458 crashed point-blank and the water boiled some more, then a line of bubbles receded and the boat rocked heavily from waves.

No words that I can remember passed as we poled a ways back down the channel, then climbed up onto an island and sat very still for a long time, waiting for our hands to quit shaking and the queasy feeling to pass. In a dozen African hunts, it was the closest call I'd ever had.

Another day we were returning to the motorboat, were almost there, when we saw two huge eyes up out of the water just 20 yards to the left. To a man we all thought "hippo," but as the eyes—and whatever they were attached to—dropped below the surface with a slight rippling, we all realized there were no ears. It was a crocodile, and those eyes were more than 10 inches apart. No one can say for sure how big a crocodile can get; like all reptiles, they continue to grow throughout their lives,

Sitatunga hunting in the Okavango meant climbing lots of trees and glassing lots of reedbeds. Although painstaking, it's actually a very pleasant way to hunt . . . unless, of course, you happen to be afraid of heights!

and they live a long time. I would have like to have seen this one stretched out on a bank; it would have pushed the upper limits of crocodiledom, and I don't like to think about what it could do to a frail *makoro*.

Aside from the occasional excitement, though, it was exhausting glassing. Had the country not been so unique and so beautiful, it might have been boring. It was frustrating. And all the while we were trying to see just one good swamp fairy, Wayne and Myron were having the time of their lives. One day they would bring in a buffalo, another a fine kudu or a lechwe or a tsessebe. If every safari could be a first safari, African hunting would be so much simpler—and the professional hunter's life so much easier!

It was the luck of the draw that gave me a sitatunga. There was a lovely, narrow island laden with sitatunga tracks. A couple of days before, we knew we had jumped unseen bulls when we had approached. This time we tried a pincer movement, with Baeti and Jack going to an adjacent island and Ronnie and I going straight to this one after they got a head start to get set up.

FROM MT. KENYA TO THE CAPE

Cape buffalo are tremendously common in Botswana's Okavango Delta, with herds of 500 strong and more roaming the savanna woodland on the edge of the marshes. Herds are smaller in the interior of the swamps, with better chances for coming across bachelor bulls.

We waded ashore and walked carefully and quietly up the center of the island, finding fresh tracks on top of day-old tracks. Once again we had been close but not close enough. No shots came from Jack's direction, so we looked for a likely tree. On this end of the island, the direction in which the tracks were heading, there was a dearth of climbable trees.

In fact, we could see just one, a dead snag that stuck up above the underbrush. Compared with what I was now used to, it wasn't very high, but that made it still much too high. Ronnie went up first, perching himself 'way up on a tiny dead limb. I found a more secure spot just below him, and we began to glass. I wasn't high enough, but from there I spotted another tree hidden in the thick foliage along the bank that would do. I signed to Ronnie what I was about and climbed down.

I had just gotten to the bottom when I heard him hiss. I looked up quickly, saw him point, and shinnied back up the tree. "It's a decent bull, maybe 27. I had hoped we could do better, but what do you think?"

There was nothing to think about, because I couldn't see him. He was just 80 yards out in the papyrus, standing in a tiny opening, and I couldn't see him. I shifted around a bit, then followed Ronnie's outstretched arm. Sun glinted off spiraling horns, and all at once he came into sharp focus—horns back, head up, looking straight at us. He wasn't huge, but he looked just fine to me.

I bent around like a contortionist getting the .338 up, but I found him in the crosshairs and he looked even better. I followed the head down to the body that was lost in the reeds, guessed where the shoulder must be, and squeezed the trigger as quickly and as steadily as I could.

He dropped at the shot, but the papyrus was moving where he had been. I could see nothing, so I passed the rifle up to Ronnie and started down, promptly falling out of the tree and losing most of the skin on one hand. I never felt it. Ronnie directed me, and I splashed out through the reeds, running now, looking for the little opening he had stood in. I found it, followed it for a few steps; he lay there dead, on his side supported by the reeds. He was the most beautiful thing I had ever seen, and I had convinced myself I would never see one up close.

During the next week we hunted sitatunga every day; if not all day then morning or afternoon. Though we saw more tracks and more females, we were never to see another bull. Never, that is, until the very last evening. The island where I shot my bull was next to the back side of Xoronari Island, the big one. We had spent a couple of days along its edges and had seen giraffe as well as lechwe and impala. Once, while walking to another tree, I crossed fresh lion spoor, and there were plenty

Botswana buffalo, though plentiful, rarely grow to extreme size. Most mature buffalo in the Okavango range from 38 to 41 inches; in the Chobe region to the northeast they get a couple inches bigger, but Botswana isn't the place for huge buffalo. It is the place for superb, exciting buffalo hunting!

of buffalo using the island. We had landed the powerboat on the other side, walking all the way across the island. Then Jack waded across the channel to the island where I had shot my sitatunga, and I stayed on Xoronari glassing a vast reedbed. I couldn't see Jack, but he was maybe 250 yards away, and I knew which tree he was in.

It was a long afternoon, and I was restless. My feet had been too wet for too long, and I had a classic case of immersion foot, with all the skin gone between the toes. In other words, I wasn't paying attention. I should have seen the bull much earlier than I did. When I did see him, there was just a flash of movement in heavy reeds 50 yards to my front, then nothing. I watched and waited, and he materialized, picking his way towards me with slow, measured steps. I was caught; he was too close for me to get out of the tree and get Jack, and there was no way I could get Jack's attention. The bull played in front of me forever. He wasn't as big as mine, maybe 22 or 23 inches, but the way things had been going he was huge. He stepped behind some thick papyrus, and I decided I must make my move. I started down, an inch at a time, and somewhere in there, when I was hanging between one branch and another, he stepped back out. I was caught, and with muscles straining I stayed still. He stepped behind another bush, and I could find a

The dugout canoes were used to get close to sitatunga haunts, but even so some wading was often required. The channels were a surprise—the water was crystal clear with few leeches, and there were very few insects.

Boddington and Jack Atcheson, Jr. with Boddington's Zambezi sitatunga, a good specimen of an unusual trophy. The rifle is a fiberglass-stocked .338, a fine choice for an all-purpose African rifle, although a bit light for dangerous game.

foothold and ease the pressure on my screaming shoulders and arms. Then he stepped out, closer yet, and there was nothing I could do but watch and will Jack to come.

He fed 20 feet below me and 15 yards out in the papyrus for over an hour. When he finally started feeding back out away from me, I saw Jack crossing the channel 300 yards down. I looked again, and saw the sitatunga's rear vanish into the reeds less than 25 yards from me. I got Jack up into my spot, but we never saw him again.

When our plane came in to take us to Maun it brought another client, a man in search of general bag who didn't know what a sitatunga was. Just for fun Ronnie took him for a canoe ride in the swamp his first evening. He shot the largest sitatunga to come out of that camp.

Between the day of my sitatunga and Jack's almost-sitatunga on the last day, we had quite a lot of fun. We hunted buffalo a bit more out in the savanna, and we took an afternoon off for some francolin shooting and bream fishing, the latter done with a .458 in one hand in case of crocodiles. There was also the matter of the leopard.

191

The African hunting dog, one of Nature's most perfect predators, is a rare sight and, if you're on foot, a chilling one. In a decade of African hunting, Boddington has seen them just twice—once in Kenya and this big male photographed in Botswana.

The MacFarlanes had a leopard quota available, and I had even purchased a license for one. But I never really expected to get one. You see, it's illegal to bait for the cats in Botswana, just as it's illegal to bait for bears in many states and provinces. But with bears there are other methods that work. With lions, there are other methods that work. With leopards, everybody knows that you either bait for them or you get them through blind luck. Since I'd spent some 40 nights waiting over good baits, I didn't have much faith in my blind leopard luck.

But from the first, as we'd been planning the hunt, the MacFarlanes had been confident we could get one. In their Kalahari and Chobe concessions, they track them with their bushmen, but in the Okavango the ground is too hard. I had no idea how they were going to pull this off, and the way the sitatunga business was going, it didn't look like I'd have a chance to find out.

The thing was, though, that we had a camp leopard. He was leaving his tracks near—sometimes *in*—the compound every night or every other night. He was stealing meat from the skinning shed and, in general, being a pest. In areas where there is no baiting, and hence very little leopard hunting, I have a feeling a camp leopard is a fairly common occurrence, tolerated for the occasional client who really wants one.

We saw this one the day after the sitatunga. It was dark, or nearly so, and he was on the wooden bridge that crossed the stream by our camp. Our headlights picked him up when we turned onto it, and we were all stunned by the sight. Now we knew two things—that he liked to pass by

After more than forty evenings spent in leopard blinds, Boddington's leopard was taken not over bait but with a predator call. This is an average-sized leopard; they come bigger, but this one is a superb trophy by any standards.

camp and that he most probably lived in the dense thornbush across the bridge from camp.

The next night, just ahead of dark, we walked out from camp and climbed a tree we had picked out. Then Jack blew a varmint call for all he was worth. It was sort of a group effort; the calls were mine, stashed in a pocket of my rucksack where they always stay. The idea was first mine, I think, since I had the calls, but Jack was the one who thought it might actually work. Ronnie picked the tree, and although he knew it wouldn't work, he had the good humor to go along with the gag.

193

I was the shooter, Ronnie the spotter, Jack the caller, and the leopard the callee. It worked on the first series. It worked too fast. A good, old-fashioned, American-style dying-rabbit scream sucked the leopard right out of the brush and into the open, and before we knew what had happened or could make a size judgment he was across the bridge and gone into the thick brush. And we looked at one another, feeling especially foolish since, just before he vanished, we had all realized that this was an eminently shootable leopard.

We saw him again the next night, just for an instant in a pale patch of sand on the edge of the heavy brush. It was too dark for a shot, and it's even possible that we only *think* we saw him.

The next night we all saw him. He stood quartered to me, in the open and clear of shadows, and he dropped like a stone without a twitch when the big, fast-moving bullet from the .338 took him on the point of his near shoulder and entered his chest. I covered him while Ronnie approached from the side with my old Boswell 12-bore loaded with buckshot, but it was just a precaution. He was stretched out where he would stay, a lovely golden leopard with clear black rosettes.

It was a perfect hunt—even for Jack, whose success was less than perfect. For Myron and Wayne, it was more than perfect, a magical first safari that will keep them coming back to Africa forever. For Jack and me, too, it had a special feeling. I had heard that, of them all, Botswana still held the safari traditions that had made East Africa what it was in days gone by. It made sense, for so many of the best English professionals migrated there in search of new hunting grounds—Harry Selby, John Kingsley-Heath, and so many others. But there's more to it than that, because our outfitter was Botswana-raised, a farmer and hunter who had never seen a safari camp until he decided to build one. And yet, even though he lacked that East African upbringing that old safari hands hold so dear, his camp was of the old school, with comfortable tents perched right on the banks of the Okavango, hippos calling nightly and hot wash water delivered in the predawn chill. It's hard hunting, harder than much African hunting, and it's a harsh land, very much the old Africa. Perhaps that brings out the best in those who like to hunt. The game was good, but certainly not better than in Zambia, or the better areas of Zimbabwe, for that matter. But it's a country one would go back to knowing the trophies might be bettered elsewhere—and not caring a whit. Perhaps it's just the spell of the emerald-green Okavango and its uniqueness. Whatever it is, it's a place that I was very sorry to leave.

CHAPTER XVI
THE VICTORIA FALLS

J ust a year before the drought conditions had made a pitiful trickle of one of the world's greatest waterfalls. Good rains had brought the the falls back quickly and now white spray rose high into the clear African sky as millions of gallons cascaded over the water-smoothed drop-off and crashed onto the rocks far below. Peter Johnstone banked the little plane in another tight turn around Victoria Falls and I clicked away with my camera until I ran out of film. The year before it hadn't been worth seeing, a bitter disappointment; this year it was in full glory, a magnificent spectacle of nature's raw power.

Peter made a couple of more passes, enjoying the feel of the airplane and showing off his falls to his American guests, then he banked to the west and headed back towards his headquarters near Matetsi. Rosslyn Safaris, with the sable-head logo, was emblazoned on the Cessna's tail, but Rosslyn himself was long gone; for more than 20 years that had been Peter Johnstone's company name and personal emblem. He had set up his headquarters at Matetsi when there was nothing there, occupying a huge concession that ran clear to the Botswana border. He had kept it, through sanctions and bush war and changes in governments, and he had outlasted his competition. Now he had the dubious distinction of being the longest-established of Zimbabwe's safari companies, still operating on the same concession after all the years and all the changes.

But he had watched his game, controlling the harvest before there were quotas and adhering to them religiously after they were instituted. After 20 years, he could still count on sable in the mid-forties, good kudu and waterbuck, and he could still bait in big leopards along the watercourses. The buffalo came and went depending on the rains, moving in and out from Wankie at their whim, but when the water was right the big herds still came. The elephant still came, too, once in a while with tusks surprising for an area not known for big ivory, and lions came and went as well. It was ideal country, rolling with mixed cover, not difficult to hunt in the way level unbroken thornbush is difficult, and vastly more interesting. It had good roads and permanent water carefully developed by Peter Johnstone. It was the kind of concession any outfitter would call heaven, and Johnstone knew well what he had.

Peter buzzed his dirt strip to clear some warthogs out of the path, then brought the Cessna in smoothly and taxied to his hangar. My partner, Jack Atcheson Jr., and I jumped out, and as soon as Peter finished doing whatever it is that pilots do—supposedly he was entering the necessary data in his logbook, but I've always suspected that was an excuse to take time for a prayer of thanks for another safe landing—we walked up the hill to Peter's sprawling lodge.

Two friends of mine from California, Tom and Margie Martin, were in the last few days of a safari with Peter, while Jack and I had arrived for a short hunt and a bit of sightseeing. Tom was just coming out of his room, rubbing his eyes after a nap, and I had to envy him. It was his first African hunt, a trip he had dreamed of and pinched pennies for over much of his adult life. We had talked about it for years, endlessly, and finally he had booked it.

Except he hadn't booked it with Peter Johnstone. He and Margie—and I as well—had booked a hunt with another outfitter in Zimbabwe, and we had made a poor choice. After making arrangements a year in advance, we found ourselves out of a hunt and out of our fortunately small deposits six months before the date. The hunt with Peter had been taken on a cancellation, an agonizing last-minute decision that must have cost Tom several years of his life, and I had gone on to Botswana with Jack, agreeing to spend a few days with Tom and Margie towards the end of their hunt.

It had been a happy decision for Tom. He looked fit and well, sunburned and happy. He should have been happy; I had seen his buffalo down at the skinning shed, a craggy-horned ancient bull, and his excellent kudu and fine sable and all the rest. I had hoped to enjoy some of the fun, but we arrived in time for only the retelling of the stories, well polished by now and skillfully embellished for a new audience. Margie looked well, too; Africa agreed with both of them and they'd be back.

Jack and I planned to do very little hunting. After God knows how many African hunts, he had never taken a sable, and now he was in the

The Victoria Falls lies in the northwestern corner of Zimbabwe, with the Zambian town of Livingstone just across the Zambezi River. It's a natural wonder well worth seeing, and it lies in some of southern Africa's best game country.

perfect place to do it. Similarly, I had never hunted elephant, and I was going to get my feet wet with one of Zimbabwe's nontrophy bull permits if we could find a suitable candidate. Other than that, we were just visiting and seeing the country, and there's no place better than Matetsi for that. Peter sent Jack off to another concession where he had a sable quota remaining, and I stayed to bum around with Tom and Margie and see what developed with the elephant.

In the late afternoon we all piled into the Land Rover and headed out, I in the back end with the trackers and Tom and Margie up front with Peter. The bush was dry, a bit too dry, but the game was moving in force. We saw a number of sable, and it strikes me that all we saw were bulls—good bulls. There was one herd of five, and the smallest was over 40. The biggest I couldn't guess at, but they were all young and still growing. Waterbuck were plentiful, and impala and warthog. All Tom needed, of course, was a zebra, and the zebra we could not get up on.

197

With elephant it's essential to get very close, both to ensure ideal shot placement and to accurately judge ivory. With this herd of bulls, finding one that qualified for the non-trophy permit was indeed a trophy hunt in reverse—until the very last moment they all appeared too large to shoot.

We made a short stalk on one herd, but the wind was fickle and we broke it off after an hour's game of unproductive tag.

Late in the day Tom did shoot a particularly fine reedbuck, as good a reedbuck as I've seen, and he shot him well. I had my shotgun along and attacked a few flocks of guinea fowl that we ran across. The results were mixed, but I think the guinea fowl pretty much carried the day.

We saw no fresh elephant tracks, but there were some elephant working the area. We did see a magnificent roan antelope, royal game in Zimbabwe. This one was a dandy, and Peter reckoned they were coming back nicely. If permits are ever offered, that's a hunt I'd drop everything and go for.

The next morning brought another clear, perfect day. We worked hard on Tom's zebra, hunting in a circle around a waterhole. We finally spotted a herd coming down to drink, and laid a careful ambush. The problem was too much game. A fine sable bull drank first, then some kudu cows and a herd of impala. The zebra, shiest of all, hung back but finally came in. Tom got a nice one with a lovely black-and-white skin, and later we had a fine picnic alongside the water with sand grouse buzzing in by the hundreds. It was truly perfect, and for a change I was happy that I wasn't hunting anything; it was more than enough just to look.

Jack came back that night with a tremendous sable, more than 45 inches of massive, well-matched, beautifully curving horns. They had ambushed him at a waterhole and had watched him fight with a younger bull, and finally they had closed in and had taken him at short range.

Peter thought there might be elephant hanging out in a deep gorge not far from the Botswana border, and the next day, towards midday, he and Jack and I went down to check it out. Peter had explained that the nontrophy permit was a real problem; legally an elephant could have no more than 22 pounds per side, and the penalties—for Peter as the professional hunter, not for me as the ignorant client—were severe if there was a mistake. "The thing is," he said, "everybody tries to push the 20-kilogram maximum to the limit, and you can't judge ivory that close. You simply must accept my judgment, and I must tell you that I'll not push the limit."

Fair enough, but I had my own reservations about the whole thing. The nontrophy concept is good in a country that must annually cull surplus elephant by the thousand. With trophy bull permits very limited and expensive, nontrophy permits give added access to elephant hunting, and it makes for a trophy hunt in reverse. If anything, one must be even more careful with a nontrophy permit and be even more sure. If a

Although his badly-broken stumps of tusks qualified this bull for a non-trophy permit, he was clearly an unusually large and very old elephant, the leader of his bachelor herd.

trophy bull is judged at 50 and goes 60, everybody is happy—but if a nontrophy bull is judged at 20 and goes 23, the professional could lose his license and livelihood.

But the real stumbling block is that it seems a crime to shoot a young bull with promise, and I'm not certain if anybody can look at an elephant in the bush and say it's a small-tusked elephant that will stay that way or if it's merely young. If we found one that qualified, I didn't know if I would shoot or walk away.

I also didn't know where I would shoot. Like all African hunters, I had read Bell and all the others, and I had seen a lot of elephant over the years. I thought I knew the basics of the brain shot, and it was a brain shot I wanted to make. I had a new bullet for the .416, a Barnes "Super Solid" that is one homogeneous piece of alloy, no jacket and no core; from a clinical aspect, I wanted to see how it would perform. And from an ego standpoint, I had been brainwashed into believing the brain shot was the only way to go.

Peter wouldn't have it. We discussed it at length, and he made it clear that he didn't allow clients to use the brain shot. Too uncertain, and too

Veteran professional hunter Peter Johnstone, Boddington, and fellow Californian Tom Martin take a lunch break—Peter Johnstone style—at Matetsi in northwestern Zimbabwe.

dicey for him to get a follow-up if the brain was missed. Bell had mentioned that the brain shot was not for a beginner, but of course I had dismissed that. Now I remembered, and we talked some more.

We discussed the heart shot, the one that he preferred, and Peter laid out the exact placement that he wanted, just at the corner of the elbow. We also talked about the brain shot, and he finally agreed that he would let me try it if the conditions were right—but I must shoot where he told me. Fair enough again.

It took a little over an hour to get into the country Peter wanted to hunt, thick mopane woodland with deep-cut brushy gorges. We left the truck on a narrow track and walked along the rim of the major canyon, looking for tracks. They were there, just a mile from the truck, the monstrous corrugated tracks of elephant bulls. It was a small herd, perhaps six or seven, and, judging from the tracks, all bulls. They had passed along the rim earlier in the day, perhaps moving from water to feed. This was good news; in a group that size, the odds were some would qualify. My palms immediately began to sweat.

We moved quickly, at least at first. The elephants were some ways ahead of us, and God knows where they might have been heading. The bush opened into more sparse mopane with a couple hundred yards visibility, and we picked up the pace a bit more. The gorge fell away off to our left, and the wind was coming up out of it. So far we could do no wrong.

Another mile or so, and Peter's Matabele tracker froze and pointed. There, just coming up out of the gorge, were great gray shapes. They were at the limit of our visibility and were moving ahead and to the right. We glassed them, saw ivory, and moved on ahead on a converging course.

There were seven, all bulls, and a couple of them were huge with ivory that stood out plainly at 200 yards. But we couldn't see them all. They moved up out of the gorge onto a brushy bench and began feeding; the sounds of brush cracking seemed deafening as we closed in slowly. At 60 yards we could see some of them clearly. One was a one-tusker, but that one tusk might go 70 pounds. On a trophy permit, you'd have to think hard about that one—I was glad that wasn't my choice to make. Another had short, thick tusks, the kind that are so hard to judge—anywhere from 40 to 60 per tusk, and anybody's guess where in that range.

Two others were borderline, but probably closer to 30 or 35 than 20. Peter ruled them out, and we had to get closer to see the rest. At 50 yards we ruled out another—more borderline yet, but still not the surety that Peter wanted. The biggest bull, the herd bull, stood a good foot taller than the rest. His tusks were hidden behind a thick mopane and a screen of dry thorn, but we dismissed him instantly.

At 40 yards we had ruled them all out. One was possible, but just barely. Peter didn't want to take the chance, and I wouldn't ask him to. We hadn't quite given up; the elephant were shifting and jockeying in the heavy brush, and several were similar enough that we weren't certain we had seen them all, but we thought we had. In a way I was relieved, perhaps because now I wouldn't have to see if I could pull it off, or perhaps because the thought of taking a young bull still bothered me. I'd prefer to think it was the latter, but I'm not at all sure.

Then the one-tusked bull moved a few yards, and behind him was the old patriarch, the monster, the one we for sure hadn't seen. Peter looked, and looked again. The bull had just a thick stub on one side and no tusk showing on the other. Peter smiled a tight smile, inclined his head slightly and whispered, "There's your bull if you want him. There may be more ivory than you think up in the skull, but it won't look like much. But man, he's huge and he's old and he's certainly legal."

The bull was leaning his forehead against a mopane now, resting. Had he developed as he should have, his tusks might have been resting on the ground. But they hadn't, and perhaps that was why he had lived to grow so huge. I wondered how many hunters in the last half-century had followed his great tracks, only to give up in disgust when they finally closed in and saw what he was carrying.

I nodded to Peter, wiping my damp palms. He motioned for Jack and the tracker to stay put, then stepped forward with me close behind.

At 30 yards another bull stepped in front and masked him. I could see the line of his back above the younger bull and realized again how huge he was. We waited, and Peter tapped his chest to indicate that I must take a heart shot.

The young bull moved slightly, and Peter eased off to the side, gaining a few more yards. I followed, stepping carefully and wincing at the slight crack of dry twigs under my feet. We moved up again, and I don't know how close we were. The bull towered above the low brush, and now his shoulder was completely clear, only his rear covered by the smaller bull. Peter slowly indicated the heart shot, and I brought up the .416.

"Wait," came the smallest whisper, "he's moving." He stepped away from the mopane, towards us, then moved ahead broadside, completely clear. "Take the brain shot. I can cover you now."

Eye, ear hole, hand's breadth forward. It was all crystal clear, and then the recoil carried me up and back and I was working the bolt. But something very strange was happening. As the rifle came back down, the elephant that was as big as a house was dropping out from under me, dropping with a great thud straight down and then rolling towards me with a crashing of brush. He was down and still, and too late I realized I should know what the other elephant were doing. But Peter was watching the whole scene, covering, and he said, "Right. Perfect brain shot. Well done. Now if you don't mind let's just back off quickly and let these other blokes sort themselves out."

And we backed away, slowly and carefully, back to a grinning Jack and a smiling tracker, and then back another hundred yards. The other bulls had lost their leader, and these were elephant that weren't accustomed to gunfire. They milled and stamped but made little noise. Finally they moved off, and we walked up to the downed monster.

Elephant meat is salvaged in Zimbabwe, and Peter had a sophisticated meat-cutting operation right there at his headquarters. He left straight away to get help, and his tracker began laying out a route to get Land Rovers to the carcass. Much later, far into the night, we would be busy skinning the elephant and boning him out in place. Ultimately he would yield more than two tons of boned meat on a continent that is chronically protein-starved.

But that would come later, and I was glad for it. Now, in the gathering twilight, I had time to look carefully at this mighty elephant, to touch him and gaze in wonder at his outsize feet and tremendous bulk. I had time to climb up onto his skull and see where the .416 solid had exited after passing through his brain and completely penetrating his huge skull of honeycombed bone. When darkness fell Jack and I gathered firewood and built a beautiful fire, both to guide Peter to us and to ward off the chill that came with darkness.

We lay back and watched the Southern Cross, telling stories and enjoying the warm fire and cold, clear air. Every few moments my eyes wandered to the great elephant that lay like a huge shadow just at the edge of the firelight.

CHAPTER XVII
THE CAPE MOUNTAINS

A frica is full of surprises. Like anyplace else, the more you've been there, the more you think you know what to expect—and the more likely you are to be thrown a curve. I was being thrown a curve, and the ball was curving ever more with each winding turn as the little pickup made its way ever deeper and ever higher into the lonely mountains of the Eastern Cape.

It wasn't a problem, really; the mountains were beautiful. It was just that I had never seen country like this before. Not in Africa, anyway. In fact, I had to speak to my professional hunter, Lew Tonks, and listen to his accented English to make sure I was still in Africa. This was familiar game country, but it wasn't like anything I'd seen in Africa; instead it was like the desolate sagebrush hills of eastern Wyoming or Montana, country just like where I'd grown up hunting pronghorn and mule deer. The elevation was about the same, the raw cold wind was the same, and while the low brush that grew amongst the sparse yellow grass wasn't sagebrush, it had to be a kissing cousin. Light blue-green in color, it blanketed the harsh landscape with familiar pale hues. Any moment now a herd of pronghorn might be skylined on a distant ridge or a mulie might jump from a ravine. Except those animals were thousands of miles away, and there didn't seem to be much of anything else up here, either—no houses, no people, and no game. We had seen a small herd of springbok in the first foothills nearly an hour before, but nothing at all since.

"This is Vaal rhebok country," said Lew, "and there's really nothing else up here. It's too high and too sparse for even the mountain reedbuck." He waved his arm towards the hills. "There used to be Vaal rhebok up here by the thousands, but the sheep ranchers tried to get rid of them. They're an odd animal, and when you cut one open it often has terrible-looking cysts under the skin. The ranchers thought they were diseased and nearly wiped them out.

"The farm we're going to hasn't been hunted for 20 years, and I'm told the rhebok have come back. We'll see. In any case, it's about the best chance I can give you for one of your little woolly bastards."

Lew, like so many ranchers in the Cape, had turned his own spread from a sheep operation to a game ranch. His own farm was a perfect mixture of plains, foothills, and a rugged mountain rising some 5,000 feet. In addition to the native kudu, bushbuck, mountain reedbuck, and springbok, he had reintroduced gemsbok, hartebeeste, Cape eland, blesbok, zebra, and more onto his acreage. I asked him why he hadn't tried Vaal rhebok.

He grinned. "Well, they tell me that of all our game, that's the one animal that can't be farmed. They require a lot of space, and the males are vicious. They fight amongst themselves, often to the death. I don't know if there ever were any on my farm or not, but I've never seen any there. We do have klipspringer far up on the mountain, and mountain reedbuck, so it seems Vaal rhebok would do well there. But no game rancher that I know of messes with them. This is where you'll find them, up here where there's nothing else, and no one but the farmers ever bothers them."

He hesitated for a moment. "To tell the truth, I'd like to take them off the game list for my operation. They're far too uncertain. Here, on this farm, I think we can get one. I've worked very hard to get permission to hunt this farm, and if there's anyplace at all to get one of these things, this is it. But I've never been able to get a Vaal rhebok for one of my hunters in the past. We've seen them, they've shot at them—often many times. But we've never brought one home."

Lew was good company, a farmer who loved his country and its game, the kind of guy who immediately becomes a good friend. But I had come a long ways just to hunt the Vaal rhebok, and I wondered what I had gotten myself into.

It was 1985; a state of emergency had recently been declared in parts of South Africa, and the American press was having a field day. Port Elizabeth, a beautiful little city on the Indian Ocean midway between Capetown and Durban, was supposed to be one of the hotbeds of unrest, and it was to that city that I flew, alone and a bit worried.

I was more worried yet when the tiny airport emptied and there was no one to meet me. A young corporal, on leave from the Angolan border, was waiting for his parents to pick him up, and he asked if he

Compass Berg—highest point in the Cape Mountains—provides a suitable backdrop in classic Vaal rhebok country. It's high and lonely, and holds virtually no other species of game.

could give me a hand. I needed one. It's a small world; I told him I was waiting for outfitter Lud de Bruijn or one of his people to meet me. The corporal grinned. "Ah, Uncle Lud. He has the farm next to ours. Let me make a phone call. We can take you there if he doesn't have someone coming."

He did. Our plane had arrived early, and even as we were speaking to Lud on the phone, a friend of his, Al Spaeth, arrived looking for me. Al was an American who had lived in Port Elizabeth—"P.E."—for nearly 10 years. The game plan was for me to spend the night there. The following morning Al would drive me up to Lud's farm at Bedford, a couple of hours inland. I thanked the corporal for his help, wished him well, and we were off.

That night I went with Al and his pretty South African wife to a brie, the barbecue so traditional in southern Africa. It was a mixed group, and it was fascinating. Just as there would have been in America, there were a couple of antihunters in the crowd, and the arguments raised were the same one might have heard at home. Politics was also a major topic, but while I felt on safe ground on the hunting issue, I simply listened when the talk turned to apartheid and emergency.

207

It was late when Al dropped me by my hotel. I slept hard until shortly after dawn, and then could sleep no more. With a couple of hours to kill, I walked out of the hotel and down to the ocean. It was a beautiful coastline, rocky and harsh with three-foot waves frothing and spraying in the brilliant sunshine. If there was a state of emergency, and indeed there was, it wasn't anything like American newspapers would have had me believe. Joggers pounded along the walkway, and fishermen cast into the surf. It could have been La Jolla or Newport Beach, and it was clearly perfectly safe to be out and about. Later, on the drive north, I kidded Al about having to step over the bodies when I left my hotel.

Al was a hunter, not a trophy hunter or a safari hunter in the way one thinks of an African hunter. He was a hunter as most American—and South African—hunters are. There's a general season for kudu and such in the Cape, and just as we would do to hunt deer in the States, he would buy a hunting license and seek permission to hunt kudu on a likely farm. He had the horns of a couple of good ones in his house, but he hunted for recreation and to put some venison in the freezer and *biltong*—jerky—in the cupboard. Like most Americans who hunt whitetail on their back 40, he didn't really understand the drive that had brought me 10,000 miles to hunt a terrier-sized antelope. He didn't approve or disapprove; he simply didn't understand. And those of us who do such crazy things don't understand it well enough to explain.

The coastal hills were lush and overgrown with dense vegetation; for all the world they were similar to California's chaparral hillsides, complete with forests of out-of-control prickly pear that some idiot had introduced to the Cape a generation ago. The vegetation thinned when we approached Lud's place. The country had more relief, with open valleys, brushy draws, and high rugged hills.

The Bedford farm, one of two large game ranches that make up Lud de Bruijn's headquarters for his East Cape and Karoo Safaris, was a showpiece. The lodge was two-story, native rock with thatched roof, and it overlooked some of the most perfect game country I'd ever seen.

In a day or so Al and I would head down to Graaff-Reinet, a historic little town that was one of the first settlements on the route when the Boers made the Great Trek northwards to escape British persecution. There we would meet Lew Tonks and commence the Vaal rhebok hunt. Now, though, Lud wanted to show me his farm. It was well worth the seeing.

With mixed cover that ranged from plain to valley to forest and hill, it was the finest example of South African game ranching I had ever seen.

It was country that could be hunted for days without one's being aware of a game fence, and its varied terrain held a tremendous variety of game. Kudu and bushbuck were native and came and went as they pleased. There were also fine herds of gemsbok and springbok, Cape hartebeeste, and common zebra. In the mountains, a rare herd of the protected and nearly extinct Cape mountain zebra, just for looking at. Lud had other "exotics" as well—red lechwe, a few scimitar-horned oryx, and some nyala.

Before we left for Graaff-Reinet we shot a kudu for camp meat, and it was good that we did. We made a careful stalk, and I held as precisely as I could low behind the shoulder to damage as little meat as possible. The kudu went down, but the big .338 bullet, from a rifle that had been so carefully sighted in, just barely broke the spine at the top of the withers. I should have worried about it more than I did; I had shot from a steady rest and the range had been under a hundred yards. The right thing would have been to check the sights immediately. I didn't.

Instead I just worried about it, and now, as Lew drove ever upward along the winding track, I worried about it even more as I realized there would likely be just one chance for a Vaal rhebok—if there was any chance at all. Lew waved his arm again, pointing to a high peak that rose above the blue hills. "We're getting close. That's Compass Berg, highest mountain in the Cape Province."

Shortly we rolled into the well-kept yard of a lonely farm, nestled in a valley with—I swear it—cottonwoods lining the stream. If they weren't cottonwoods, they were identical, and they were the only trees in those wind-swept hills. We had coffee with the farmer and his wife, a middle-aged couple of English extraction who had spent a lifetime raising sheep in this inhospitable land. He confirmed that there were plenty of Vaal rhebok and that it had been many years since anyone had hunted them. He suggested a place where we might start to look, and I finally figured I'd best resolve the problem of my rifle. I asked if we might put up some kind of a target in the streambed and check it out.

It was good that I did. Our "target" was a Coke can, and at 100 paced yards the rifle was three feet high. I moved it down until I could hit the top of the big C with a center hold. It seemed fine, and I didn't think about it again; there was nothing more I could do, so there was no reason to worry about it further. Later, back home, I discovered that one of the screws holding the scope in its rings had sheared off. I don't know why it held zero for even a single shot, but back home it was *still* in zero, although the groups had opened up a bit.

The Vaal rhebok seemed too far for a shot, but there was a nice shelf of rock for a rest and it was unlikely there would be another chance. Professional hunter Lew Tonks thought at first the bullet had gone high, but it had actually passed through the tiny animal, and after two safaris for Vaal rhebok Boddington had one.

The Vaal rhebok were indeed there; we found a herd on the far side of a long valley, and there seemed to be a nice male—though at nearly half a mile the pencil horns were hard to see, let alone judge. I have to take it on faith that these animals hadn't been hunted for several of their generations for they were as wild as March hares, on the run when we first saw them. Lew commented that he didn't understand it, either. But we had a good male out there, and we could either look for a better one or try to get this fellow. He looked good, and nobody was willing to bet on the odds of finding another, let alone a bigger head.

They had angled up a long sidehill and gone out of sight over a false crest. We moved one valley over and started up, thinking that they might slow down once out of sight and we just might get in front of them.

The Vaal rhebok is one of Africa's few true mountain species, and you hunt it as you hunt all mountain game—on foot and with binoculars. Those little things had beaten me before, and as we started up the steep slope I fully expected to be beaten again.

It was just like Wyoming mule deer hunting, open and cold with a raw wind coming from, instead of the Arctic, straight out of Antarctica. Underfoot was crumbling rock with just a hint of ancient rimrock along the tops. We worked our way up as quickly as we could, puffing from the 7,000-foot elevation.

Of course we glassed as we went. We had a high saddle in front of us as our goal, but there might be another herd hidden in any fold,and in any case the stops to glass made a good excuse to get our wind back. We were two thirds of the way up and had seen nothing. The yellow pickup was just a dot on the flats far below; we had come up much farther and more quickly than I had realized. Gasping, I flopped down with my back against a crumbling ledge and took a few ragged breaths before lifting my little Zeiss glasses.

Nearly nine inches in length, this is a superb Vaal rhebok. With their woolly coats and impossibly long needle horns, they're a lovely trophy and quite possibly South Africa's most difficult trophy to obtain. Lew Tonks, left, looks as pleased as Boddington—this is the first (though not the last) that he's guided a client to.

Hunting camps in South Africa are often extremely comfortable, but Lud de Bruijn's headquarters for his East Cape and Karoo Safaris in the eastern Cape Province is simply spectacular. The eastern Cape offers an incredible range of species, and the hunting is usually leisurely and very pleasant.

I don't recall who saw them first; either Al or Lew, certainly not I. They were on the far side of the cut, just coming over the top in a line, running but running towards us. They were too far to consider a shot, just little moving dots. Several females came over, then finally the male. It may have been the same one, but whether it was or not, he was very good.

The Vaal rhebok is an odd creature, very gray with a thick woolly coat. He might weigh 40 pounds and a bit, and he has sharp, thin, coal-black horns that, on a good specimen, appear tremendously long—out of all proportion to his body size. The world record is something over 12 inches and must look magnificent. They go into Rowland Ward's at eight inches, and anything much over that is most unusual today. This one looked good enough, but at the distance didn't have the outsized appearance I'd seen on the mounted heads of really big ones.

They came on, and when they dropped into a little cut I took the rucksack off my back and made a makeshift bench-rest on the crumbling rock. When they came back up and into sight again they stopped and the male was broadside to me. I should have shot right then, but it was too damned far and I thought they just might keep coming.

They didn't. The wind was wrong, and even at that great distance perhaps they smelled us. I'm not prepared to say that they didn't see us, but few animals will spook on sight at 300 yards. For whatever reason they spooked and ran, angling away from us. I kicked myself; that was the end of that.

And then they stopped again, just on the crest of a little cut. I had followed them with my crosshairs and now had the male lined up, broadside. But Lord, where to hold? I made the best guess I could, held a foot over his backline, and finished the squeeze.

The bullet impacted in rock behind him, and Lew said, "You're high. Shoot again." But that was the one chance. He was running now, and at that distance another shot would be pointless. I followed him and realized that I'd heard the bullet hit flesh and bone, the unmistakable whack of a heavy bullet striking at high velocity. I told Lew, "No, it went through him," and I followed with the scope, watching. He ran 20 yards straight off the end of a boulder, rolled when he hit, and vanished into the brush.

Al stayed to mark the spot while Lew and I worked our way across, slowly and carefully. There was blood where he had stood, and more blood on the rock, and he lay where he had come to rest, a lovely little buck with needle-sharp horns, well matched and well over nine inches. With Compass Berg as a backdrop, we propped him up on the boulder and admired him as we took photographs. He would have been unimposing next to so many of Africa's great game animals, but he was pretty and petite and totally unique, and I reckoned I had one of South Africa's finest trophies.

CHAPTER XVIII
THE PALALA RIVER

The battered Land Rover trailed a plume of white dust as Willem van Dyk guided it expertly over the rock-strewn track. I was watching the dry, thornbush-studded hills with the special excitement of the first day on safari, waiting for my first glimpse of an African animal in nearly a year. It came quickly enough and was predictable: A small herd of reddish-gold impala froze at our noisy approach, then scampered into the thick thorn with their impossible, bounding leaps. We weren't hunting impala, and in days to come would scarcely stop to look at those we encountered. But on the first day one looks at *everything*. Willem knew the feeling and gently brought the Land Rover to a stop while I got my binoculars on the herd ram and watched him vanish into the thorn.

As we started up again I glanced at Willem for a moment. He had been my first African professional hunter, and he had been very good. On one's first safari one has little to compare with; that first professional hunter is bound to leave a deep and lasting impression, and if that first hunter happens to be particularly competent, he becomes the yardstick against which all others are judged. Willem had been that good.

A full 10 years had passed since I had laid eyes on Willem van Dyk, a busy decade that had taken me to many parts of Africa on safari with many fine professional hunters. Against Willem's yardstick, few had come up lacking—but none had dispelled the special memory of, almost reverence for, the man who had first introduced me to Africa. It was that memory, as much as the circumstances of the hunt, that had drawn me here to the northern Transvaal.

I had been very young on that first Kenya safari. I think it's fair to say that I had grown up in the ensuing years; certainly, biologically, I *was* a decade older, if not any wiser. I don't know what Willem's impression had been of me when my wife, Paula, and I arrived in camp late the

The hills above the Palala River were rugged and steep, classic thorn-bush country virtually untouched by man. Species such as eland, wildebeeste, impala, zebra, and kudu do well in such habitat.

preceding evening. Certainly I had changed. In the years since I had seen him I had divorced, remarried, and now had left a one-year-old at home with her grandparents. In Kenya I had been in desperate hope of selling a few freelance stories to help cover part of the trip; now the writing had long since become a profession, satisfying if not particularly lucrative.

Whatever his impression of me, it was clear that time had wrought her changes on Willem—and perhaps in the way I viewed him. Although he still had more of his hair than I had of mine, he had advanced towards middle age, and the years had graved new lines in his craggy features. The odd thing was that he wasn't as tall as I had remembered, nor were his shoulders as broad. But his confidence remained, clear in his sure step and firm grip on the steering wheel and gear shift.

There are many guides, outfitters, and professional hunters—in North America as well as Africa—with whom I've hunted only once, although I hope to hunt with several of them again. Everyone establishes his own hunting goals, and mine has been to experience as much of it as possible. I'm not a true species collector, though I like to hunt for new and unfamiliar animals. Nor am I a true record book hunter, though I appreciate a particularly fine trophy when chance throws one my way. But I do like to see new country, and that has meant that I've returned to the same hunting grounds only rarely. Had the hunting world remained the same, it's likely that I would have returned to Kenya, perhaps several times, and certainly I would have again hunted with van Dyk long before.

But the world hadn't remained the same. Kenya banned all hunting shortly after my initial safari there, and that ban undoubtedly altered the course of my hunting career. But whatever slight effect it had on me, that ban irrevocably changed Willem's life, as it did the lives of all the great Kenya professionals. Willem's grandfather had trekked to Kenya by ox-wagon. Willem had been born there, and he had farmed in the White Highlands until independence and the nationalization of his farm. He had then become a professional hunter, first in Tanzania and later in Kenya after Tanzania closed hunting the first time. For many seasons he had worked for other outfitters, but in the mid-seventies had started his own hunting company—Trophy Hunting Safaris. On the eve of the hunting ban he was starting to see light at the end of the tunnel. Bookings were good, and eventually there might even be a small profit. He had been in the States, booking hunters for the next season, when he read of the ban in the newspaper. I had seen him during those dark days but had not seen him since.

The ensuing decade had been very good to me, but for Willem and his family it had brought years of disappointment and struggle. He had hunted in the Sudan for several seasons, doing well on bongo and elephant until the situation there began to deteriorate. He had operated camera safaris in Kenya for a time, even foot and camel safaris into the trackless Samburu country. Finally he decided that the rumors of Kenya's reopening hunting were just that—rumors. He and his family pulled up stakes and headed to South Africa.

He had managed a game ranch or two and had guided for several outfits, ultimately coming to work for John van der Meulen's North-Western Safaris. Here he would manage and develop a lovely game ranch on the Limpopo River in the northern Transvaal and would guide hunters both there and on van der Meulen's other concessions. Unlike many South African situations, the concessions were very large and the thornbush dense. It wasn't the wide-open spaces of Kenya, but the game was there and the hunting could be done the way it should be done.

Over the years I had lost track of Willem, but with confidence in his new situation and what it could offer, he began writing to all his old clients. It took nearly a year of planning and correspondence, but when I got that introductory letter I knew that I would hunt with Willem again.

One of these days I will return to Africa for a true general-bag hunt, both to try to relive the excitement of the early safaris and to do away with the pressure that a specialized, limited-objective hunt brings. But for now, the rarities and the oddities beckon, and the trip I was planning with van Dyk would be the most limited in scope of any I had taken.

It would not be a difficult hunt, for Paula had never been to Africa, and one of the objectives was to introduce her to that strange land that had become so important to me. Part of it would be a journey into the past, for I wanted to hunt bushbuck with Willem again as we had done on Mount Kenya, and part of it would be just for fun—to see if we could find a truly monstrous kudu, much better than anything I had taken in the past. But the real objective was to take a rhino, and to take one the right way—on foot in completely fair chase.

The rhino was something I had simply waited too long to do, and the sands of time had run out. I could have hunted a black rhino in Kenya, but at that time the animal held no interest for me. I could have taken a white rhino in Zululand in 1979—for the kind of trophy fee some charge for a kudu today. But I wasn't yet interested in rhino hunting. And then time ran out. Kenya closed and the black rhino there closed with it. Tanzania reopened and offered rhino hunting for just a couple of seasons. Then, as poaching escalated, they shut down rhino hunting. Zambia, too, halted black rhino hunting in the early 1980s. Suddenly, if you wanted a rhino, it would have to be the much larger but more docile white rhino, and you would have to take him in South Africa.

Hunting is a supply and demand business, and nowhere is this more true than in South Africa, where game on private lands is private property and may be charged for at the landowner's discretion. Although all species of rhino are classed as endangered under the Endangered Species Act, properly documented white rhinos from South Africa may be imported to the U.S. With this ruling, average trophy fees for white rhino took a quantum leap, with the trophy fee alone currently much higher than the total cost of many good safaris. I had waited too long; if I took a rhino now, it would be far and away the most expensive animal I had ever laid eyes on.

The problem was that now I wanted one. These throwbacks from a prehistoric era fascinated me, as bison fascinate North American hunters. And there are many parallels. The rhino was always the easiest of the Big Five to find and shoot; perhaps that's one reason why so few remain across Africa—they have been all too easy prey for poachers. Likewise the bison. He's not a great challenge to hunt, and in just 20 years, from 1860 to 1880, a population numbering over 60 million was all but wiped out. Yet the bison has built back, slowly and steadily and under controlled conditions. So has the white rhino in South Africa, and like the bison, he can be hunted today without doing any harm to the species. The catch in both cases is that phrase "controlled conditions."

It's easy to find a good bison trophy in many parts of North America; there is a surplus that must be harvested in some fashion. But it's very hard to find a bison *hunt* today; few herds exist on large enough acreage to allow true fair-chase hunting and the opportunity to experience bison hunting as it once was. It is the same with the rhino. Once one accepts the inevitability of paying an inordinate amount of money for the privilege of taking a rhino, one must accept the fact that it will be a collection, not a hunt. Relatively few game ranches have true breeding populations of rhinoceros. Few, in fact, are large enough for such a concept to be possible. Instead, surplus rhino from parks and nature conservancy areas are purchased and brought in for the express purpose of hunting. That's neither good nor bad; it's simply the truth. It's unfortunate in that the hunter—or shooter, if you prefer—loses the opportunity to seek a truly great game animal on proper terms. On the other hand, it's a very good thing for the rhino, since his tremendous value as a trophy has exponentially expanded breeding programs for his tribe.

I had decided that I wanted to hunt a rhino, and I had accepted that it would cost a fortune. But I hadn't accepted that I would have to shoot one on small acreage in a fish-in-a-barrel situation. I was hoping that Willem would come up with something, and unless his ethics had drastically changed from his Kenya days, I thought he could.

It took the better part of a year, but he did. I had been corresponding with Willem, and I had met his employer, John van der Meulen, at the Safari Club Convention in Las Vegas. I told him what I wanted, and after the convention he wrote me about a new concession he had acquired.

It was on the Palala River, a tributary of the Limpopo that winds its way through rugged hills cut by deep canyons. It's an arid, thornbush country made up of large cattle ranches where the game has been developed very little. Their own concession, some 40,000 acres, holds a large number of eland, numerous zebra, wildebeeste and impala, a few mountain reedbuck, and good numbers of klipspringer. There are a few kudu, including some fine bulls, and a scattering of waterbuck and bushbuck. A few huge leopards roam the hills and prey at will. Lion, elephant, and buffalo are gone, but essentially the game is as it was 80 years ago. With one exception. About 25 years ago the Nature Conservancy department reintroduced a number of white rhino into the district, and they've done well. They've essentially been left alone and wander at will as feed and water conditions dictate. On van der Meulen's concession and the neighboring ranches there are believed to be about 34 white rhino, including several cows and calves.

Van der Meulen told me there was a fence breaker, a wandering old bull rhino who came and went as he pleased and had a bad habit of destroying cattle gates in his passage. If I wanted, I could try for him, and he would offer the most genuine fair-chase rhino hunt remaining in Africa. Of course, I could have van Dyk as my guide. That was the good news.

The bad news was twofold. First, a couple of other hunters had tried for this beast and had given up after several days of effort. Second, it was believed that the fence breaker was a large bull, but according to local herdsmen he was thought to be a bull that had broken his front horn off a number of years before. It had regrown to some extent but was still not a great trophy and never would be; the locals called him the "stump-nosed bull."

I thought about that and decided it didn't matter. I would hunt for him with van Dyk, and if we could find that bull under those circumstances the size of the horn didn't really matter.

Now, just 12 hours after arriving in Johannesburg and with my eyes feeling as though they'd been sandpapered, we were starting our search for the tracks of Old Stump-Nose. I had never been in this part of South Africa before, and it proved quite a pleasant surprise. It wasn't the verdant rolling hills of Natal or the manicured estates of the Cape. It was true thornbush, characterized by high plateaus falling steeply to rimrocked canyons and lush riverine growth. Willem had warned me that there wasn't very much game, and indeed he was correct. In a day's time one might see a few zebra, a few more impala, and once in a while the fawn-colored flash of an eland, but there was little game to be viewed. Most of the clients who were brought here came in search of the specific trophies that grew to excellent proportions—eland, klipspringer, and mountain reedbuck. I had no interest in those three; our purpose was to find one specific rhino who might be literally anywhere in a total of some 100,000 acres.

We found his tracks readily enough, or at least the tracks of a lone bull rhino of very large proportions. But the tracks were three days old, and they led onto a neighboring farm. (Once again the word *farm*, nowhere more misleading than here. The farm we were on was some 20,000 acres, just a portion of our concession, and the tracks led onto another farm of about the same size—a roadless expanse of rocky hills and dense thorn.) For the moment, there was little we could do, save look around for other fresh tracks and hope to bump into a good kudu or perhaps a bushbuck in the process.

As the days passed we covered seemingly endless stretches of country. The evenings were cool, but it was September and spring was coming on quickly. The days heated up with a vengeance, and had we not just left the height of California's summer it might have been uncomfortably hot. As it was the weather was pleasant enough, but during the midday heat hours would pass with no sign of game.

Rhino had been here, and more than just the one bull. Months had

Boddington and Willem van Dyk's first trophy taken together after 10 years was a big Burchell's zebra stallion. This is a nice skin, but clearly shows the shadow striping prevalent with most southern zebras.

221

passed since the last rain, and the huge oval tracks were deeply etched alongside dried-up pools and watercourses, and large middens of dried dung were common. But nowhere could we find fresh tracks. Lack of water was the problem. Only a few pools remained on the Palala, and the waterholes were mostly dry. There were better water sources on the neighboring ranches and across the river in the Nature Conservancy area; Willem theorized that the bulk of the rhino had moved out and would only return after the rains. Fortunately, we didn't want a lot of rhino; we needed only one. The local herdsmen reported that the tracks we had seen were indeed those of the bull that we sought and he, together with a cow and calf, was presently staying along a well-watered valley on the neighbor's farm. They hadn't seen him, but they had seen his tracks and his calling card in the form of a demolished gate.

We had some time, so for now we would wait him out. It was really very pleasant; the country was magnificent and challenging, and I had no large list of things that I wanted to do. We explored little pockets of riverine growth for bushbuck and kudu and looked over a score of klipspringer in hopes of a new world's record. One evening I shot a fine zebra stallion, an easy shot but well placed. Willem had been raised speaking both Afrikaans and English, and in his childhood had added Wakamaba, Kikuyu, German, and a smattering of Samburu as well as Swahili. In South Africa he had added a smattering of northern Sutu, a prevalent dialect in the northern Transvaal. As we skinned the zebra I could almost follow his hand signals as he explained to the trackers in this new language that I had hunted with him in Kenya; he told them that it was always one shot, one animal. They probably didn't believe him, but they grinned enthusiastically. Come to think of it, I didn't believe him—Willem's memory had been even more selective than mine, blotting out the bad shots in favor of the good ones.

During our frequent breaks for coffee—van Dyk is as much a caffeine addict as I am—we talked endlessly of Kenya and the Sudan, and Willem wistfully recalled his trackers and skinners. In Kenya he had been very careful to play the part of Bwana, a part his camp staff helped him to play. But I always suspected there was much more than an employer-employee relationship, and indeed there was. The trackers, Muindi and Musili, the old skinner Ngili, and all the rest, had in fact been good friends, each respecting the others' abilities. When Willem had gone to the Sudan he had taken his entire crew with him for the six-month season, had gotten them all passports. And every one of them had wanted to go. The South African blacks who were assisting us now were good people and willing to learn. But they were herdsmen, not hunters. The bush that was an open book to the hunting tribes of East Africa was a strange and frightening place to them.

We were doing good hunting in good country, and Willem was doing a fine job. But he was haunted by memories, perhaps brought on by my presence, the first of his Kenya clients to hunt with him in South Africa. Once Willem pointed out a fresh leopard track, then looked at his hand. "You remember that Musili never pointed at a track with his finger." He held up his hand with the folded knuckle of his index finger extended. "He pointed thusly, believing if you pointed your finger at a track you would never see that animal."

Once, when we descended a narrow track to some pools along the Palala, a magnificent bushbuck barked and ran across our front. He was a fine ram, nearly black with long spiraling horns. We still-hunted for him carefully, both then and on subsequent days, but never saw him again. I checked the game log for their concession and noted that no hunter had yet taken a bushbuck, and I wanted badly to be the first.

There were also a few Sharpe's grysbok in the area, a lovely little antelope confined mostly to the Rhodesias, with just a tiny arm of his range extending into this part of South Africa. We were to see only flashes of these little beasts, never enough to make out horns. Paula had come down with a flu of some sort after our arrival, and that first week went out with us only rarely. The one time she was with us on the part of the concession where the grysbok might be found she caught the only clear glimpse of this rare little beast. We had rounded a corner high on a wooded hillside. Our tracker was driving, and Willem, Paula, and I were in the back of the Land Rover on a raised seat. I was looking to the right, Willem to the left. Paula was looking straight ahead and saw a small reddish antelope rise from his bed at 50 yards, stretch, and stand broadside. She even saw sharp little horns extending above the prominent forelock, making it a very fine grysbok indeed. She got our attention—just in time to see a magnificent trophy bolt into the waving grass. After that we spent hours looking for grysbok on purpose and never saw another.

Ultimately though, the pressure started to wear on us. It wasn't that we were short on time; we still had plenty. Rather, it was a matter of our knowing, through process of elimination, exactly where the rhino was but not being able to do anything about it. Nor did there seem much likelihood of his coming to us. He had plenty of water and good grass, and the cow and calf he was running with had been in that area for years. The private land situation made things a bit ticklish; my license allowed me to take a rhino on the property we were hunting, not next door. The ownership of the rhino was also in question. He had unquestionably come from our concession, but now that he was living on the next farm, whom did he belong to? Some high-powered negotiations were in order, and it proved no problem to work them out. It seems that this particular rhino had been a problem animal for much too long. The herdsmen were terrified of him, and all the neighboring ranchers were tired of replacing gates. This last was obvious—virtually all the cattle gates we passed through had been repaired extensively, and lying alongside many of them were rusted old gates with rhino-sized openings. The permit was reissued for the neighboring farm with that land-owner's permission, and we were cleared to go in and get Old Stump-Nose.

The animal we were seeking was, of course, a southern white rhino. He is believed to be the largest land mammal after the elephant, with a mature bull weighing in excess of three tons. The black rhino and the white rhino are of exactly the same color, a uniform battleship gray with sparse body hair. The white rhino gets its name from the Afrikaans sobriquet *wyd*, meaning "wide." That refers to the square muzzle, as opposed to the sharply hooked muzzle of the black rhino; the white rhino is often (and properly) called the square-lipped rhinoceros. Actually, the black rhino and the white rhino are only distantly related. The former is a browsing animal, while the latter is a grazer. As such, the white rhino is generally an animal of open savannas and disappeared from Africa's game country much more quickly than the brush-dwelling black rhino. It's perhaps a unique accident that has made the white rhino so plentiful today. The bulk of his population was always in South Africa, but he was in severe danger of extinction just a few decades ago. He was saved by last-minute efforts at a time when black rhino elsewhere on the continent were still quite plentiful. Thanks to those efforts, South Africa suddenly found herself with a population of more than 2,000 white rhino, and just as suddenly the black rhinoceros was virtually gone.

It has been said that the black rhino truly ranks as a member of the Big Five, while the unquestionably more docile (but much larger) white rhino does not. Since the Big Five is merely a grouping of Africa's large and dangerous animals made up by hunters, there's really no truth or untruth to this. It should be noted that when hunters first began speaking of the Big Five, there were no white rhino to hunt. In an odd paradox of history, today, when so many hunters would like to say that they have collected the Big Five, there are no black rhino left to hunt—but the white rhino is readily available. Since the grouping is made up by hunters, I think it's a moot point.

If it pleases one to exclude the white rhino from the Big Five, so be it. If it pleases one to include it, that's fine too. The Big Five is, after all, an extremely artificial grouping that lumps together animals from widely divergent taxonomic orders, hardly an exact or scientific listing. While many hunters will split hairs between black and white rhino, it's interesting to note that only the Cape buffalo has traditionally been included as a member of the Big Five. No one has ever debated whether the Nile buffalo, northwestern buffalo, or the vicious little dwarf forest buffalo are part of that illustrious grouping. Since neither I nor any other hunter of my generation is ever likely to hunt the black rhinoceros, it seems a useless argument. If the Big Five can still be said to exist, then the white rhino is part of it. If the white rhino isn't part of it, then the Big Five as hunters have known it no longer exists.

But whether Old Stump-Nose considered himself a member of the Big Five or not, as sunrise came over the eastern hills we were headed into new country in search of his tracks. On this ranch the hills slanted sharply down to a marshy streambed, fed by springs in this driest part of the year. Here, for the first time, was fresh rhino sign—clear prints in the dust and still-wet dung atop the much-used middens. We noticed the demolished—and painstakingly repaired—cattle gate leading to the largest pool, and near the water we could clearly pick out the tracks of three rhino. There was a very small calf accompanied by a mature rhino, surely the cow, and off to the side was a very large track, just as surely the old fence breaker himself. The rangy African cattle were coming in to water, and we couldn't discern last night's tracks or their direction. We cast around on the hillside, but the ground was rocky and only rarely surrendered a clear print. Finally the herdsman who had repaired this gate and so many other gates over the last few years came up with a clear spoor a quarter mile up the hill. For the first time I uncased the double .470 and slipped in two of the cigar-sized cartridges. At the same time Willem pulled out his old Model 70 in .458, checked the loads, and he led the way as we took the tracks.

It would seem to be no great problem to track a rhino, but this was rocky country, and even a 6,000 pound animal left little impression. Slowly, a few yards at a time, we followed the spoor uphill, often casting a hundred yards ahead to softer ground to find the odd three-toed track. It *appeared* that the bull was still traveling with the cow and calf, but now there were no clear prints at all, just dislodged rocks and crushed grass to mark their passage. It was warm now and the big double was getting heavy, but time was on our side. The rhino would be looking for a place to lay up, and if we could just keep the tracks and hold the breeze in our faces we would find them.

Another half mile, and we were fairly certain that somewhere, somehow, we had lost the track of the bull. But perhaps not; there just wasn't enough to go on. Willem was staying directly on what spoor there was, while our two trackers—really just herdsmen who knew cattle far better than they knew game—ranged ahead to either side. One of them pointed, and Willem and I duck-walked ahead. The cow was there, with a very small calf, and although her weak eyes couldn't possibly have picked us out, she had heard us and was up and looking. We watched carefully for several minutes, peering into the surrounding bush. This was a very good cow with a long, sharp front horn, but for the moment she and her calf were alone.

After a time we left them in peace, backing off carefully to a safe distance before discussing tactics. We had lost the bull somewhere along

The Palala country was very dry, with just a couple of waterholes still holding water. Checking for fresh rhino tracks was a daily ritual, but the bulk of the rhinos had moved out.

The Palala rhino was an old bull with the marks from many demolished gates and broken fences deeply graven on the back curve of his front horn. With a length of 23 inches, the front horn was average; it had been broken many times and soon would have broken again. But the circumference of 31 inches was incredible, making him a much better trophy than Boddington had expected.

the way, probably in one of the many fields of slab rock. The one chance for today was to circle well to the left and work back into the crosswind, hoping for either a fresh track or a chance sighting.

The hillside was very dense thornbush and far too rocky to track. But this time Lady Luck smiled on us. We had circled around and descended partway down the hill, then sidehilled along straight into the wind. We stopped frequently to glass the thornbush ahead, and on one such occasion Willem stepped up on a flat-topped boulder to get above the brush. I stepped up beside him, and together we saw the rhino, ambling straight away from us like a great gray dreadnought. He was about 250 yards away, but at that angle we could tell he was a bull. From the tracks we had seen, the fact that he was a bull meant that he had to be our bull. He was moving and feeding, unaware of our presence, and we had the wind exactly right.

227

Willem looked at me and nodded. "Right, that's your rhino. We have the wind, so we'll close up now. We may want to follow him for a bit and let him get to a place where we can get a vehicle in to him."

I checked the rifle, made sure I had solids in both barrels, and stepped off after Willem as he motioned for the trackers to stay put. We closed the distance rapidly, moving quickly and quietly on the rhino's blind rear. Perhaps he was headed for a favorite laying-up spot; he never wavered right nor left, and I never saw his head. We waited while he moved across a great slab of barren rock not 50 yards in front of us, and once again I could see his great testicles swaying below his naked tail. With rhinos, it's easy to mistake a cow for a bull—but not this time! He crossed the slab, and Willem motioned to a low bush growing right out of the rock. My tennis shoes seemed to scrape horribly as we half-crouched, half-ran across the slab, then sank down behind the sparse cover. The rhino was dead ahead, not 20 yards.

"The wind could shift at any moment. If he turns at all, take him," Willem whispered.

There was nothing to it; the animal was unaware of our presence, and at that distance he was as big as a house. So why were my palms sweating and my heart beating uncontrollably? I slipped the safety, wincing at the slight click, raised the rifle, rested my elbow on one knee, and waited him out. His head was down as he took a mouthful of grass, and I saw just a hint of horn as he swung slightly. He took another step forward, then started to turn to the right. The great mass of his front horn registered in my brain, but my eyes were for his shoulder. I buried the bead in its shallow V, held low behind the shoulder as he quartered away from me, and pressed the front trigger.

Even as the recoil rocked me up and back I could see him falter and sag, then recover himself and gather his legs under him. I found the rear trigger and fired again, holding a bit higher for the lungs, then stood and fumbled for more shells as the rhino began his death run down the slanting hillside. Just as he went into the brush I got a third unneeded solid alongside his tail, and we felt as much as saw him pile up about 60 yards away.

We moved up slowly and carefully, but the rhino was finished. The first shot had taken him cleanly through the center of the heart and the second had gone squarely through the lungs. He was the fence breaker we had sought; the back side of his front horn was deeply grooved from a quarter-century of snapped fence wires. But he wasn't Old Stump-Nose; he was a grand bull with a long, massive front horn fully 31 inches and more in circumference and a typically short rear horn a monstrous 27 inches around. He had been in the district all his life—surely more than 20 years—ranging at will, and no human save the odd herdsman had ever seen him.

Eventually we hiked back to the truck, then went back to the sprawling old farmhouse that served as our camp to get Paula so she could see him and so we could take the interminable photographs. But for the moment I could only stare at him and run my hands over his scarred horn. More than any other animal, he symbolized to me the Africa that is going so quickly, and I felt so very fortunate to have been a part of what remains today.

In a few days we would shift to the main concessions on the Limpopo, but now we had no pressure at all—just time to explore the Palala country a little more. The day after the rhino we climbed some hilly country above the Palala looking for whatever. We saw a few klipspringer, fewer warthogs, and a scattering of kudu tracks. We jumped a couple of waterbuck females, a rare sight in that area. It really was an amazing range of hills, perfect country to sit and glass the day away. It was clear that the game was scarce, but it was the kind of country in which any animal sighted was likely to be a fine trophy. But that day we saw nothing of interest.

Not far from the house was a deep canyon choked with heavy brush and holding numerous small caves in the rimrock walls. We had dropped down into it early in the hunt looking for rhino sign and hoping for remnant pools of water. The rhino sign had been there, but it was very old. The water we didn't find, but fresh bushbuck and bushpig tracks told us there must be water nearby.

The next day we went back to that deep canyon, hoping for a bushbuck or the rare sight of a bushpig. It was still very early when we crept to the rimrock; the sun was just touching the opposite slope. We glassed for a moment, then started down. Something caught my eye, a patch of bush that had a definite shape. I put my glasses on it, then gave Willem a low whistle as the throat patch and spiraling horns of a bushbuck shone in the morning rays.

Willem crept backwards to me and I pointed across the deep canyon to the opposite sidehill. I had lost him now, just a black blob in the thorn, but Willem picked him up instantly. "Well spotted," he whispered. Then, "I think it's a very good ram."

I picked him out again. He was moving very slowly, working his way downhill, and there was a reddish female just downslope from him.

They were something over 200 yards away, and finding an opening to shoot through would be the very devil.

Both bushbuck disappeared into a thick patch of thorn. I had a few seconds now before they emerged into a clearing below. At that point a shot must be taken; farther down was more heavy thorn, and then they would be in the bottom, shielded by the roll of the slope. I tried to rest over a couple of different branches, but foliage was in the way. Bushbuck unglue me far too badly to attempt an offhand shot at that distance. I backed up a few yards, getting still higher on the slope, sat down carefully and looped my arm into a tight sling. I wasn't steady enough, but it would have to do.

The female came out, right on schedule, but she didn't hesitate. Nervously she trotted on down and out of sight. And then nothing. Time passed and the .375 grew heavy. We could have missed him on any one of a dozen brush-covered escape routes; there was no real reason for him to step into the one opening where I could shoot him, but he did. Willem and I saw him at the same time, very dark and heavy-horned. He was moving, but not quickly. I saw the crosshairs steady just behind the shoulder as the rifle went off, and I have a recollection of seeing him plunge headlong into the thorny tangle of vines below.

The shot had struck a couple of inches too far back, but the big Sierra boat-tail had done its work well. We followed on hands and knees in the thorn, first a few drops of blood, then large splotches on both sides, and finally torn and stained leaves where he had plunged straight through without taking the turnings of the faint game trail. He was down and dead 75 yards into the tangle, stretched out in full flight. He was a very old bushbuck with few teeth remaining and unusually thick bases. His tips were worn, placing him lower in the record listings than the Masai bushbuck of 10 years before, but he was every bit as fine a trophy.

Willem and I had gone down alone, shouting back to our driver and local tracker waiting above after we found the ram. They came down to help us carry out the meat and in the deep echoing canyon somehow overshot us. They had continued up the far side before turning back to finally locate Willem and me—and just as they realized they had gone too far they jumped a magnificent kudu bull. Or they reported him as magnificent.

Willem asked them how many spirals, and the answer was three. "Well," Willem said, "we'll never know until we come up to him. We'll take the bushbuck back, make a big circle around and try to pick up the tracks. They said he wasn't too spooked, that he just trotted off into the

The white rhino is a huge beast, much larger than the black. He's a grazing animal, and the square snout indicates his more proper name of square-lipped rhinoceros. It's said that a big bull can weigh five tons; certainly three tons or more is in the ballpark for this monster.

231

brush. It's ten o'clock now; we can be on the tracks ahead of noon, when he's sure to be lying up.''

Kudu were scarce on this farm, very scarce. But a neighbor had shot a 65-incher by Rowland Ward measurement just a few weeks before, an old bull that appeared to be dying. Willem knew what I wanted—not a 60-incher (let's be reasonable!), but at least 55. This bull was worth a try; the driver worked for Willem on the Limpopo and he had seen many good kudu. Although they were scarce, there was no hunting pressure; any bull spotted could be very large. Even so, I never expected to see this bull, and I couldn't tell if Willem was doing it for the exercise or if he really believed we would find him.

First we had to find his tracks. We circled in from the opposite direction, had the Land Rover drop us off, and with just Willem and I and the local herdsman-cum-tracker we took a line towards the canyon in which we had shot the bushbuck. We overshot the track the first time, but Willem picked it up on the second pass. To me it was just a kudu track, barely distinguishable from other tracks of varying age. To Willem, it was a big bull track of exactly the right age to belong to the kudu we sought.

From there developed the most magnificent job of tracking I have ever seen. The ground was hard-baked red clay interspersed with rocks. Only here and there would a little dust give up a clean imprint. For all of these years I had thought the Wakamba trackers had imparted some of their skills to Willem. Now I wonder who taught who. Oh, to be sure, I could pick up the odd track, and so could our local herdsman, a good man and very willing. But I couldn't have tracked that kudu 200 yards.

Van Dyk tracked him for hours, until the zenith had come and gone and the track had been lost, cast for, and relocated a dozen times. Several times he went forward on blind faith and feel, and always—though not often—the heart-shaped spoor was there. The wind shifted radically as the afternoon wore on, but until the very end it never quite got behind us. Baboons barked off to the right, downwind, and like a U-turn sign the tracks led around in an arc towards them. Protected by wind and ever-alert baboons, high on a hogback ridge in some of the densest thorn we had yet seen, the bull had finally bedded for his midday rest.

We should have seen him in his bed, but it was too thick. We got to within 20 yards before he jumped, but the wind was just slightly across and he couldn't quite make us out. He gave two great floating leaps to the left and put himself completely in the clear, then swapped ends and quartered back to the right.

He was a big bull and a very old bull. The crosshairs of the .375 were on him all the way, and part of me wanted him very badly as a remembrance of the fine tracking I had witnessed. But I could see his horns clearly, as if in slow motion. There was no third turn, nor were there the outlandishly deep curls that gave added length. There was just the normal horn growth of a very mature kudu, and I had no real reason to shoot him. He floated away out of sight, circling until he had the wind.

The deep, vegetation-choked canyons of the Palala country are ideal bushbuck habitat—so ideal that the animals are rarely seen, and none had been taken by sportsmen until van Dyk and Boddington caught this one feeding on a sidehill. This old ram is of the Limpopo bushbuck variety.

He stopped there, barked, and crashed off again. I'm still very glad I didn't shoot him—but equally glad that we saw him, for it was tracking that I wouldn't have believed possible.

We were really finished on the Palala now. The rhino and bushbuck were well in hand, and the kudu were much more plentiful along the Limpopo. We closed up the camp and drove north, Willem and I in the Land Rover, Paula in the Nissan pickup with Willem's wife, Rosemary. On the way we stopped by the neighbor's, he who had let us hunt the rhino, and Willem picked up a puppy, a tiny terrier of the type favored to protect one's yard against snakes. The little tyke started out on the seat between Willem and me, but somehow, after a stop for gas, wound up spending the rest of the three-hour drive in my old felt hat on Paula's lap.

CHAPTER XIX
ON THE LIMPOPO

Home territory was a vastly different situation from the "spike camp" on the Palala. We drove to John and Pam van der Meulen's home on Mmabolela Estates, a huge holding with several miles of Limpopo frontage backed by a vast expanse of thornbush-covered plain. The property that van Dyk managed as North-Western Safaris was called Montera; it lay several miles to the northeast, also bordering the Limpopo. The setup was a little complex, but I deduced that the van der Meulens—John, Pam, and their son, David—had different partners between the Mmabolela and North-Western operations. To a client it mattered little; there were not only these and the Palala but also numerous other concessions and farms where one might be taken to find a specific trophy. Somewhere on one of these areas should live the kind of kudu I was looking for.

Pam and John showed us to a comfortable room in one wing of their sprawling farmhouse while Rosemary headed home to Montera; she had been with us on the Palala and was no doubt long overdue in putting her own house back in order. Only after she left did I discover that we still had the puppy, and I began to wonder how I was going to explain him to the customs inspectors.

By the time we got organized we had just a couple of hours of daylight left. Willem took us for a drive, mainly to see the difference in the country. And what a difference! In those two hours we saw more game than we had seen the entire time on the Palala. Here were impala, there kudu females and young bulls, then gemsbok, warthog, wildebeeste, and waterbuck by the score. We began out in the thornbush well away from the river line, then spent the last few moments of light cruising slowly along the edge of the thick riverine jungle that marked the winding line of the Limpopo. Here the border with

Botswana was essentially open; the river wasn't flowing but had dried into a series of pools, and only a flimsy veterinarian fence separated the two countries.

At about this time of year, the height of the dry, the border farms received an influx of kudu from Botswana, making the river line and the islands on the South African side of the channel a prime place to hunt. We saw no big bulls that evening, but I saw enough country and enough game to excite anyone. I knew a big kudu would be hit or miss at best. I didn't want just a good one, which would have been no problem; I wanted a great one, and even in the best country the odds weren't good for finding him. As the days passed, I came to understand how slim the chances really were. Kudu were extremely common, and rarely did we go more than a quarter hour or so without seeing cows and youngsters, and every so often a twist-horned bull—often in a bachelor group—would peer out of the brush. We saw several bulls that were shootable, but never one that was great. In addition to the kudu, we saw a number of truly great trophies of other species. The waterbuck here were exceptional, the gemsbok surprisingly good, the impala absolutely incredible, the steinbok amazing.

We shared the dinner table with an Australian couple that David van der Meulen was guiding. This was their first hunt in this region of Africa, and both of them were shooting. Each and every day they brought in some magnificent trophy or other, and it was really good fun to watch them at work. Meantime, we plugged away looking for that one stubborn kudu, and several times walked away from trophies of a lifetime of other species.

The waterbuck were particularly large on Mmabolela, and indeed this particular region—extreme northwestern Transvaal and the adjoining Tuli Block of Botswana—has long produced some of Africa's finest common waterbuck. But although we saw several that were very good, I didn't see one quite big enough to sidetrack me. Somewhere in there we did shoot a very fine southern impala, my best to date.

Impala, of course, were extremely numerous and the trophy quality overall was outstanding. It's odd; shooting an impala is generally quite easy, but when you see a particular impala and then try to shoot *him*, it can get to be quite a trick. We saw this one towards midday as we were returning to camp after yet another unsuccessful try for kudu. He was part of a bachelor herd and gave us just a quick glimpse before darting into some particularly heavy brush. Willem and I bailed out, and I whispered to Paula that we'd be back in just a few minutes. We weren't.

The mighty Limpopo, one of southern Africa's great boundary rivers, had dried into a series of isolated pools and channel islands. The islands held a variety of game, including kudu, while many of the pools held crocodiles and hippo.

An hour and a half later we were still playing cat-and-mouse in the thick stuff and had never been able to sort the big fellow from his buddies long enough for a shot.

The chase had moved quite a distance by now, and we were heading towards another road. Willem sent Lucas, our driver, back to get the truck, and we moved ahead for one last try. The impala were understandably spooked by now, and neither of us expected to get a shot. But we finally lucked out. We were off to the side to keep the wind right and chanced upon a long open tunnel in the brush. We waited a few moments, and the big ram stepped into the open and stood for just an instant, long enough to get the crosshairs on him. The big 300-grain Sierra from the .375 put him down where he stood, and he really was a beautiful impala. Had I had the interest, I suppose I could have taken trophies of similar quality of several species, but the kudu—the one animal I really wanted—simply wouldn't cooperate.

Over dinner, after a frustrating evening hunt during which virtually every animal on Mmabolela except a single outsize kudu was up and

237

moving, John van der Meulen announced that we would leave early in the morning and try some new country a considerable distance away. Here, he said, was the greatest concentration of big kudu he knew of. It was on this farm, earlier in the season, that his American partner had missed a grand bull well over 60 inches.

A change of pace seemed in order, so I was all for it. Lucas (John's tracker, driver and right-hand man), Willem, John, and I piled into John's new Toyota Land Cruiser and headed back south well ahead of dawn. This farm, as it turned out, wasn't too far from the Palala country. But while kudu had been extremely scarce on the Palala, this farm was part of a pocket that had an unusual concentration.

It was a large farm that rose into two great sugarloaves of mountains with a broad valley between—rough, rocky country in the main with good browse on the hillsides and broad, grassy flats below. It was game fenced, a fact of life on a hunting ranch in South Africa, but once we entered the gate we never saw another fence. The kudu were abundant, as were impala and gemsbok. Through the course of the day we also saw a number of shy eland and some spooky Cape hartebeeste, and the flats held immense herds of blesbok. In short, it was a classic example of good habitat properly managed for game.

We drove a winding track up the first mountain, seeing a number of animals, including some young kudu bulls, as we went. The track eventually descended to the central valley, then wandered along the base of the second mountain. Above us a kudu bull paused on a shelf of rimrock, then vanished over the edge. He was big enough to be more than interesting, so wm left the truck and took his track.

The tracking here wasn't as difficult as on the Palala; there was much more soft earth between the abundant rocks. Which is to say the tracking appeared possible, if just barely. This bull may or may not have been the kind of kudu we sought—we never got a good look at him. He was big enough to have been hunted before and old enough to understand what tracking was all about. His tracks wound up and over the mountain, circling wide until he got our scent, then cutting deep into the red earth where he had run downwind just out of sight. It was a warm day, and the light breeze shifted several times and allowed us to get tantalizingly close. But never close enough. By now we had sorted the bull's tracks from numerous groups of cows and calves, and our bull had joined at least two other equally invisible kudu bulls. We were spread out on a rimrocked face overlooking the central valley, having momentarily lost the spoor, when the three bulls came out underneath Lucas and trotted casually across the grassy opening. When we finally got to Lucas it was much too late. The last bull had long since crossed the valley and was just going over the far mountain more than a mile away. With difficulty we found him in our binoculars as he wove his way through the thorn, and through shimmering heat waves we could just make out a hint of the great corkscrew horns laid back along his flanks.

And that, in spite of the obvious concentration of kudu and John's assurances—which I fully believe—about the numbers of big bulls, was the best look we had at a trophy kudu that day. We simply couldn't put it together, though we hunted hard until black dark. It was a quiet crew on the long drive back to Mmabolela.

The next morning we tried a foot hunt on some of the islands on the Limpopo. It was still a bit early for the major influx of kudu from Botswana, but the dense bush of the islands was a whole different world—a world in which one never knew what might pop up. There were just scattered pools remaining in the deep, boulder-strewn channels, and these would continue to dwindle until the rains started in early November—provided, of course, they arrived on time. But each sizable puddle held crocodiles, and just the ears and nostrils of a submerged hippo protruded from one of the larger pools.

The riverine growth was extremely dense on the islands, impenetrable tangles of thornbush and vines. It was perfect cover for bushbuck, of which there were many, and also a perfect haunt for warthog and the nocturnal bushpig. It was prime leopard habitat, too, and there were several known to be hunting up and down the river.

We moved slowly, into the wind, nearly stepping on an outraged warthog who squealed and crashed away through the thorn. We slipped up on a young bushbuck ram as well, and I hoped for the sight of one of the 16-inch-plus rams that just might be found in such country.

But we found just one kudu bull, a fine youngster with great promise in his just-maturing horns. We had come to the end of one brushy island, and he stood on the bank of the next across a narrow channel. The sunlight glinted on his gray hide and his horns were thrown back so only the deep spiral of the first turn could be seen. For a long moment we thought we had something, and then he turned and showed us what he really was—a bull who would be great if no one made a mistake like we could easily have made, but a bull who was not yet great. Finally he crashed into the brush. We moved on, covering another mile or so of the endless islands, but saw no more kudu and few of their heart-shaped tracks. These islands could undoubtedly be the right place to look at any

Boddington and his wife, Paula, with a fine southern impala taken near the Limpopo River. The impala is a lovely antelope, generally the most prevalent species in southern thornbush regions. This one is just over 24 inches, an excellent specimen.

given time, but the sign told us this wasn't the time.

There were just a couple of days left, and there was really just one place left to try. That was on Montera, Willem's farm a few miles down the Limpopo. The game there was being carefully developed and built up, and the hunting had been extremely limited so far. Few clients had been on the farm, and they had hunted specifically for a couple of surplus blesbok, gemsbok, and Cape hartebeeste. No kudu had been taken there in recent years, and although the total herd was much smaller than on Mmabolela, there were a few very big bulls. With most other possibilities exhausted, John agreed to let us have a go at kudu on Montera.

Paula and I packed a few things quickly so that, for simplicity, we could stay with Willem and Rosemary for the last days of the trip. We also packed up the puppy in his wicker basket and brought him to his new home. I had grown to like the little rascal, but I still hadn't figured out how to get him through customs.

Though not nearly so grand as the big house on Mmabolela, the ranch house on Montera was also large and sprawling. Crafted of native rock, it was decorated with countless mementos of the van Dyks' life in Kenya: wood carvings, basketry, a large collection of seashells picked up along the coast near Mombasa, and just a few East African heads—a fine Kenya impala, a defassa waterbuck, and a monstrous 48-inch Cape buffalo taken on Willem's farm near Mount Kenya.

We had a quick cup of coffee, then headed into Montera to continue the search for kudu. Although only 20 minutes by dirt road from Mmabolela, the country had changed significantly. We had entered a belt of much heavier thornbush, with visibility much reduced from the bush on Mmabolela away from the river line. There was a type of yellow acacia found here, and the trees were in full bloom, announcing the coming of the African spring. It was a beautiful farm, and the game was quite tame. Big herds of blesbok stood and gaped at us, and the normally wary zebra just faded into the brush a few yards. There were kudu here as well, and seemingly good numbers—from the start we saw cows, calves, and young bulls—but as they had every place else, the big bulls kept out of sight.

Kudu hunting was mostly done by tracking, a painstaking and time-consuming technique on dry ground. The Africans who are good at it—black or white—can follow tracks where there seem to be no tracks at all, but it's hunting wizardry that is totally foreign to most Americans.

Still, it was a lovely piece of classic thornbush and provided a good opportunity to view game and take some pictures. We were getting short on time, and with the incredible thickness of the brush the best tactic seemed to be to cover as much ground as possible and hope to chance across the kind of bull we were looking for. So we drove the endless tracks slowly and carefully, stopping often to look. It was the weekend, and young Willem van Dyk was home from school. In Kenya Rosemary had brought him down to our camp at Tsavo for a few days. He had been a toddler then; now he was a tall teenager. He drove the Land Rover for us, and we stopped often so Paula or I could take pictures or just look at the animals.

On Sunday morning we found the herd of some dozen giraffe, and they posed beautifully for us. Towards midday we found the fresh tracks of a big bull rhino, one of a small herd they were trying to establish. We followed him up, hoping to shoot some photos, but we bumped him out of his bed in impossible thorn. We followed him for a ways, but nobody had told him how docile white rhino were supposed to be, and we broke off after jumping him a couple more times.

Young Willem had to go back to school at noon, and since it was Sunday Willem's staff had the day off. For the afternoon hunt, our very last chance, Rosemary drove with Paula while Willem and I sat in the back. It was a perfect afternoon, just starting to cool after the heat of the day, and the sun was brilliant. The game was moving well, and we saw many zebra, blesbok, impala, and waterbuck, and several more kudu—family groups of cows and calves and the occasional young bull. The sun was getting lower before we spotted a mature bull, but he was more of the same—about 48 inches with tight spirals, not a bad kudu, but not a great one. It was just a few minutes afterwards that I caught a flash of gray hide in dense thorn to the left of the road.

Willem tapped and Rosemary stopped. I had seen an immature bull, but just then the big bull behind him turned and whirled into the thorn, giving us just a glimpse of wide spread, deep spirals, and great length. This, at long last, might be the kudu we were looking for. No world record, to be sure, but he appeared to hit the 55-inch mark we had set, perhaps with a little bit to spare.

We climbed out carefully and Willem told Rosemary to drive a few hundred yards down the road and stop. Just possibly the bull wouldn't go far, especially if he heard the truck drive away. He hadn't stopped, but his prints were clear in the hard earth. We took them, Willem watching the trail and I trying to peer through the heavy thorn. The

Much of the Limpopo country is flat thornbush, with little relief and few vantage points to glass from. Where a kopje can be found, it's a good place to sit and glass for kudu bulls.

wind was right, but the bush was nearly impossible. The tracks showed that he had trotted for a few hundred yards, then slowed to a walk.

I got ready, but I wasn't ready enough. When he jumped all we could see was horn tips and flashes of white-striped gray hide. And then we began all over again.

He was starting to circle to get the wind, but the wind was shifting erratically. The game wasn't quite over, but the sun was getting uncomfortably low. Still, he felt secure in the thick bush—as well he should have—and again his tracks slowed after a short dash. This time we never saw him when he jumped, just heard him crash away. The next time we neither heard nor saw him, just saw the deep tracks where he had jumped and the marks of the long running stride that carried him away.

We followed the tracks quickly until he slowed down, then moved ahead with ever more caution. The wind was holding from our right, and the brush was starting to open slightly. The faint game trail pinched us in slightly, putting Willem directly ahead of me. He froze, staring

The greater kudu is one of Africa's most regal trophies, and like exceptional trophies of most species, a really big kudu is a hard-won prize. The Limpopo region produces some of Africa's finest kudu, but, as Boddington discovered, getting one of them isn't always that easy. (Photo by Bob Robb).

ahead, but I could see nothing. I took half a step to the right to get clear, and in that instant the kudu jumped. He had been standing behind a thick thornbush, and this time his flight took him across the open. I got the rifle up and could see his monstrous horns clearly for the first time—black, polished corkscrews with deep curls and ivory tips that seemed to touch his rump as he laid them back. In two jumps he was gone into the brush, but in those two jumps there had been a chance for a shot. I hadn't taken it, and I don't know why. I had the light rifle, the .30-06, and the shot would have been a marginal rear-end attempt. Perhaps subconsciously I was unwilling to risk a wounded animal at dusk on the last day. Perhaps I was too busy trying to size up the horns, for until that moment I hadn't known for sure that I would take the bull if presented a shot. Or perhaps I was quite simply too slow. Perhaps with the .375, perhaps with just a slight quartering angle, perhaps with a half-second more time, we would have had this kudu that we had been seeking for so many days. As it was, we now knew for sure he was the kind of bull we wanted, and we were fast running out of daylight.

Willem paused for a moment where he had stood behind the thorn. "The brush opens up nicely just ahead. He's going to make a mistake one of these times—he almost did here. We'll stay with him, and I think we can get him."

But I knew, deep down, that the bull had made a mistake—and I hadn't taken advantage of it. It's rare for a great trophy such as this to give you more than one chance, and although we took the trail again in the deepening dusk, I wasn't surprised by what happened next.

This time it wasn't our lack of skill that finished the game, nor was it the craftiness of the bull that proved too much for us. It was Africa herself, deciding that we had had our opportunity, however marginal it might have been, and ruling in favor of the kudu. The bull had run in a straight line for just a hundred yards, then once again had slowed to a walk. The brush had indeed opened nicely, and on the edge of the thick stuff the tracks told us the story. He had walked right into a big herd of zebra, and they had scattered in all directions. Somewhere underneath, between, or on top of their horseshoe spoor was the track of our bull, but we couldn't find it.

We cast in all directions, but the ground was harder here and the kudu spoor had vanished. After searching carefully in the gathering gloom, we gave it up and took a line back to the truck. Oh, we would use the last few moments of shooting light to circle around and try to catch the bull coming out on the far side, but I think Willem knew as well as I did that this kudu had won the game fair and square. He had given us a good look when he flashed across the narrow opening with the low sun glinting from his twisting horns, and that glimpse would have to suffice until I returned to try again another year. We had turned from the confused muddle of indistinct tracks, and Willem van Dyk had led the way back, heading directly towards the crimson African sunset. It was there, with the chill of evening just coming on, that my first 10 years of African hunting came to an end.

APPENDIX A
AFRICAN RIFLES AND CARTRIDGES

It's been written and said countless times that African game is much tougher and harder to bring down, pound for pound, than similar-sized species in North America or Europe. There is some truth to that, but personally I feel it is a gross oversimplification. There are literally scores of African game animals ranging in size from the 10-pound suni and dik dik to the seven-ton elephant, and each species of African game is unique in its habits, habitat, and in its reaction to the strike of a bullet. African game is generally more keyed up than game in other regions. I have always believed that to be a result of the large numbers of predators present in most African game country, keeping the prey species always on edge. Whatever the reason, it's quite true that most species of African game, if poorly hit with the first shot, will exhibit unusual tenacity.

However, it's not that cut and dried. Kudu, for example, are often likened to the American elk and are indeed quite similar in size. But the elk is an extremely tough animal, certainly hardier and more difficult to bring down than the much larger moose. Kudu are actually quite soft, succumbing readily to a well-placed bullet and rarely traveling far before lying up after a marginal hit. The sable-roan-oryx clan, on the other hand, are a good deal smaller than both elk and kudu, but are extremely tough and tenacious of life. They're also quite dangerous when wounded. Bushbuck, though of the same general family as kudu, are much tougher pound for pound, and are also extremely vicious when wounded and cornered. In the dense cover where they're often hunted, numerous hunters over the years have been badly gored by a wounded ram.

However, none of that is to imply that African plains game is dangerous, nor is it armor-plated. As is the case with all hunting

247

everywhere, the idea is to place a properly constructed bullet from an adequate cartridge in the right place with the first shot. If that is done, there will be meat in camp—it's as simple as that. In terms of defining an adequate rifle and cartridge, there are literally dozens of fine choices. For the smaller and midsized plains game, any cartridge deemed adequate for North American deer will work just fine; for the larger plains species—heavyweights like zebra and eland, and tough animals like oryx, sable, and wildebeeste (these ungainly animals are legendary for being impervious to bullet shock)—any cartridge considered adequate for American elk will do just fine. The dangerous game rifle—the one used for the cats and thick-skinned game—opens up a whole new set of parameters, and we'll discuss it later.

In most African hunting, the game list includes a broad array of animals of widely differing sizes. Typically, the soft-skinned or plains species will range from tiny antelope such as steinbok or duiker, go up through the deer-sized antelope such as impala and reedbuck, larger antelope such as hartebeeste or nyala, and probably include heavyweights such as zebra, kudu and eland. Buffalo and other thick-skinned game may be included, as may one or both of the cats. Now that's a wide range of hunting, and several radically different rifle/cartridge combinations could prove extremely useful.

A .22 Magnum or .22 Hornet, for example, would be great for the tiny antelope and perhaps guinea fowl for the pot, and would be lots of fun for shooting varmints such as spring hares and dassies—the plentiful rock hyrax. A hotter .22 centerfire would also be useful, and could be used for slightly larger antelope such as mountain reedbuck or springbok. A .243, 6mm Remington or .257 Roberts would be superb for impala, bushbuck, and such; I took a .250 Savage once, and had great fun using it on smaller antelope.

A .270, .280, .30-06 or 7mm magnum would be ideal for the medium-sized plains game and could take the larger antelope just fine with good bullets, and of course the various .300 magnums, .338 Winchester and .340 Weatherby Magnums, and the .375 H&H are well suited for the largest of the plains game. The .375 would also come into play for the cats and even the thick-skinned game, and there could also be a big bore—.416, .458, .460 Weatherby, or perhaps a big double—exclusively for the elephant, buffalo, rhino, and hippo. On an extensive general-bag safari of three weeks or longer, it would be easy to make good use of half a dozen different rifles and certainly a shotgun as well.

The obvious problem is that it's a real pain in the neck to transport more than two guns. More than that requires two guncases, so if two guncases must be taken, then four guns are as easy to haul as three. But that fourth gun should probably be a shotgun, not a rifle. All too often I've missed out on some superb birdshooting for want of a scattergun. Less obvious than the impracticality of transporting all the rifles that might be useful is the fact that most hunting days aren't all that specialized.

You may start from camp looking for a good bushbuck, but that could be the day that you run into the kind of buffalo you've been dreaming about. Even if you manage to haul a half-dozen rifles all the way to Africa, you simply can't carry that many in the safari car. Two, a light or medium rifle and a heavy, are about all that's reasonable. On foot, you'll carry one rifle yourself, and chances are one of the trackers will carry another, but even that isn't always practical.

Therefore versatility is one of the key considerations in planning an African battery. With the possible exception of the dangerous game rifle, African rifles shouldn't be specialized but should have the power and trajectory to handle a wide range of game and shooting circumstances. In general, choices should favor the heavier animals that might be encountered—being overgunned seems a much less costly mistake than being undergunned!

There are many circumstances in which one can do very nicely with a single rifle, especially on safaris that will not include any dangerous game. In such cases, the choice should be a rifle and cartridge that will be plenty of gun for the largest game that might be hunted. Excluding dangerous game, the various .300 magnums, the .338 Winchester Magnum, and the .340 Weatherby Magnums are fine choices. If dangerous game is included, then the choice for a one-rifle safari is quite narrow. Only the .375 H&H and its various "improved" versions and the mighty .378 Weatherby, to my mind, offer the needed combination of flat trajectory for the plains game and power for the dangerous game.

A single rifle and perhaps a shotgun make a lot of sense and such a selection certainly simplifies things, but few hunters travel to Africa with just a single rifle. Although the concept has great merit, I'm not much in favor of it. Africa is a long ways off, and it makes good sense to take at least two rifles, even if the second is only a spare. I landed at Jan Smuts Airport in Johannesburg once to find the stock of my .30-06 broken off at the wrist. I had brought three rifles—the .30-06, a .375, and a .470 double. Before the safari was over I was able to get the broken stock put back together, but aside from being a heartbreaker—it had been a beautiful piece of walnut—there was really no problem. The .375 simply inherited the duties of the .30-06, and business went on as usual. Just on the off-chance that something horrible like that happens, I think it's all right, perhaps even best, if there is some overlap amongst the rifles that are selected.

Traditional safari batteries consist of a "light," a "medium," and a "heavy" rifle, and for hunts that will include very large and/or dangerous game, this remains the best way to build a battery. The light rifle is generally in a caliber that would be considered good for deer, and it should have enough power to come up into the elk class. It will be used for animals ranging from the tiny up through the very large, if not dangerous, so it needs to have the utmost in versatility. It should be flat-shooting and accurate, and should wear a scope of moderate power—a 4X or a mid-range variable in the 1 1/2-5X or 2-7X range. Because of the need for versatility, I believe the .270 Winchester should be the absolute minimum choice for a light rifle. These days the 7mm Remington Magnum and the good old .30-06 are probably American hunters' most popular choices for a light rifle, with the .300 magnums falling right behind. All are extremely good choices. With some of the excellent 200 and 220-grain bullets available, the .300 magnum can actually be used on the largest of game in a pinch. A colleague of mine recently had a customs foulup that prevented her from getting her .375 into Zambia. She used her .300 magnum for everything, including a one shot kill on a Cape buffalo.

In spite of what the light rifle can do when it has to, its purpose is for essentially the full range of plains species. The medium rifle is a bit more specialized. It might be used on the very largest or toughest of the plains game, it will certainly be used on cats, and it might actually take the place of a true heavy for thick-skinned dangerous game.

Some countries still have caliber restrictions for various types of game. If they exist, then generally the .375 H&H Magnum will be the minimum for dangerous game. I think that's a sensible minimum whether it's legislated or not, so if there is to be no true heavy rifle, the .375 H&H is virtually the only choice as a medium rifle. The .378 Weatherby Magnum is another possibility. On the other hand, if there will be a heavier rifle on hand, the medium rifle could well be a .338 or .340 Weatherby.

Like the light rifle, the medium should wear a scope, and the rifle should have the capability for fairly long range shooting. Unlike the

African game comes in all shapes and sizes, and good trophies—like this record-book Kirk's dik dik—can come in small packages. Given the great range of African game, it's ridiculous to say that African game is super-tough. However, the great size variance in game that might be encountered in a single day indicates that the light or medium African rifle must be very versatile and very accurate. Only the dangerous game rifle can be a special purpose outfit.

light rifle, though, it's important that the medium rifle be fast-handling and quick-pointing, and that the hunter be totally familiar with and have total confidence in it.

Finally we get to the heavy rifle, the rifle that is generally used the least by a wide margin but receives the most attention by an equally wide margin. And after all, the romance of the heavy rifle is really part and parcel to the mystique of African hunting. On most safaris today, it's the rifle that might not be fired more than once—but it's the rifle that, when fired, lives are staked on, and while the other rifles are perhaps deserving of more attention than they often get, the heavy rifle unquestionably deserves the utmost in care and consideration.

The heavy rifle is by its nature a specialized gun. It will be something over .40 caliber, and it won't be designed for long range work. It will generally push a bullet of some 400 to 500 grains somewhere between 2,100 and 2,400 feet per second, giving it a modest trajectory but plenty of stopping power. Schools of thought on scopes are mixed. The traditional heavy rifle carries open express sights, and for the purpose this rifle is designed for, they are adequate. However, most hunters today grew up in a scope generation. Most of us aren't as confident with open sights, don't align them as quickly, and quite simply don't shoot as well with them as we do with scope sights. Most of us would actually be best served by a low-powered scope of, say, 2 1/2 or 3X, on the heavy rifle.

There are really just three action types—the single shot, the bolt action, and the double. Ruger's Number One in .458 makes a fine heavy rifle, but most hunters would prefer to have at least a second shot available. In days gone by, the double was the odds-on choice. I personally like a heavy double very much. They're fast, give an instant and reliable second shot, and the old cartridges such as the .470 and .450-3 1/4 offer the same outstanding performance they always did. However, I must admit that the nostalgia of the double is a very large reason for my preference for them. In use, the bolt action is every bit as good, in some ways better, and the cost of the very best bolt action is a fraction of the cost of even a plain, much-used double today.

Even for the professional hunters, the guys who actually have the most use for a charge-stopping rifle, the bolt action has become the most popular choice. In all the African hunting that I've done, I have seen a total of seven double rifles in use. Willem van Dyk used an over/under Kreighoff .458 in Kenya; Bill Illingworth used another German over/under .470 in Zambia; Geoff Broom carried a side-by-side .500 of Continental make; Ian MacFarlane in Botswana carried a Cogswell & Harrison .475 No. 2; John van der Meulen carried a Gibbs .470; and I have used two .470s—a lovely Wilkes .470 that was stolen from me, and a new Heym .470 side-by-side which I used to hunt my rhino. And that's it for doubles. In the same period of time I've seen innumerable .458s, a few .460 Weatherbys, a couple of .416s in various wildcat configurations as well as the original .416 Rigby, a couple of .404 Jeffreys, and a few other wildcat big bores.

Of course, many hunters choose not to use a true heavy at all but instead use the great .375 H&H as both a medium and a heavy rifle. To be sure, the .375 is adequate for buffalo and elephant. It always was and always will be. The hunting client will undoubtedly be backed up by a professional hunter, and under those circumstances the .375 H&H is enough gun. However, at the risk of inviting a flood of hate mail, I believe the .375 is marginal for both buffalo and elephant under today's hunting conditions.

In the old days, the thick-skinned game was rarely hunted in the most

In a typical day, the same rifle might be asked to account for a tiny dik dik or steinbok and an 800-pound zebra—and zebra are one of the tough ones. A rifle in the .30-06 or 7mm magnum class will handle this range of game, but anything much lighter could cause problems.

dense bush. On the savannas it was possible to wait for the best shot placement, and follow-up shots were usually possible if they were needed. Not today. Both elephant and buffalo have been poached and harried, and today's hunter must often go into the worst thornbush or most dense forest imaginable. Classic pinpoint shot placement may not be possible, and in the thick stuff follow-up shots must be taken as they're presented. Under such conditions, I think today's hunter is best served by a true heavy rifle.

Just a few years ago the .458 Winchester Magnum and the .460 Weatherby Magnum were the only two choices available. Today there seems to be a tremendous resurgence of interest in the big bores, and there are some additions to these two. KDF in Texas makes a .411 available over the counter, and there are a number of good .416 wildcats; .416 Rigby ammunition is also available. A-Square markets a full line of rifles and ammunition for "proprietary" big-bore cartridges, and both B.E.L.L. and A-Square offer fresh ammunition for many old Nitro Express cartridges. Several European firms are now making .470

doubles again, and there are several good .458-caliber wildcats that better the performance of the .458 Winchester. It really doesn't matter what cartridge you choose, so long as you're looking at a bullet of about 500 grains with a velocity of 2,100 to about 2,300 feet per second or, in the .4ll or .416, a 400-grain bullet in the 2,300 to 2,400 fps range.

What are some sensible African batteries? The rifles chosen should be arms that the hunter is familiar with and has confidence in, and as long as those criteria are met the choices are endless. On my most recent safari, I took a .30-06 and a .375, both bolt actions, and a double .470. Oddly enough, that's exactly the combination Ruark chose in 1952. There are many combinations just as good, but in the last 35 years I'm not sure any have come along that are any better. The .375 is really the mainstay, but as has been mentioned, there are numerous good cartridges that could replace the .30-06 as a light rifle or the .470 as a heavy.

I've experimented with a lot of different combinations, and have usually taken just two rifles. On my first safari, they were a .30-06 and a .375—but if dangerous game is on the list, I believe a heavy rifle should be added. On one trip to Zambia, I left out the light rifle and took just a .375 and a wildcat .458 Lott. That's actually not a bad way to go, since the .375 works perfectly well as a light rifle. On another trip I took just a

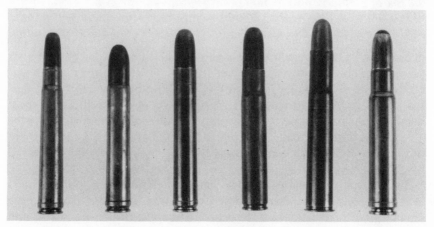

There are a wide range of choices for a dangerous game rifle. Left to right are a few common choices: .375 H&H; .458 Win. Mag.; wildcat .458 Lott; .404 Jeffrey; .470 Nitro-Express; .460 Wby. Mag. The .375 H&H is a bare bones minimum for dangerous game in today's Africa. Not shown are the various .4ll and .416 wildcats and the old .416 Rigby—all good choices.

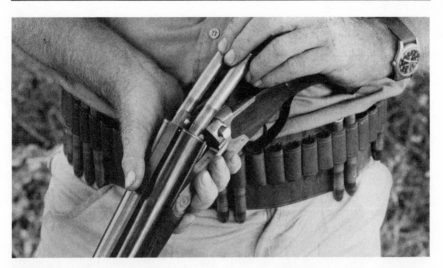

The side-by-side double is the classic stopping rifle, offering an in-stantaneous second shot, great reliability, and the fast-handling characteristics of a fine shotgun. This one is a new Heym in .470, certainly a superb choice. However, the guy who really needs such a rifle is the professional hunter; the hunting client is probably just as well off with an accurate, scope-sighted bolt action.

.300 Weatherby and a .460 Weatherby—not a bad combination—but I greatly missed the versatility of a .375, and borrowed my partner's on several occasions.

I had an unusual but really super combination on a couple of hunts—a pair of Remington 700s in fiberglass stocks, one in .338 Winchester Magnum and the other in the wildcat .416 Hoffman. Both were scoped, and that's a combination I will most definitely use again.

While the exact rifles and cartridges selected are, within sensible guidelines, largely a matter of personal preference, there are several important considerations in getting them ready for the hunt.

First is the rifles themselves. Africa is not the place to test-fire a brand new rifle, especially the dangerous game rifle. Most of us, if the truth were known, are a little bit afraid of hard-kicking rifles, though few will admit it. Wear plenty of padding, and don't shoot the darn thing off the bench any more than you have to—and then only with a thick sandbag between you and the butt. But shoot it offhand plenty, and make certain, on bolt actions, that you run through several full magazines of the exact type of ammunition you will use on safari. It may single-load just fine, but bolt actions chambered for big cartridges can be a bit finicky on feeding. I have two that were, lovely custom jobs that were finished literally days before the start of a hunt—and neither fed properly from the magazine. Fortunately I found it out on the range, and Jack Lott, a true wizard with big bores, worked his magic and got them both to feed before I left.

If you purchase a new big bore for a hunt, have a good gunsmith take it apart and look it over before you even fire it. Many good rifle manufacturers simply don't understand the bedding and reinforcement that are necessary to keep an extremely powerful, hard-kicking rifle from recoiling clear out of its stock. A little extra bedding and reinforcement are often needed to shortstop the possibility of stock splitting.

Of course, practice with all the rifles you will take as much as you can before the hunt, and practice with the exact type of ammunition you will use. Some professional hunters are astute firearms enthusiasts, but most are not. After you arrive in camp from your overseas flight, insist on checking the sights on all your rifles. Chances are they'll be fine, but you'll feel better and shoot better knowing for sure.

Scopes and sights, like the rifles themselves, are largely a matter of personal preference. Shooting in Africa can be very long in the deserts and savannas or very short in the thornbush. Usually a 4X scope is adequate, but for those who prefer variables, the low range 1 1/2-5X or 2-7X is plenty. Both the medium rifle and the heavy rifle (if it's scoped at all) should wear good open sights in addition to the glass. Odds are you won't use the irons if you have a scope in place, but they should be there just in case. I'm personally not a big fan of detachable scope mounts. I love the *idea* of them, but I've seen very few that work with heavy-recoiling rifles. Chances are, if you have occasion to take the scope off, you'll have plenty of time to put it back on. Just make sure that you have the right screwdriver to handle the job. If you have more than one scoped rifle with you, it's a very good idea to use the same mounts, then have a spare scope in compatible rings in your gun case.

It's essential to select the bullets for your African hunt with the same care you show the rifles themselves. Your bullet may be asked to handle a 10 pound dik dik one moment and a 1,500-pound eland the next. Obviously no bullet is ideal for such diverse tasks, but the bullet should be of controlled-expansion design and should be constructed to provide deep penetration on the largest game you might possibly take with that rifle.

Because of the keyed-up nature mentioned previously, most African

In Botswana the author used a widlcat .416 Hoffman in a Chet Brown fiberglass stock. Propelling a 400-grain bullet at nearly 2,400 feet per second, this and similar .411 and .416 wildcats are more than adequate for African dangerous game—and are much flatter-shooting than .458-class cartridges. The fiberglass stock makes a lot of sense for swamp and rainy-season hunts.

257

animals are somewhat resistant to raw bullet shock. However, like all game everywhere, they will succumb quickly to extensive damage to vital organs. The idea is to get a bullet into those vitals. Penetration, not the shock of rapid expansion, is the key. I usually use relatively heavy-for-caliber bullets of controlled expansion design—Nosler Partitions, Speer Grand Slams, Hornady Interlocks, heavy-jacketed Barnes bullets, and the like. In the .30-06, I usually stay with 180-grain bullets; in the .300 Weatherby, 200-grain bullets; for the 7mm, 160 or 175. In the .375, I almost always use 300-grain bullets since I will invariably have some 300-grain solids in addition to the softpoints and am thus certain of at least similar points of impact. Of course, accuracy is the key, so priority should be given to selecting a load that shoots well in your rifle. All things being equal, however, go with the heavier bullet and forget the more impressive velocities of the lighter bullets. It is terribly important to test-fire some of the ammunition from the exact batch you will be hunting with, checking it for reliable feeding as well as firing. Here the older doubles are a definite problem. I have had batches of old Kynoch .470 ammo that had erratic ignition, and in the past year I've heard a couple of horror stories of near-misses with dangerous game caused by old ammo for old doubles. The postwar Kynoch ammo *should* still be reliable, but regardless of its value (.600 Nitro ammo, for example, is worth up to $50 per cartridge!) a few cartridges from the lot you will be using must be test-fired.

For the cats, of course, one will definitely want to use an expanding bullet. The .375 remains near-perfect lion medicine, and the .375 will usually be the choice for leopard. The leopard is really quite a small animal—150 pounds is a good-sized leopard—and the .375 is needlessly powerful. A more rapidly-expanding, faster-moving bullet from a 7mm magnum, .30-06, .300, or .338 may actually produce quicker kills than the .375, although the latter may be the legal minimum. In any case, shot placement is the key on leopard, and nowhere is it more critical, especially since the shot will almost always be taken in fading light with little time to follow up.

On buffalo, opinion is sharply divided as to whether a softpoint or solid is the better choice. The hunter should have both solids and soft-points for the rifle that will be used on buffalo, and since most professional hunters have strong opinions on the subject, the best advice is to follow your professional's suggestion. Given a choice, I usually hedge my bets. I prefer a good, stoutly constructed expanding bullet for the first shot on buffalo. I almost invariably try for a chest shot, and I want the added shock of an expanding bullet. Usually, though, I back up the softpoint with a solid for the second and subsequent shots.

Buffalo are tough, and unless the spine is broken a one-shot kill is very rare in my experience. The usual scenario is the first shot to the shoulder or chest, preferably the former. Charges from the first shot are almost as rare as unprovoked charges; usually the buffalo will turn to run, and the second shot with a solid will be a raking shot behind the last rib or a shot into one hip or between the hams—that's where the solid is really essential. Then the buffalo is gone, everything becomes very quiet, and you wonder if you've started something that the buffalo will finish. You'll wait awhile, and if the first shot was good you'll find your buffalo down and dead. If the second shot was as good as or better than the first, you'll find the same thing. If both shots were off, all you can hope for is that either shot slowed your bull down enough for you to finish the job when he comes . . . .

The .375 H&H is an extremely useful African rifle, after 75 years still virtually the only choice for a one-rifle safari. Here Boddington takes a rest on an anthill to shoot a big Livingstone's eland, the moose-sized antelope that really rates the power of a .375.

While actual injuries from dangerous game are rare, they can and do happen. It just makes good sense to use an adequate rifle, concentrate on shot placement, and don't shoot at all if you aren't sure of a good hit. The old saying "it's the dead ones that kill" you is quite true—any down animal must be approached with caution, but most especially the ones that can gore, trample, or eat you.

Elephant and rhino, of course, are game for solid bullets only. Both animals are too big to shock with anything less than a cannon, and here you're looking for precise shot placement and penetration. It's wise to study as many photographs of African animals as possible before a safari, and it's also wise to discuss shot placement at some length with your professional hunter before you go after dangerous game.

Americans on the whole shoot fairly well, though rarely as well as we should. Those of us who do shoot well often develop a bad habit through years of experience with nondangerous game: We tend to "admire" the shot, waiting to see the first shot take effect before firing the second and subsequent. On Africa's dangerous game, it's a habit that can be fatal. Spend time on the range working the action and getting off second and third shots rapidly. Place the first shot as well as you possibly can; it's the one that matters the most. But don't wait around to see what happens. Whether there seems to be immediate effect from the first bullet or not, on dangerous game get another one in as quickly as possible.

Most of us want to drop the animal ourselves, with no collaboration from the professional hunter. However, a dangerous situation with a dangerous animal is no place for vanity. The professional hunter is charged with your safety, and it's part of his job to ensure that wounded animals—particularly dangerous ones—are recovered. He shouldn't have to back you up, and the good ones will never fire their rifles unless it's absolutely necessary. Hopefully you'll have picked a professional that you trust, and you should leave the shoot/don't shoot decision up to him alone.

You're the guy who will fire the first shot, and to that extent you're charged with *his* safety. If the animal gets into the brush, it's the professional who's responsible for digging it out, and it's altogether his call as to whether you'll go with him or not. Worse, the trackers who will go in with him will be unarmed. Their very lives depend on your ability to place the first shot well. Unfortunately, no matter how careful you are and how well you normally shoot, sooner or later that first shot won't be where you want it. It's part of the game that bad shots come with the good, but don't compound a poor shot by being the kind of client who insists on no collaboration no matter what. Most professional hunters won't pay any attention anyway on dangerous game—but the inexperienced ones might, once. That once, when a wounded animal could have been stopped before it got into the thick stuff, could cost somebody his life, and in all likelihood it won't be you as the hunting client.

That's why I have to draw the line on shooting dangerous game with inadequate arms, be they rifles that are smaller in caliber than they should be, handguns, bows, or whatever. A clean kill is the object in any hunting, and equipment other than modern sporting rifles has proven adequate, even devastating, over a wide variety of hunting situations. But not with Africa's dangerous game, where chances are all too good that someone else may pay with his life for your folly. The .375 H&H minimum for dangerous game came in a time when far more hunters knew a great deal more about dangerous game than anyone knows today, and it remains a good rule to follow.

APPENDIX B
PLANNING THE SAFARI

The actual starting point for any African hunt is usually many months before the fact. That's the way it should be, for the more planning and preparation that goes into it, the better the chances for the safari to live up to expectations. Africa is a real place, and in the real world things aren't always perfect. Unfortunately, most hunters have dreams of Africa based on sources that are somewhat removed from reality—Tarzan movies, adventure novels, even sporting literature that's more than a few years old. Africa *is* a magnificent place, and in spite of expectations I've never talked to anyone who was exactly *disappointed*, but I've talked to a lot of people who were surprised at what they found. No amount of research or planning is likely to change anyone's preconceived notions about Africa, but they will ensure a good hunt for the animals that are most important, and Africa herself will take care of the rest.

African hunting has produced an incredible body of excellent literature, and while a few authors tend to place maneating lions behind every bush, most writing on Africa and African hunting is honest, although it becomes dated very quickly. For background material, just to get the "feel" of Africa, Hemingway's *Green Hills of Africa* and Ruark's *Horn of the Hunter* and *Something of Value* are essentials; no one should go to Africa without first reading them. Wilbur Smith, the fine South African novelist, has turned out a number of historical novels set in southern Africa. Smith's dates and places are accurate, and if he describes it, he's been there. Most of my writing friends and I eagerly await a new Wilbur Smith novel, and it never disappoints. For more specific information on African hunting, especially books that will help you to choose the right safari, the real bible is unquestionably James Mellon's *African Hunter*. Just remember that it's getting a bit out of date—anything written about African hunting, including these words will be dated within months of publication. Things change too fast in Africa today. For help in deciding what animals are most important, try to find a copy of Russell B. Aitken's *Great Game Animals.* The record books are an invaluable source of data both on animals and hunting areas. Safari Club International's record book has developed into a magnificent reference, complete with articles on various areas and outfitters' names listed with the hunters they guided to the top trophies. Rowland Ward's *Records of Big Game,* now produced by Game Conservation International, remains a standard reference. The list could go on indefinitely, but suffice it to say that there's a wealth of good reading on Africa—and I strongly believe in reading up on a place before traveling halfway 'round the world to get there!

If you're planning your first safari, perhaps such reading will help you make some decisions about animals and areas. If you've been to Africa before, then most probably you already know what you want to go after next. In any case, some decisions as to what animals have the highest priority—or what part of Africa you would most like to visit—should be made before the safari is more than a thought. If there are no priority animals—if you really just wish to see a bit of Africa and don't care what winds up in the bag—your planning is greatly simplified. However, most hunters, whether first timers or old hands, usually have something in mind that they'd like for their den or trophy room.

It's best to be honest with yourself at this stage, and then be specific when you query outfitters and their references. Don't book a general bag-hunt if what you really want is a lion. If the lion is of prime importance, and you're willing to shoot nothing else until you have him, make sure your outfitter understands that, and do your homework to ensure that you're in a good cat area at the right time.

In establishing priorities, it's also important to understand African hunting today, and most of the reading will be a bit misleading. Elephant used to come along quite naturally as part of a general-bag hunt. Today good elephant are perhaps Africa's most specialized animal. The ultra-unique antelope are probably next: bongo, mountain nyala, sitatunga, Derby eland. Entire safaris are planned around the taking of such animals. Other game is usually present and may be taken as well, but on the animals that are both localized *and* difficult to hunt, as opposed to easily hunted local rarities like the lechwe, the difference is that if you let yourself get sidetracked once too often you will go home without your primary animal. Today both cats require exactly the same level of concentration.

True, in a baiting situation other things can be hunted while the baits are being checked. But again, it's all too easy to get sidetracked, and those baits simply must be checked. If either lion or leopard is truly your Number One trophy, then by all means go for it. But in general, unless one has available at least three weeks in top cat country, I don't recommend lion or leopard on the the first safari. Far better to work on a good buffalo and a general bag of plains game. Of course, buffalo are also starting to get a bit expensive in some areas. Plains-game-only hunts aren't to be scoffed at; they're a lot of fun and can yield some truly outstanding trophies. Zimbabwe, South Africa, and South West Africa all have outstanding hunts of this type.

Wherever you decide to hunt, establish your priorities, if you have any, and be prepared to spend the needed time to fill those priorities. On the other hand, don't overlook the local rarities, even if they don't seem important at the moment. In the Luangwa Valley, for instance, taking a good puku is no problem at all—but in a lifetime of hunting that may very well be the only time you'll lay eyes on a puku. Virtually every African area has some species that, if not unique, grow to the best proportions only there.

Hopefully you've decided what you would like to hunt, and some careful reading and studying of the record books have given you some idea of where to go. Sometimes such decisions are dictated by budgetary considerations, but given a choice I lean towards the traditional safari in the more remote areas, especially for a first safari. The old Africa is going quickly, and while I think the ranch hunting is often excellent, it will be available for some time to come. I like to see a hunter go for the traditional African hunt—or as close an approximation as possible—the first time around.

Now it's time to locate a professional hunter that you can trust to do a good job. Of course, you may have a specific outfitter that you simply want to hunt with, and to heck with what's on the game list. That makes things nice and simple. Usually though, a hunter goes shopping for a lion hunt, or a sable hunt, or an elephant hunt. In general, you get what you pay for. However, a high price may not be any guarantee of a good hunt. Prices in Zambia are essentially the same from one outfit to another; likewise in Botswana, Zimbabwe, and even Tanzania. Provided the area is good for the game you are seeking, it's really your individual professional hunter who makes the difference.

Most African hunting takes place in pleasant weather, and camp laundry service makes clothing requirements minimal. There are plenty of thorns, so whether shorts or long trousers are chosen is a matter of personal choice. Shorts are quieter and generally more comfortable, but their use is occasionally painful. Good binoculars are an absolute necessity!

For that reason I personally don't care to hunt with very large outfits, where you simply are assigned a professional hunter. Of course, there's a simple way around that. Find out what professionals hunt for that company, check references on several of them, and don't book the hunt unless you can get a professional hunter of your choice.

In the main, finding a good outfit or a good guide is just the same as it is the world over—a painstaking process of checking references. In general, most African professionals are pretty darned good. On the average, I think one's chances of getting a bad hunt are much lower in Africa than anywhere else in the world. In fact, no matter what happens I can't imagine a bad African hunt. But some careful checking can ensure that it's what you have in mind.

Hunting conventions—Safari Club, GameCoin, M'Zuri, Dallas and Houston Safari Clubs, and others (sure are a lot of them these days!)—are great places to meet outfitters and their agents. In the convention atmosphere, it's important to remember that everybody is trying to sell and the promises can come hot and heavy. Balanced against this, it's awfully nice to meet your outfitter or guide face to face and sit down over a drink to discuss specifics. The newsletters and magazines of these various organizations are often good sources of information about outfitters, as are hunting magazines and the New York-based *Hunting Report*.

Use of a booking agent can save a great deal of legwork. I've had very good luck with several, and many in that business—Jack Atcheson and Dan Thimmes, to name a couple—are extremely close friends. However, I've had equally good luck planning hunts on my own. It just takes longer.

Most safaris usually begin the planning phase a year ahead. Sometimes there are last-minute openings, and once in a while a late cancellation can be had at a bargain. But it's usually wise to start planning something like a year ahead—and with the best and most popular outfitters, the best dates could be spoken for several seasons in advance. It's also wise to remain a bit flexible for as long as possible. Obviously there will come a time when the commitment must be made and the

A tented safari camp—rare in today's Africa—is the ultimate safari experience. Mornings can be quite cold, so long trousers and long sleeves—and often a sweater or down jacket—are needed to start out the day. By midday, though, the weather is usually quite warm and pleasant.

deposit paid, and then let the chips fall where they may. Don't lose a good date with a good outfitter, but keep some measure of flexibility as long as possible. In fact, as you're planning, it's wise to have a backup plan in another country, even if it's only in the back of your mind.

In 1986 I was literally on my way out the door enroute to Tanzania for, I thought, a 21-day hunt including elephant, buffalo, cats and plains game—a dream safari. It turned out to be a pipe dream. My outfitter ran afoul of the government there and at the very last moment cabled me not to come. The South African safari that forms the last two chapters of this book wasn't exactly a backup plan, but it had been planned for a bit later on. I did some scurrying around, made some overseas phone calls, was able to move up the date, and enjoyed an absolutely fantastic safari.

Cancellations like that can happen, and the more exotic the destination, the more exotic the potential problems. In any African hunt, some degree of flexibility is essential. There will be delays, there will be flat tires, vehicles will break down. It's all part of the game. It isn't part of the game for a hunt to be jerked out from under you at the last moment, but in Africa anything can happen at any time. When Kenya closed there were safaris actually in the field. Too bad—all those licenses you purchased yesterday aren't any good today. In planning any African hunt it's important that disasters such as that be remembered. We hope that nothing like that will happen again, but keep in mind flexibility in everything dealing with Africa.

The paperwork required for an African hunt is really quite simple, but it should be started a couple of months in advance. Check your passport and make certain it doesn't expire within six months after your planned safari. If it does, time to get a new one. Check with your travel agent or the consulates of the various countries involved and find out whether you need a visa. Chances are that you do, and you will need to apply in plenty of time. If you are passing through any countries enroute, you may also need visas there.

Talk to your taxidermist and see if you need a CITES permit for any of the animals you plan to hunt. If you do, you can get them from the U.S. Fish & Wildlife Service, but it will take a couple of months. For leopard, white rhino, and such, it isn't required to have this permit before the safari—but you must have it before you attempt to import the animal or any of its parts into the U.S. While you're talking to your taxidermist, you may want to discuss shipment of trophies. He may have a customs broker who can clear the shipment when it arrives, you

In the Okavango, or any other swamp region, foot care is extremely important. Quick-drying canvas shoes are best for most African hunting, as there is really no way to keep your feet completely dry. Boddington suffered from immersion foot in the Okavango; the only answer is to dry your feet as often as possible.

may have a broker, or you may prefer to clear the shipment yourself. I've done it all three ways, and I don't think I'll clear another one myself. It isn't difficult, but it's a bureaucratic hassle that's too hard on one's blood pressure.

Of course, many hunters these days are having their animals mounted in Africa. The taxidermy is generally good, faster than in the U.S., and much cheaper. However, the shipment of mounted heads is a great deal more expensive. I think the most important consideration is to choose a taxidermist whose work you like and whose integrity can be relied on. Beyond that it doesn't matter what continent he's on. There are, however, two strikes against using an African taxidermist. First, right at the conclusion of a safari—in the heat of the moment, so to speak—isn't the best time to decide what should be mounted and what shouldn't be. Trust me on this one; I've gone this route! Right at the conclusion of the hunt the natural tendency is to have everything mounted, but some the animals will be better than others. Unless space and budget are unlimited, it's far wiser to consider very carefully which animals should be mounted and which might be best as European or skull mounts. The other drawback to using African taxidermists is that, because of the chronic uncertainties in Africa and the vast distances involved, you want to get your trophies home as quickly as possible. At this writing the economic sanctions against South Africa have hundreds of hunting trophies tied up. It will be resolved, but in the meantime I have a trophy shipment stuck there that, had I had the paperwork three days earlier, could have gotten home under the wire.

In most African countries you will need to send ahead serial numbers of your firearms and number of cartridges. Make certain this information gets there *correctly*; send it by two or three means, and don't change your mind. There may be restrictions on numbers of cartridges. Depending on that, something between 50 and 60 rounds should be adequate for the light rifle; 30 to 40 for the medium, including 10 solids; 20

Proper trophy care is an essential—and occasionally neglected—part of any safari. Most African outfits are pretty good in this regard, but a few are sloppy or just don't know how to do it right. Before the hunt, have a talk with a good taxidermist about field trophy care in warm climates. Then, make sure you at least check on the skinning shed periodically during your safari. It's a good idea to take personalized tags and supervise their attachment to your trophies.

for the heavy—10 solid, 10 soft. That amount of ammo should do for even a very extensive safari.

Packing for the safari isn't difficult. Daily laundry is virtually a fact of life on safari, so three changes of hunting clothes is probably one more than is absolutely required. Some hotels throughout Africa do require a coat and tie in their dining rooms, so we casual-minded Americans may go hungry without them! I prefer to hunt in shorts, but that's very much a matter of taste. Shorts are cool and quiet, but the thorns will cut the hell out of your legs. Depending on preference, two pairs of short trousers and one of longs or vice versa will be right. Conversely, I prefer long-sleeved shirts—I can always roll up the sleeves. Three shirts to hunt in is adequate. Khaki *was* the color when African hunting meant the open savannas of East Africa. In the thornbush and forest where most hunting is done today, green is *the* color. Camouflage is pretty much out, even illegal in many countries. It would be useful but carries far too many connotations of guerrilla warfare. Stay strictly away from it.

Boots should be light and quiet. Modern boots that are part Cordura nylon with leather reinforcing are good, but I've worn nothing but high-topped green canvas tennis shoes for years and have been quite pleased with them. In the mountainous regions, of course, conventional climbing boots with better support are called for.

The midday sun gets fierce, so some kind of a hat is needed, plus sunscreen and sunglasses. Felt hats get too darned hot to be comfortable, but I need more than a baseball cap to keep the sun off. The canvas "floppy" hat is a good way to go; I bought two of them in Johannesburg last trip and am retiring the old felt safari hat.

In the African winter (our summer months) it gets incredibly cold, particularly in the high country or when riding in an open vehicle early in the morning. Sweaters, down vests, windbreakers, and even gloves are called for. I wear a sweater a great deal while hunting; they're warm but above all they're quiet in the bush.

Rain is very rare except during the rainy season, but almost never impossible. A light rainsuit weighs nothing and just makes sense. Raingear certainly isn't essential, but the best insect repellent you can buy *is*! In general there are few bugs, but in a leopard blind those few bugs drive you crazy, and in tsetse fly country, you need the best there is. I've had pretty good luck with a couple of brands advertised to be 100 percent DEET. That stuff will take the chrome off a trailer hitch—or the finish off a gunstock—but it keeps off the tsetses.

Good optics are important. It's relatively rare to need a spotting scope, though I always take one. Binoculars, on the other hand, are a must. You simply can't do without them, and you should have the best you can afford in something like 7X or 8X.

Most of us, myself included, show up on safari with far more clothing and equipment than is needed. After all, packing just the right gear is part of the fun. But the less gear you have the easier it is to keep your tent or rondavel in order, to keep track of everything, and to travel back and forth. You need a good hard gun case; you should get by with one large duffel bag easily; and then all you need is a carry-on bag that will hold your cameras, binoculars, film in a lead bag, toilet articles, and a change of clothes. If everybody showed up on safari with that amount of luggage, there'd be a whole bunch of happy professionals!

AUTHOR'S NOTE

I hope it will be clear to readers of this book that I've had a heck of a good time seeing and hunting in Africa over the past 10 years. I've been fortunate to see a pretty good chunk of that vast continent, and I've enjoyed every second of every minute I've been able to spend there—in spite of the occasional heat, cold, biting insect, and very rare close call with four-legged or two-legged predator. I'm sure it will be equally clear that there's a good deal of Africa that I haven't seen, and certainly there's a great deal more of it that I would like to see, if the good Lord gives me the time, energy, and resources. But no matter how much of Africa I eventually get to see, I'll never be a real expert on that fascinating continent. Rather, I'm just a casual observer, and this is a book of personal observations written from the standpoint of admittedly limited personal experience. It isn't a "how to" book, nor a "where to"book, although some of that information—at least the way I see it—may be gleaned. Instead, it's strictly a personal account of my own African hunting in the past decade.

There are, of course, real experts on African hunting—not just casual observers, but men who live it every day of their lives. They're the professional hunters out in the field, and I've been fortunate to know and hunt with—and learn from—a number of very good ones. To them I owe a special debt of gratitude, not only for the existence of this book, but for the direction my life has taken. Specifically, that debt is owed to Willem van Dyk, Barrie Duckworth, Roger Whittal, Ben Nolte, Ed Hannon, Garry Kelly, Ray Torr, Raymond Theron, Joof Lamprecht, Bill Illingworth, Geoff and Russ Broom, Ronnie MacFarlane, Peter Johnstone, Lud de Bruijn, Lew Tonks, and John and David van der Meulen; good professional hunters all. But that debt is also owed to every professional hunter plying his trade across the vast continent that

273

is Africa—not only the many that I've been fortunate to meet, but all who have created both the legend and reality of African hunting, and are still doing so today. A simple thanks is not enough.

A debt is also acknowledged to HUNTING's Managing Editor, Jeanne Frissell, who spent her weekends on the initial editing of this manuscript—and, as always, offered sound advice that was generally followed, and likewise to this volume's publisher, Ludo Wurfbain—a good hunter and good friend—who held my feet to the fire to get finished.

But most of all, my special gratitude goes to my wife, Paula, who puts up with my all-too-frequent absences, accepts the mounted trophies strewn all through her house, suffers through a chattering typewriter in the middle of the night, and above all gives me that extra measure of support that a writer has to have.

Craig Boddington
Los Angeles
January 1987